Catholic Teaching Brothers

Historical Studies in Education

Edited by William J. Reese and John L. Rury

William J. Reese, Carl F. Kaestle WARF Professor of Educational Policy Studies and History, the University of Wisconsin-Madison

John L. Rury, Professor of Education and (by courtesy) History, the University of Kansas

This series features new scholarship on the historical development of education, defined broadly, in the United States and elsewhere. Interdisciplinary in orientation and comprehensive in scope, it spans methodological boundaries and interpretive traditions. Imaginative and thoughtful, history can contribute to the global conversation about educational change. Inspired history lends itself to continued hope for reform, and to realizing the potential for progress in all educational experiences.

Published by Palgrave Macmillan:

Democracy and Schooling in California: The Legacy of Helen Heffernan and Corinne Seeds
By Kathleen Weiler

The Global University: Past, Present, and Future Perspectives
Edited by Adam R. Nelson and Ian P. Wei

Catholic Teaching Brothers: Their Life in the English-Speaking World, 1891–1965
By Tom O'Donoghue

Science Education and Citizenship: Fairs, Clubs, and Talent Searches for American Youth, 1918–1958
By Sevan G. Terzian

Catholic Teaching Brothers

Their Life in the English-Speaking World, 1891–1965

Tom O'Donoghue

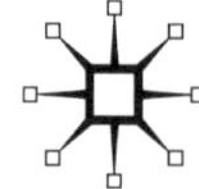

CATHOLIC TEACHING BROTHERS

First published in 2012 by
PALGRAVE MACMILLAN®
in the United States—a division of St. Martin's Press LLC,
175 Fifth Avenue, New York, NY 10010.

Where this book is distributed in the UK, Europe and the rest of the world, this is by Palgrave Macmillan, a division of Macmillan Publishers Limited, registered in England, company number 785998, of Houndmills, Basingstoke, Hampshire RG21 6XS.

Palgrave Macmillan is the global academic imprint of the above companies and has companies and representatives throughout the world.

Palgrave® and Macmillan® are registered trademarks in the United States, the United Kingdom, Europe and other countries.

ISBN: 978–1–137–26904–1

Library of Congress Cataloging-in-Publication Data

O'Donoghue, T. A. (Tom A.), 1953–
Catholic teaching brothers : their life in the English-speaking world, 1891–1965 / Thomas O'Donoghue.
p. cm.—(Historical studies in education)
Includes bibliographical references and index.
ISBN 978–1–137–26904–1
1. Brothers (Religious)—English-speaking countries—History—20th century. 2. Catholic Church—Education—English-speaking countries—History—20th century. I. Title.

LC490.O35 2012
271′.03017521—dc23 2012011551

A catalogue record of the book is available from the British Library.

Design by Newgen Imaging Systems (P) Ltd., Chennai, India.

First edition: October 2012

10 9 8 7 6 5 4 3 2 1

Printed in the United States of America.

Contents

Foreword

Throughout history, religious communities recognized that their survival and expansion depended upon an ability to inculcate the precepts of their faith in the young. This was not to be left to chance. It is a truism that teaching and learning occur in many contexts, formal and informal. The home, family, and community are always important educators. But adults have often turned to schools as one of the most direct ways to preserve their values and shape the future.

Through the millennia, Roman Catholics established seminaries, monasteries, institutes, and a variety of schools to extend their legitimacy, power, and authority. From the establishment of cathedral schools and universities in the Middle Ages to the creation of numerous parish schools in many nations in the centuries to come, Catholic control over what students learned helped sustain the priesthood, spread the faith, and root out heresy. As Tom O'Donoghue demonstrates in his riveting history of religious teaching brothers, the eighteenth century witnessed an important development in the history of Catholic education. Starting with the pioneering efforts of Jean-Baptiste de La Salle, diverse groups of nonordained teachers lived in their own self-contained religious communities, took vows of obedience, poverty, and celibacy, and, with priests and nuns, ultimately played an integral role in Catholic schools.

Catholic Teaching Brothers offers a sweeping panoramic account of its subject, focusing on five English-speaking countries: Ireland, England, the United States, New Zealand, and Australia. The focus is on the late nineteenth century through the 1960s, when the Catholic church, recognizing the need to combat socialism and seemingly confront the modern world more rationally, built an impressive array of schools, including those operated by the teaching brothers, most notably De La Salle, Irish Christian, and Marist. The schools aimed to raise the status of Catholicism, a worldview in retreat after the French Revolution and the rise of a more secular civil society. With great clarity, however, O'Donoghue describes how the brothers were recruited and socialized, as well as the main features of the rigid authoritarian institutions in which they labored, which contributed to untold physical and sexual abuses in a variety of schools and residential institutions.

By the time of Vatican II (1962–1965), Catholic schools had reached a crossroads: their teachers would increasingly be drawn from the laity, as fewer people aspired to become priests, nuns, or teaching brothers, whose status seriously declined. O'Donoghue provides general readers and scholars alike with a wide-ranging exploration of the history of the teaching brothers. His hard-hitting prose insightfully explains how their schools operated, often out of public view or effective oversight, with sometimes horrific consequences for children, making *Catholic Teaching Brothers* the starting point for future research in the field.

William J. Reese and John L. Rury

Acknowledgments

I am grateful to many colleagues and friends for their advice and assistance, and for listening to my expositions on my favourite subject. Within the Graduate School of Education, The University of Western Australia, these include Anne Chapman, Elaine Chapman, Simon Clarke, Di Gardiner, Elaine Lopes, Ian Melville, Marnie O'Neill, Tim Pitman, and Clive Whitehead. In Ireland I benefited from the encouragement of Michael Barry, John Coolahan, Tom Farrelly, Peg Hanafin, Noel Kelly, and John Logan. Fellow historians of education around the world have, in various ways, motivated me to continue with my lines of research. These include Elizabeth Smyth in Canada, Bill Reece and Richard Altenbaugh in the United States, Gary McCulloch and Jane McDermid in the United Kingdom, Denis McLaughlin, Geoffrey Sherington and Tony Potts in Australia, and Jenny Collins, Greg Lee, and Howard Lee in New Zealand. Responsibility for viewpoints and errors of fact, however, lie entirely with me.

I am particularly grateful to my colleague Anne Chapman for permission to rework material already published by us in Chapman, Anne and O'Donoghue, Tom, "The Recruitment of Religious as Teachers: A Case Study from 1960s Australia," *Cambridge Journal of Education*, 37, no. 4 (December 2007): 561–577. The *Cambridge Journal of Education* is published by the Taylor and Francis Group, and the reworking of the material is in accordance with the group's copyright policy.

I wish to express my gratitude for assistance given to me by the staff members of the various libraries where I have worked. I am also pleased to record my thanks to The University of Western Australia for giving me generous study leave and financial assistance to undertake the necessary research.

Finally, I wish to thank my wife, Margaret, for her support and for maintaining a cheerful disposition as I launched, once again, into a new project.

CHAPTER 1

Introduction

Teaching was a life-long commitment. Teaching was not a means of gaining economic stability or advantage; it was a commitment to a life in community where the community not the individual gained the financial remuneration. Teaching was not a job; it was a vocation—a call to serve God.[1]

Throughout the world, thousands of Catholic men and women have, over centuries, lived in single-sex communities as members of what were, and still are, popularly known as religious orders. Here they constructed their professional lives as integral to their religious vocation. As described in the opening quotation, this particular notion of vocation embodies a spiritual belief in being called *by* God, to work *for* God, as a priest, a religious brother (a brother), or a nun—collectively known as "the religious"—within a religious order, and taking vows of poverty, chastity, and obedience. For many priests, religious brothers (brothers), and nuns, the work in question was "teaching."

This book is concerned with the life of brothers who were teachers (teaching brothers), especially during the period 1891–1965. The central theme running through the work is that the commitment of teaching brothers was, first and foremost, to their religious life, and that teaching, while deemed to be a very important role, was always in accord with, and where necessary took second place to, that life. The central period of concern here is what is regarded as the heyday of the religious orders, both numerically and in terms of their influence in the schools. It also constitutes a distinct era in the history of the Catholic Church internationally. The year 1891, which was the beginning of this era, saw a shift in the attitude on the part of the papacy, which up to this point had steadfastly opposed Modernism, but now placed an emphasis on confronting it head-on by attempting to shape society in accordance with Catholic social teaching. The year 1965, which marks the closing point of the era, constitutes another watershed in the history of the church, as it witnessed the end of the Second Vatican Council and the emergence of a host of enormous challenges to the "traditional" Catholic mind-set and religious practices.

Religious orders have been in existence for more than 16 centuries, during which time they experienced cycles of expansion, stagnation, and even collapse due to various upheavals. One great period of upheaval in the modern era was caused by the French Revolution of 1789; yet by 1850, the decline that had set in was reversed. Indeed, over the nineteenth century as a whole, more than six hundred new religious orders were founded within the Catholic Church (the church) worldwide.[2] A distinguishing feature of these new orders, along with some of the older ones that were reconstituted, was that they were oriented around specific areas of work. Teaching was one of the most prominent of such works, so much so that, as Wittberg has pointed out, the century has been designated by some authorities as "the age of the teaching orders within the history of the Church."[3]

The staffing of Catholic schools throughout much of the nineteenth and twentieth centuries with teachers who were members of religious orders (the teaching religious) was crucial to the church's educational project during this era. As teaching was constructed by the church as a vocation rather than as a career, they were able to ensure that Catholic schooling was shaped in a manner that served the church's interests. Overriding all else was the interest in making sure that religious instruction was provided in the schools. The outcome was the provision of special lessons in which Catholic prayers and doctrines were taught. In addition, great stress was placed on using every opportunity to promote Catholic principles and ideals when teaching the various subjects on the secular curriculum, while religious pictures, statues, and extracurricular activities were harnessed to great effect to create an all-pervasive religious atmosphere in the schools.

The church also stressed the importance of providing a basic elementary education in reading, writing, and arithmetic for the majority of Catholic children. Viewed in the widest sense, this great expansion in the nineteenth century can be seen as having been part of a major social effort driven by the middle classes in various European countries, which cut across religious denominations and was aimed at pacifying and regulating the lower classes.[4] The Catholic Church, however, had its own additional motivation, driven by its mood of intransigent defiance as it responded internationally to what it saw as a hostile world. In other words, schools came to be seen by the church as one of its instruments for holding on to, and reestablishing its control over, the faithful at a time when it was rapidly losing its temporal influence. Intimately related to this was the view of the Catholic Hierarchy (the hierarchy),[5] in countries where Catholicism was not the religion of the majority, that education was important in elevating the status of Catholics so that, in turn, the status of the church itself would be elevated. For this reason also, the Church expanded its efforts in secondary schooling with the advent across many Western countries of mass state secondary school education.

Given the extent of the involvement of the teaching religious in Catholic education for over 150 years since the beginning of the nineteenth century, their demise throughout the English-speaking world today is most striking. Young people being educated in Catholic schools nowadays are usually taught by lay teachers and, more often than not, the school principals are lay men and women. Also, lay people tend to be in the majority on the boards of Catholic schools. Equally, the presence of nuns, religious brothers, and priests as teachers and administrators in the schools is minimal. The turning point was the middle of the 1960s and the opening up of the Catholic Church to the modern world as a result of the proceedings of the Second Vatican Council (1962–1965). This development resulted in a very significant exodus of the existing religious from their orders to return to the world as "lay people," a major decline in the average number of new recruits, and a consequent need to employ ever-greater numbers of lay teachers.[6]

Cognizance of the rapid disappearance of the religious from the schools provided one stimulus to write this book on Catholic teaching brothers throughout the English-speaking world, which concentrates on the period 1891–1965. I have been able to relate to this disappearance in a very personal manner because of the influence that the religious had on me for a significant portion of my life. This influence was brought to bear for the most part, though not totally, during much of my primary and all of my secondary school education in the Republic of Ireland, where I was born in 1953. This was the heyday of the "triumphalist Catholic Church"[7] within the country. It was a time when, as Inglis[8] has put it:

> There was a priest, nun and brother in every corner of society. They presided over schools, hospitals and a wide variety of social welfare institutions...Like all good authority figures, their supervision and

> control persisted even in their absence. In the most subtle and yet penetrative forms of power, the supervisory eye of the Church was internalized in the minds and hearts of Irish Catholics.

The education sector was one area in which the supervisory eye of the religious was most prominent. While a national department of education oversaw primary, secondary, and technical education throughout the nation, it was administered, in the main, by loyal conservative Catholics who had no desire to threaten the dominance that the church had achieved in the provision of schooling for the majority Catholic population in the latter days of British rule in the country, and that was reinforced in the decades after independence in 1922.[9] Church personnel were also centrally involved in the development of curricula, which had a strong religious ethos, for primary and secondary schools in newly independent Ireland.[10] Primary schools sought to develop basic skills of literacy and numeracy, while the focus at the secondary school level was on a general academic education in the grammar school tradition, with an emphasis on rote memory work and lower cognitive skills.[11] A major emphasis was also placed on nation building through the promotion of the Irish language.[12]

Most of my primary and all of my secondary schooling within this system took place in Lismore, County Waterford, under the tutelage of those I referred to then as "the Christian Brothers"; it was not until the very end of my secondary school days I discovered that they were known internationally as "the Irish Christian Brothers" and also that other orders of brothers existed. I commenced school when I was four years old. For the first three years, I went to the primary school around the corner from my home. Here, I was taught in a coeducational setting. This was the "nuns' school," run by the Presentation Sisters. At seven years of age, like many generations of boys before me, and many more after, my male peers and I were transferred to the all-boys' primary school run by the brothers,[13] which was located at the other end of the town. This was a two-teacher primary school in which multigrade teaching was the norm; one brother taught grades two, three, and four, and another taught grades five and six. The regime was stern, and day after day we were slapped for failing to provide the correct answers in tests in "mental arithmetic" and spelling, for poor penmanship, and for talking in class without permission. Yet, I have no memory of the "slaps," or "fops," as we termed them, being brutal. Neither have I any memory of my peers, or I, ever expressing to each other that it was an inappropriate practice. I think we just got used to it, accepting it as part of what schooling by the brothers was about. Occasionally, however, we did hear stories of boys in some of the much larger urban schools getting terrible beatings with hurley sticks, and I distinctly recall conversations during which we expressed to each other how lucky we were that such activity was unheard of in our own little small-town school. Also, I must say that I was never subjected to any kind of sexual abuse in primary, or secondary school, never witnessed it, and never heard any whisperings of it taking place.

Besides following the state-prescribed primary-school syllabus, life in primary school involved receiving daily religious instruction, being prepared for confirmation, and being trained to be an altar boy. We were also encouraged to become members of the local junior branch of the Legion of Mary,[14] which met every Sunday for prayer and to motivate us to engage in charitable work with the sick and the elderly in the local area. Each year we received a visit from a brother, whose particular job it was to present talks in schools with the aim of trying to gain recruits for the order. He spoke to us during school religious instruction periods on the important work of the order throughout the country, but I cannot recall any mention being made of work overseas, including those on the mission fields.

In my final year in primary school, I was one of a small group in my class who received additional instruction by way of preparation for the very competitive Waterford County Council scholarship examinations. Success in these examinations meant that I was able to join the ranks of the privileged 25 percent of those proceeding nationally from primary to secondary school, with the additional benefit of having my school fees paid by the state. The physical act of proceeding to secondary school meant a journey of about 30 meters; the primary school was housed in two big ground-floor rooms of a two-story building, and the secondary school was located upstairs in four smaller rooms. Our five-year program of secondary schooling was conducted by four teachers, two of them brothers and two lay teachers. There were separate classrooms for pupils in each of the first three grades, but those in the fourth and fifth grades were taught as a unit on a multigrade teaching model.

My memory of secondary schooling is that the brothers controlled all operations, with the lay teachers being concerned solely with teaching their subject specialism. This reflected the pattern throughout the nation of lay teachers being a clearly marginalized educational interest group.[15] The religious secondary school authorities excluded them from school policy development by identifying them merely as "assistant teachers." The standard argument of the religious was that they themselves were eminently more suited to determining policy and administering the schools because of their religious commitment, their total devotion to their work, and the fact that they were not distracted by family demands and problems. In addition, religious authorities defended the employment of those priests, brothers, and nuns in schools who were not registered teachers, on the grounds that while they did not have university degrees, they were much more suitable than lay university graduates because of their greater religious, moral, and social convictions. Nevertheless, as far as I know, the brothers who taught me in secondary school all did have university degrees, while they had also been trained as primary school teachers.

Daily religious instruction continued in secondary school. Wednesday was the most loved day of the school week because in the afternoons we went to the local sports field to play the traditional Irish game of hurling; soccer, rugby, cricket, and hockey were definitely off the agenda, being, we were told, the games of the British Army, who had ensured that Ireland remained a colony of Britain for centuries. As in primary school, the regime in secondary school was stern, although the ritualistic daily punishment slowly diminished as we proceeded through the grades. The annual visits from the recruiting brother continued, and I remember welcoming them simply because the talks he gave broke the monotony of the daily routine of school. I never once seriously considered joining the order. Neither did I ever seriously consider joining any of the various orders of priests with which we were familiar, although we got plenty of encouragement from their particular "recruitment personnel," who also visited the school regularly and were given time slots to speak to us about their way of life. Unlike the brothers' own recruitment personnel, those representing different religious orders of missionary priests spent most of their time eulogizing the work of their peers on the mission fields of Africa and other exotic locations where, they stated, "the need was great."

As I approached my final secondary school examinations, the brother superior engaged me in various conversations at recess time on my plans for the future, encouraged me to become a teacher, made me aware of the existence of various higher education scholarships for which I subsequently applied, and wrote references and letters of commendation for me. He also told me that once I graduated as a teacher, I should seek him out and he would help me to obtain my first teaching post. Four years later, in 1975, I acted on his advice, and in September I took up a position as a high school teacher in Dublin, at a Christian Brothers' school. There were three brothers on the staff, and they were very welcoming. In that year I recall living in the hope of getting an opportunity to ask them to explain to me a number of observations about their way of life that I had made during my secondary school years, and that had prompted various questions that still remained with me. Now, I thought, I had the chance to find out why the brothers in my local town had always walked in single file, about 30 meters apart from each other, as they traveled from their monastery to the local convent to attend daily mass. I had for some time been perplexed as to why they did not travel at least in pairs and converse with each other along the way, like the way my pals and I did as we headed off for school each morning.

For a long time I had also been perplexed as to why the brothers, who demonstrated their prowess on the playing field when taking us for games on Wednesday afternoons, had not been regular playing members on the local hurling and Gaelic football teams. This, to me, had seemed to be a situation of wasted opportunities as our local town-based team vied with those of neighboring towns and villages to win the regional tournaments promoted by the Gaelic Athletic Association. However, the opportunities that could yield answers did not arise. I had to wait quite a number of years before I gained enlightenment, and then it was through engaging in historical research on primary source documents, rather than through conversations with any brothers.

In 1976, I moved back to my hometown to take up a teaching position in the neighboring town of Cappoquin. While the position in question, which I held for 12 years, interspersed by lengthy periods of absence on postgraduate study, was at a coeducational school run by the Sisters of Mercy, I became friends with those who comprised the brothers' community in my hometown. By now, following the liberating influence of the Second Vatican Council (1962–1965), social relations between the religious and lay people were freer than they had been in my own school days. For example, for quite a number of years, one particular brother accompanied my three friends and I on our daily punishing ten-mile runs as we prepared for a series of annual marathon races, and he was a regular participant in all of the good-humored banter in which we engaged. Then, in 1989, when my wife and I decided to investigate the possibility of spending a number of years as volunteer workers in a developing country, my main source of information was the Christian Brothers. The outcome was that we spent two years on a Catholic mission station on the Gazelle Peninsula on the island of New Britain in Papua New Guinea, where I was head of a small department of education studies in a teachers' college that trained women primary schoolteachers. While this college was run by an order of teaching nuns and was where I spent the bulk of my time, I became closely associated with a nearby teachers' college for Papua New Guinean men run by the Christian Brothers. Along with working with some of the resident brothers in the provision of professional development programs for lecturing staff in both colleges, my family and I were regularly invited to their house for meals and social conversation, and we always liked to reciprocate, as the resident Australian brothers proved to be great company. Occasionally, we exchanged stories on the accounts of the sex-abuse scandals involving the teaching religious, including brothers, which were beginning to be reported in various places around the world, and I have a vivid memory of the brothers with whom I mixed expressing horror, sadness, and shame about what had taken place.

Once I left Papua New Guinea, in 1991, and moved to Australia to take up an academic position at university level, my contact with the brothers diminished greatly, but their influence continued to be central within my own conceptual framework for understanding, and engaging with, the world. By now, I was beginning to develop a research agenda on the history of the role of the religious in Catholic education internationally and present papers in the field at various conferences regarding the history of education. The presentations seemed to provoke a certain amount of interest, especially among those who had never experienced a Catholic education themselves, and many very engaging follow-up conversations ensued. These ranged across a variety of topics, but there was one recurring set of questions year after year. Time and again, fellow historians of education would point out to me that they felt they had an understanding of what characterized priests and nuns who were teachers, but they had no idea about what was distinctive about teaching brothers, apart from realizing that they lived in community, were not ordained priests and, consequently, were not empowered to administer the Seven Sacraments of the church. Is it, they asked, that they are the male equivalent of nuns? Or, are they some kind of second-class priests, perhaps those who have not quite made the grade? I always did my best to provide explanations during coffee breaks and afternoon tea, but the more I tried, the more I came to realize that the understandings I took for granted because of the role that the brothers had played in my own life required the provision of extensive explanations for those who had had no such experiences. Increasingly, I was urged by academic peers to find some way to disseminate these explanations so that they would be available to a wide audience. This work is the product of my attempt to respond to their urgings.

As I started to engage in the initial research for this book, I quickly became aware that no similar work had been written before that would be instructive for the "general" reader. This situation contrasts greatly with the growth in recent years of more specialized historical expositions on individual orders of the teaching religious in Catholic schools in particular countries, especially in the last 150 years. Since many of these works have been produced by the teaching religious themselves, to document the activities of their predecessors, they tend, in the main, to be largely hagiographic, with very little attention being paid to the nature of the daily life within the cloister and the classroom. This is unfortunate, given the potential of such expositions to contribute to our understanding of the history of religion and that of Catholic education. In addition, I have long held that expositions of such a nature could be instructive for the contemporary teaching profession and for those interested in alternative perspectives on teachers' lives. In particular, they could be used to promote reflection on the possibility that teaching can be influenced by discourses of "vocation" and "the giving of service," every bit as much as it can be by positions based on "industrial" and "labor" perspectives.

This book on the life of teaching brothers throughout the English-speaking world during the period 1891–1965, therefore, grew out of a desire to make a scholarly contribution aimed both at addressing the deficit in the corpus of historical work noted earlier and at providing contemporary educational professionals with some food for thought regarding how teaching can be viewed in ways other than the stereotypical. The decision to focus specifically on the brothers was influenced by two factors. First, there was a realization, as has already been pointed out, that of the three broad "types" of the teaching religious—priests, brothers, and nuns—the brothers are the least understood. This is not to argue that, generally, nuns and priests are understood correctly; far from it, as will be made clear in later chapters. Rather, it is to contend that, however inaccurate such an understanding may be, there is at least a fairly wide "popular" understanding of what constitutes a priest and a nun, but the nature of what constitutes a brother is a mystery to many.

The second reason for focusing on the teaching brothers is that, of the three groups of the teaching religious they are by far the most neglected within the body of historical scholarship on Catholic education generally, particularly when one keeps in mind the level of attention paid to nuns in the literature in recent years.[16]

A major paradigm shift within the church following the Second Vatican Council facilitated this attention, with nuns being given opportunities to question the long-standing view that they were unequal to the professional caste of the priesthood.[17] It also allowed them to depart from a self-definition of their historical identity as one of silent serving and to put aside their reluctance to promote their achievements.[18] The new openness created also resulted in the religious communities of nuns making their private archives more accessible to scholars. Religious brothers, for whatever reason, did not respond with the same degree of enthusiasm to the opportunities presented.

Among the most significant of the works to appear on nuns is McNamara's *Sisters in Arms: Catholic Nuns through Two Millennia*,[19] which argues that the experience of the women religious has been one of struggle to gain power and recognition within the church for their contributions, and Wittberg's *The Rise and Fall of Catholic Religious Orders: A Social Movement Perspective*,[20] which analyzes the impact of the women religious on the history of the United States. Specifically in relation to Canada, a rich body of comparable research emerged in the late 1990s in relation to French-speaking Quebec, while for the predominantly English-speaking provinces in Canada a complementary body of scholarship also began to appear.[21] Burley[22] identified the emergence of a corresponding literature in Australia, while Collins[23] responded for the New Zealand scene to Perko's[24] point regarding scholarship in the United States, where he concluded that studies of the "lived experience" of religious teachers are very much in their infancy. Major works on the role of nuns in Ireland, including in education, are those of Clear[25] and Peckham-Margay,[26] while Walsh[27] and Mangion[28] have produced complementary volumes on the situation in England and Wales.

Such accounts of nuns have not been matched by similar accounts of teaching brothers, or priests, as teachers. Indeed, brothers are almost invisible in the general scholarly literature, largely appearing only in works produced for internal circulation by individual orders on the origins and development of their communities in various times and places.[29] With regard to the United States, for example, it was concluded in the year 2000 that while Roman Catholic religious brothers have been highly influential, their lives and work have been "overshadowed by those of their female opposite numbers."[30] Similarly, it has been made clear about the Australian scene that a most glaring gap in the study of Catholic religious teachers is the paucity of research focusing on male religious teachers, particularly teaching brothers.[31] The situation also applies to much of the remainder of the English-speaking world.

This book is offered as a contribution toward addressing this need. The focus of the book is on the "traditional" English-speaking countries with Catholic populations, and on their emigrant communities, in the United States, Ireland, England, Australia, and New Zealand, during the period 1891–1965. However, some attention is given also to the missionary work of brothers, work that was defined within the church as that particular evangelization, or special activity, disposed toward those who had never heard the Gospel. Finally, the book ends with some attention being paid to the period from 1965 onward, the year that marked the end of the Second Vatican Council and the emergence of a host of enormous challenges to the "traditional" Catholic mind-set and religious practices. This situation, as has already been pointed out, was accompanied by a major departure of the existing religious, including the teaching brothers, a rapid decline in the average number of new recruits, and a consequent employment of lay teachers in order to maintain the Catholic schools in existence.

The research project, which culminated in this book, was conceptualized in very basic terms. It took a lead from Clear's contention that such foundational works should concern themselves with "the whats, the wheres, the whos and, to some extent, the whys."[32] In other words, it was felt that an approach guided by a set of general questions, rather than by any specific hypothesis, would be the most productive one to adopt in seeking to produce a pioneering account that would relate to the work of a range of religious orders of the teaching brothers in various countries throughout the English-speaking world, and it would also address the life cycle of "typical" members of the orders for much of the period. Equally, it was recognized that, as the work unfolded, various specific areas worthy of research in greater detail by others would be likely to present themselves and should be outlined. Also, I consider it important to make it clear that I have already explored different aspects of a number of issues dealt with in this book in a range of previously published works, the titles of which appear in the bibliography. Where I have quoted extensively from these works, as well as revisited some of the expositions within them, I give full attribution in related endnotes. These draw attention to various issues I have examined in relation not only to the lives of religious teaching brothers, but also to the lives of priests and nuns, and to the fact that treatment has usually related to specific religious orders, geographical contexts, and relatively short time periods. What makes this work different is that it pertains to religious teaching brothers more specifically, to a longer time period, and to a broader sweep of the English-speaking world.

It is essential to explicitly state at this point that while the book is concerned primarily with the life of religious teaching brothers, the emphasis is more on delineating the broad parameters within which that life was constructed and regulated, rather than with capturing lived experience. There are two reasons for this. First, I held from the commencement of the project upon which it is based that the broad outlines of the system within which the religious life was conceptualized, constructed, and regulated needs to be accurately outlined, and the various influences on that outline need to be determined before further research can be undertaken. Along with consulting a range of secondary sources on the general history of the period, as well as on the more specific history of the Catholic Church, it was necessary to this end to interrogate documentary evidence on the vision, or moral purpose, of the orders. Particular attention was paid to the "constitutions" of the orders as they elaborated on how their shared vision was to be realized, and the "books of customs" that described adaptations to local circumstances. Second, while some source material does exist on the lived experience of religious teaching brothers, and while I use it to full effect throughout the book, it is a very slim corpus of work indeed. This is partly because a religious brother was explicitly trained not to reflect on his life as an individual, and partly because he was most definitely expected not to document any of the inner, private, and perhaps divergent, thoughts regarding his life. Nevertheless, as the final chapter of this book indicates, there are a number of avenues that scholars could take in addressing at least some aspects of this deficit in future work.

As has already been pointed out, the central theme that was generated as a result ot taking the research approach outlined so far, is that the commitment of the teaching brothers was, first and foremost, to their religious life, and that teaching, while deemed to be a very important role, was always in accord with, and where necessary took second place to, that life. This theme is elaborated on in various ways in the remaining eight chapters that follow. Chapter Two provides a broad historical background. Chapter Three is concerned with how teaching brothers were constructed by the church as being different both from lay people and their fellow religious. Chapter Four deals with the avenues utilized by the church in recruiting members for the religious orders of brothers. Chapter Five provides an exposition on one of the most distinguishing characteristics of the life of a teaching brother, as with all fellow religious, namely, that it was conducted within a very authoritarian framework. Chapter Six is concerned largely with the manner in which the worldview into which brothers were immersed influenced the process of education that they adopted in their schools. Chapter Seven deals with the momentous changes brought about by the Second Vatican Council (1962–1965). Chapter Eight examines another radical turn within the history of the church, namely, the exposure of a host of child-abuse scandals within schools, including schools of brothers. Finally, Chapter Nine, provides an overview on the book and indicates what the future seems to hold for the religious orders of teaching brothers.

CHAPTER 2

The Church and Its Teaching Orders

Since the Middle Ages religious orders have played critical roles in the internal struggles of the Catholic Church. The mendicant orders—the Dominicans and the Franciscans—have fought to maintain Catholic orthodoxy and religious devotion to poverty. As Italy entered the Renaissance, friars from both orders were in the forefront of those excoriating the spread of what they called epicureanism or worldliness. Their interventions, of course, were not always appreciated by secular and ecclesiastical princes devoted to the culture of ancient Greece and Rome. The Dominicans have maintained an institutional base in the Inquisition and its successor congregations (presently CDF), while the Franciscans have continued to represent papal interests in the Holy Land.[1]

The work of the teaching orders can be added to this list of the long and extensive involvement of the religious orders in the affairs of the world over the centuries. This chapter outlines some broad parameters within which such work took place. It opens with an account of the involvement of the Catholic Church in education from the early days of Christianity, with particular attention being given to the great expansion in the teaching orders and their work in the period from the early decades of the nineteenth century until the immediate years after the Second Vatican Council (1962–1965). The second part of the chapter sketches out developments in Catholic education and the presence of teaching brothers in the enterprise in the United States, England, Ireland, Australia, and New Zealand, which are the principal English-speaking countries in which the orders were active over the period 1891–1965.[2] Finally, there is a broad outline of the origins of, and developments within, some of the major religious orders of teaching brothers.

The Church, Education, and the Expansion of the Teaching Orders

Brock and Tulasiewicz[3] have categorized the nature of the early provision of education by the church into three "types." The first of these types was education for the good of the soul. This has been defined as "schooling exclusively designed to assist salvation with articles of faith and rules of conduct, although from the very outset associated with basic literacy and numeracy."[4] The second type of education provided by the church has been defined as "preparation for secular administrative service in the converted society in which the Church was all powerful, or was allowed to hold power by a secular ruler."[5] The third type was "education for the priesthood."[6] This subsumed the first type and, in various instances, also included elements of the second. Brock and Tulasiewicz concluded by arguing that all three types of education were aimed at preserving the status quo in society and, thus, the hegemony of the church.

During the Middle Ages, the church and the state cooperated in the provision of education for the clergy in cathedral schools and for the laity in parochial schools. The emphasis was primarily on religion, with considerable time being devoted to the study of the scriptures. Associated with the work of St. Thomas Aquinas that sought to reconcile Christianity with Aristotle's realism was the development of training in systematic thought aimed at harmonizing the findings of reason and the "truths" of divine revelation. The outcome was an approach to learning that permeated the medieval schools and universities until the advent of the Renaissance and the growth of Protestantism. A prominent place within the curriculum was given to instruction based on the seven liberal arts.[7]

The Catholic Church's hegemony was rocked by the Reformation and the Age of Enlightenment. From the time of the Council of Trent (1545–1563) until the First Vatican Council in 1869, its influence ebbed and flowed. Members of the Society of Jesus (the Jesuits), established in 1534, played a major role in trying to stem the tide. They codified their curriculum and pedagogical approach in a document entitled the *ratio studiorum*, first printed in 1586. This approach has been summarized as follows:

> It specified a curriculum and teaching method organized by classes and grade levels. Patterned after Renaissance humanism, the program of classical studies spanned approximately seven years of instruction roughly equivalent to secondary and college education. The *studia*

> *imperiora* (secondary) curriculum emphasized the study of the classics (Latin and Greek), grammar and rhetoric. The *studia superiora* (college) curriculum emphasized philosophy, mathematics and science...The *ratio* emphasized a mental training in logical argument: thesis, evidence, objections, discussion, and final proof.[8]

Nearly 150 years later, a very different approach aimed at providing guidance in basic elementary education was provided by Jean Baptiste De La Salle, who founded an order of teaching brothers, which became popularly known as the De La Salle Brothers. First printed in 1720, his *Conduct of the Schools* specified a curriculum of reading, writing, arithmetic, and religion, with whole-class recitation as a favored method.[9]

Notwithstanding the educational work of the Jesuits, the De La Salle Brothers, and other teaching religious, both female and male, the church became further weakened with the advent of the French Revolution and the growth of liberal thought. Its response was to adopt a fortress mentality.[10] In particular, it engaged in an all-out war on Liberalism, viewing it as a doctrine fueling a desire to strip it of its worldly influence. Pope Pius IX clearly expressed this position when he articulated the Catholic denunciation of all things modern in his *Syllabus of Errors* of 1864.[11] This *Syllabus* condemned propositions favoring the withdrawal of state-supported schools from church control, the separation of the church and the state, and the abolition of the temporal power of the papacy.

The church, however, was fighting battles that it was losing rapidly, including those aimed at maintaining its power over its territories. The Franco-Prussian War was particularly devastating for the papacy, with Napoleon III being forced to withdraw his troops from Italy in August 1870, and Rome then surrendering to the Italian troops in September. A month later, Pope Pius IX suspended the First Vatican Council, which had been meeting since the preceding December. This council had been summoned to "restate the faith in certain matters where it had been attacked or misunderstood; to review the whole matter of clerical life and its needs," to provide new safeguards for Christian marriage and the Christian education of youth, and "to take up in this new age the ancient problems of the relations of Church and State and provide appropriate guidance, so as to promote peace and prosperity in the national life everywhere."[12] The council concluded with the promulgation of papal infallibility. Thus, as Hanson puts it, "The Pope received his strongest religious legitimacy as his temporal empire crumbled."[13]

The church, despite having the Papal States now reduced to no more than 108.7 acres, continued to react to the challenge of an increasingly pluralist and rationalistic society by a vigorous assertion of its exclusive claims to truth and authority.[14] In doing so, it was, at a time when it was unable to maintain its civil power over large tracts of territory, asserting that it was determined to tighten its spiritual power over the hearts and minds of its flock. The ideology underpinning the range of practices developed to this effect was termed "ultramontanism" by contemporaries, the reference being to "the man beyond the mountain living in Italy" (the pope) and to an assertion of the superiority of papal authority over that of local temporal, or spiritual, hierarchies. This ideology was distinguished, as Connolly suggests, "by its political conservatism, its exaltation of papal authority, and its acceptance of a dogmatic, combatative theology."[15] It also promoted a highly organized system of ecclesiastical administration that was clerically dominated, hierarchical, and strongly centralized.

Ultramontanism signaled a radical departure from the Gallicanism which for long had held sway within the Church. Strictly speaking, the term Gallicanism was used to characterize the state control that the French monarchy had established over national Catholicism prior to the French Revolution. A number of related trends, however, also came to be viewed as reflecting Gallicanism.[16] These included the variety of ways in which church officials in various countries had become supporters of their respective states, and the growth of ideas emphasizing the right of the church authorities within individual states to manage their affairs with minimal interference from Rome. A consequence of all of this activity, particularly during the eighteenth century, was the papacy suffering a severe loss of influence throughout Europe.

Ultramontanist activity set out not only to reverse this situation, but to strengthen the hand of Rome as well. An outcome of this was a reinvigoration of Catholicism in various parts of the world. The United States, where the Catholic proportion of the population increased from just over 8 percent in 1880, to over 22 percent by 1963, was one front that witnessed this development.[17] The church also flourished in Germany showing an increase in numbers and through involvement in social life, up to the end of the Weimar Republic.[18] In Britain, Catholics were particularly successful in achieving new levels of organizational strength and popular adherence in a society where, for centuries, they had been viewed as potential subversives of the Protestant constitution. Here, since 1829, they had full political rights as citizens of the state and were able to avail of government grants introduced to assist in the building of schools at a time when mass primary school education was being promoted to maintain social stability.[19]

The activity of the Catholic population in Britain that resulted in state financial assistance for the provision of schools so that the church could increase its control over the hearts and minds of its "flock" was part of its wider strategy in many parts of continental Europe aimed at increasing its influence over the faithful. This involved building on its very long tradition of involvement in education by placing a major emphasis on extending the provision of mass schooling for the lower classes. In this, it was facilitated greatly by the emergence and growth of a group of new socially active religious orders alongside those with a very old tradition of commitment to teaching and caring for the poor, the sick, and the aged.[20] Focusing on this development, Smyth has pointed out that the two groupings of religious orders were composed of communities, which had practical and moral purposes as well. She categorized them under the single term "religious" and explained their common characteristics as follows:

> They are enacted under Codes of Canon Law—the law of the Roman Catholic Church. Religious are groups of individuals who freely come together to enter into a vowed life within a community which is both formally recognised and regulated by the Church. Generally members take vows of poverty, chastity and obedience, pledging to uphold the charism, or mission, of the community. This shared vision of mission and the personal commitment to work collaboratively towards it within community life are fundamental characteristics of religious life.[21]

She went on to state that the vision, or moral purpose, of the "religious" was actualized through practical activities that shaped daily community life. Instructions as to what these activities should be, and how they should be carried out, have traditionally been codified in various manuals. Particularly important in this regard have been the "constitutions" that elaborated on how the charism, or shared vision of the organization's purpose, was to be realized, and the "books of customs" that described adaptations to local circumstances.

Catholic religious teaching orders were at the forefront in the expansion of Catholic schools not only in the traditional Catholic countries, but also in the great new wave of missionary work in the evangelization of non-Christians in Africa and Asia. Religious orders from France, Italy, Belgium, and Holland were particularly prominent in this movement.[22] They also served the church in its extensive outreach to emigrant communities.[23]

By the latter half of the nineteenth century, nuns, religious brothers, and priests, who staffed a growing number of Catholic schools throughout the English-speaking world, were significantly different from lay teachers in a number of ways. They were known not only because of their distinctive religious attire and their commitment to the teaching of religion, but also because of the range of work practices in which they engaged. As I have outlined elsewhere, their duties included the following:

> Cleaning the school, taking care of the surroundings, training various teams for competitions in sport, giving extra tuition to "slow-learners," conducting the work of the various religious "sodalities" for pupils and adults, organizing school concerts, engaging in a variety of fund-raising activities, and preparing pupils for the Sacraments of Confession, Communion and Confirmation. Where schools catered for boarders, it was often the classroom teacher who also supervised them after school hours and at weekends. Further, it was common, particularly in the case of nuns in religious orders teaching the poorer sections of society, for music lessons and speech lessons to be offered after school hours, often to Catholics and non-Catholics alike, to supplement the income which the particular communities derived from low school fees.[24]

While much of this work throughout the English-speaking world was carried out by nuns, teaching brothers were also prominent. Indeed, in some countries they, as with nuns, outnumbered the priests teaching in the schools.

Developments in Catholic Education in English-Speaking Countries and the Growth and Demise of the Religious Teaching Orders

From the early years of the nineteenth to the early decades of the twentieth century, there was a steady increase in Catholic education throughout much of the English-speaking world.[25] Concurrently, there was an increase in membership of the religious orders, including teaching orders. This development was particularly important to the church as it meant that the schools could be staffed by those most trusted for the enterprise. From the 1960s onward, however, a rapid decline was seen in the number of religious overall, including the teaching religious, throughout these same countries. In Britain, for example, the number of female religious fell by 43 percent, male religious by 82 percent, and male seminarians (those preparing to become religious) by 54 percent.[26] The situation in Canada and a number of Western European countries, which traditionally had supplied a large number of members for the religious orders, was along comparable lines.[27] Stark and Fink portray a similar situation for the United States as follows:

> In 1965 there were 181,421 nuns, 12,255 brothers and 48,046 male seminarians in the United States. Just five years later, in 1970, there were only 153,645 American nuns...the number of seminarians had declined to 28,819 and the number of brothers had dropped to 11,623.[28]

Furthermore, by 1995, the number of nuns in the United States had dropped to 92,107, brothers to 6,578, and seminarians to 5,083.

The overall decline in the number of religious in the United States represented a significant turning point in the history of Catholic education in that country. It is standard practice to trace this history back to the seventeenth century.[29] Parish schools were established under the leadership of John Carroll, who, in 1790, became the first bishop in the United States. By the end of his episcopacy in 1815, educational provision for Catholics had significantly expanded in the east coast states. In 1829, a decree was issued by the First Provincial Council of Baltimore requiring every parish to provide a school for the children in the area.[30] This became a major challenge, particularly with the great upsurge in Catholic immigration from the early 1800s from Ireland, Germany, Italy, and Eastern Europe.

Large numbers of parochial schools were established in New York, Massachusetts, Philadelphia, Kentucky, and Cincinnati, so that by the 1860s a network of Catholic schools was in place across the country.[31] By now, the number of public schools established by local political authorities was also increasing. Catholics expressed their opposition to the associated "common school movement," arguing that it was underpinned by an ideology that was mainly Protestant, and that the associated curriculum was deeply influenced by Protestant traditions.[32] The outcome was an increased determination on the part of most of the bishops to provide a Catholic education for children of Catholic parents.

The church pronounced officially on education at the various plenary councils of Baltimore. At the first council in 1852, the bishops called for the establishment of Catholic schools for Catholic children. Particular interest groups were also active. For example, Grant and

Hunt note that German Catholic bishops in the United States, "utilizing the appeal of the preservation of culture," were outspoken in their conviction "of the need for Catholic schools to preserve the faith and other customs of their flocks."[33] Meanwhile, the Catholic population of the United States had continued to grow due to immigration; the situation pertaining to the period between 1851 and 1870 has been summarized thus:

> A total of 1,349,897 Irish, almost all Catholic, and 1,739,135 Germans, many of whom were Catholic, landed in the United States, making up about 64 percent of the immigrants during the two decades.[34]

One major consequence of this growth was a continuing expansion in Catholic school enrolments. For example, in 1880, of the 6,143,222 Catholics in the United States, 405,234 were enrolled in 2,246 parish schools.[35] The relatively widespread growth of private Catholic secondary schools, operated directly by the religious orders, also originates from around this time.

Growth in Catholic education from the early 1900s took place against a background that witnessed a more planned approach to provision.[36] Greater uniformity was brought about at the diocesan level through the establishment of school boards and the appointment of superintendents. This was accompanied by the introduction of a clearer vision at the national level through the establishment of both the Catholic Educational Association and the National Catholic Welfare Conference.

The continuing growth in Catholic education in the United States could not have taken place without the very large teaching input of the religious orders. When, in 1790, John Carroll became the first bishop in the United States, there were no religious orders in the country, apart from the Jesuits. In his work aimed at establishing parish schools, Carroll encouraged the introduction of religious teaching orders from Europe. Then, in 1866, the Second Baltimore Conference stated that, as far as possible, all teachers in Catholic parish schools should be religious, with lay teachers being hired only as a last resort. So successful was the implementation of this policy that, by 1966, the number of priests teaching full-time in Catholic schools at all levels totaled over 12,000, that of brothers was nearly 6,000, and that of nuns was over 104,000.[37] This meant that the number of full-time religious teaching in the schools outnumbered that of the full-time lay teachers, which stood at 75,000. Taking this situation into consideration, and also the fact that a very large number of priests served as chaplains in schools and took time away from parish duties to teach part-time, it is not an overstatement to say that the religious exerted an enormous influence in Catholic schools in the United States.[38]

At the same time, however, it must be kept in mind that very soon the numbers attending Catholic schools began to decline, largely because of a declining birth rate. Furthermore, by the early 1990s, it was clear that a huge reduction in the number of teachers who were priests, brothers, and nuns, had taken place over the previous 25 years. The origins of this decline went back at least three decades. As Judge has put it:

> Between 1966 and 1978, fully ten thousand men left the priesthood, while the number of seminarians, or priests in training, declined by over 70 percent in the twenty years between 1964 and 1984. Between 1966 and 1980 the number of women religious dropped by 30 percent. In the three years immediately after the convening ofVatican II, 4,332 women in America left their religious orders.[39]

He concluded that the greatest single change had probably been in the composition of the teaching force; of the 150,000 teachers then employed in Catholic schools across the United States, only 7.8 percent happened to be members of religious orders. This was a very great change from the days when the schools were dependent on the religious for so much of their teaching.

Religious orders have had a much longer presence in England than in the United States. Indeed, White notes that, for 600 years before the Reformation, the religious houses "were the principal perpetuators of learning."[40] By the end of the reign of Elizabeth I, in 1603, however, the monastic houses had passed into the hands of the state, or of private individuals, and very few Catholic schools existed. It was nearly 200 years before the tide began to turn slowly in favor of Catholics once again. In 1829, they gained full political rights as citizens of the state, including the right to vote. Now, they set out to develop a separate educational system. Despite the hostile environment that still existed, they, like other religious denominations, were soon able to avail of government grants introduced to assist in the building of schools, as mass elementary education was promoted to maintain social stability. Development was such that by 1870 there were 770 Catholic elementary schools, of which 350 received some financial support from the state.[41]

A major landmark in Catholic education in England and Wales[42] was the passing of the 1944 Education Act. The church accepted what was termed "aided" status, whereby 50 percent of the capital expenditure would be paid by the local education authority, but governors would be appointed by the trustees of the school.[43] The bishops found themselves still having to raise large amounts of funding for their schools. Nevertheless, as O'Keefe has argued,[44] the passing of the act and the introduction of "secondary education for all" resulted in the Catholic school network in England and Wales experiencing continuous growth until the middle of the 1970s. Also, within the wider education scene, Catholic schools from the late 1950s underwent reorganization along comprehensive lines. By now, the Catholic population in England and Wales had grown extensively, having risen from 1,890,018 in 1918 to 2,392,983 in 1945; the figure was to reach 3,956,500 by 1965.[45] The number of Catholic schools and the numbers attending these schools had also grown—from 1,623 elementary and secondary schools with 39,000 pupils in 1918, to 1,990 elementary and secondary schools with 426,000 pupils in 1945.[46]

By the early 1950s, the Catholic population of 4.7 million, or 10.7 percent of the total population of England and Wales, had within it four distinct strands: the "recusant" Catholics who had retained their Catholicism from pre-Reformation days; the converts; Irish immigrants and their descendants, who constituted the largest strand; and the other immigrants, including the large number of refugees from Europe following the Second World War.[47] The great majority of this Catholic population "could reasonably be characterized as predominantly working class" and "overwhelmingly concentrated in the large urban-centres."[48] A new Catholic middle class was, however, emerging,[49] thanks partly to the effects of education. Furthermore, the potential of this effect was increased when, first, the passing of the Education Act of 1959 resulted in the granting of 75 percent of the capital costs of schools to the church,[50] and then, in February 1966, when the Secretary of State for Education and Science announced that grants for denominational schools would be increased to 80 percent to implement the reorganized schemes, and that applications for these would be invited from the church.

Notwithstanding the substantial financial support from the state, the advances in Catholic education in England and Wales, as in most of the English-speaking world, would not have been possible but for the work of the religious orders.[51] Indeed, as Buchanan has put it, "the religious orders played a disproportionately large role in all areas of Catholic life"[52] in England and Wales. Following trends throughout the English-speaking world, however, their presence in the schools began to seriously wane from the late 1960s. For example, between 1964 and 1974, the religious staff in schools declined from 5,857 to 3,813, a drop of 65 percent.[53] This decline continued; by the middle of the 1990s, the religious orders provided only 1 percent of the teachers in Catholic primary schools and less than 1 percent within the secondary school sector. Ironically, this situation prevailed at a time when Catholic schools constituted the largest number of fully denominational schools (2,102 compared to 2,031 for the Established Church) in England, formed 10 percent of the total number of schools in the country, and educated close to 10 percent of the total school population of 7,483,780.[54]

Over the centuries, Catholicism in Ireland remained stronger than it did in England, being the church of the majority despite being subjected to constant threat from outside forces. This threat was most severe during the seventeenth and eighteenth centuries when a series of "penal laws" was passed aimed at the removal of all rights to property, religion, and education from the "native" Irish. These laws were substantially relaxed in the latter half of the eighteenth century. Toward the beginning of the nineteenth century, a variety of Catholic schools established by individuals and religious orders grew alongside Protestant schools run by various voluntary groups.

A state-sponsored national (primary) school system, overseen by a board of commissioners, was established in Ireland in 1831, but by the late 1870s it had become an almost totally religious-managed system.[55] Because Catholics were in the majority throughout the country, the manager in the case of the majority of the national schools was the local Catholic priest, while ownership was vested in trustees who included the local Catholic bishop. A small number of Catholic schools, especially in urban areas, were managed by religious orders, whose members also staffed them. Regardless of the management, however, the schools were the property of the church bodies, while the state paid the bulk of the capital costs. For their part, the schools operated a state-prescribed timetable and curriculum, and religious instruction was permitted as a school subject. This situation continued in postindependent Ireland.

From the passing of the Intermediate Education (Ireland) Act of 1878, through to independence in 1922, direct government influence in secondary school education was kept to a minimum, primarily because of the opposition of the Catholic Church. While the secondary schools continued to receive government aid in independent Ireland from 1924 onward, they remained firmly in private hands, which, in the vast majority of cases, were those of diocesan priests, or members of religious orders.[56] The State Department of Education inspected schools and exercised a certain degree of supervision through its powers to sanction grants to secondary schools based on the inspection, but it was not concerned with founding secondary schools, or financing their building.

By the early 1960s, there were 3,789 primary schools in the country under the management of a local priest and staffed by 8,776 lay Catholic teachers.[57] Alongside these schools were the Catholic primary schools managed by priests and brothers whose staff consisted of 1,990 lay teachers and 2,948 religious. The latter included 442 Irish Christian Brothers, 114 De La Salle Brothers, 62 Presentation Brothers, 51 Patrician Brothers, 29 Franciscan Brothers, and 26 Marist Brothers.[58] Also, of the 4,110 secondary school teachers in the country in 1965, 2,384 were religious.[59] Of these religious, 340 were Irish Christian Brothers, 86 were De La Salle Brothers, 31 were Presentation Brothers, 30 were Patrician Brothers, 20 were Marist Brothers, and 10 were Franciscan Brothers.

This situation was about to change significantly as in the rest of the English-speaking world. Between 1970 and 1981, there was a dramatic decline in the number of individuals opting for the religious life in Ireland. This decline was particularly marked in the case of teaching orders, with the number of sisters engaged in primary school teaching declining by one third and those engaged in secondary school teaching by a quarter.[60] Overall, the decline in the number of brothers in the country was even more noticeable; in 1970 there were 2,540 brothers, but by 1995 this number was down to 1,479. This situation reflected an overall waning of the power of the Catholic Church in Ireland. The lack of members of religious orders had forced the withdrawal of the religious from many of the institutions they had established and a retreat to merely a token presence in others. To all, it was becoming apparent that the religious, who for so long had had such a high profile in Irish schools, were rapidly fading from the scene. The consequence of this for the church was that while it has lost little ground in the funding and control of its schools, its religious habitus has been undermined.[61]

The same can be concluded regarding Australia, where Irish Catholics have been influential throughout public life for over 200 years. A British penal colony was established in the late 1780s, and eventually six colonies emerged, with the government and administration of each being centralized in the capital cities. However, while the colonies were very strongly British and Protestant, both socially and culturally, they also had a significant Irish-Catholic minority. The general pattern by 1850 regarding educational provision was a mixture of government enterprise, occasional voluntary effort, and state aid to denominational schools. This situation was brought about through the insistence of the Anglican, Presbyterian, and Catholic churches that the control of schooling was their responsibility. Pressure from them resulted in grants being paid to religious societies to assist in payment of teachers' salaries and the cost of school buildings.

At the time of federation, in 1901, each Australian state had established a system of primary schools providing free, compulsory, and secular primary school education, which was controlled by government departments.[62] By now, financial aid to denominational schools had been abolished in each of the colonies. Catholic education was particularly badly hit by the associated acts,[63] and it was not until the 1950s and 1960s that Catholic schools once again began to benefit from even a small amount of government financial assistance. Developments following the deliberations of the Karmel Committee in 1972, however, turned the tide.[64] Soon the great majority of Catholic schools obtained 80 percent of their costs from the Australian state, or federal, governments, and also were able to apply for capital grants for refurbishing, or extending, schools.

In insisting on having its own schools, the Catholic Church in Australia reflected the mood of intransigent defiance of the church internationally to what it saw as a hostile world. In addition, throughout the nineteenth century, the great majority of Catholics in Australia were Irish born, or of Irish descent, and saw the schools as a mechanism for asserting their separate cultural identity. After the formation of the federation, the situation slowly began to change as Irish migration to Australia declined, while the number of Catholics from various parts of the rest of Europe slowly increased. Catholic schools continued to teach religion on their own terms, infuse other school subjects with a religious tone, and ensure that a religious ethos pervaded daily events. At the same time, Catholic primary schools adopted the various syllabi prescribed for state schools, with their emphasis on reading, writing, and arithmetic, while Catholic secondary schools came to be dominated by state public examinations.

The teaching religious played a central role in all of this activity. In the latter half of the nineteenth century, Australian bishops had succeeded in persuading a number of religious orders in European Catholic countries to send their members to Australia in order to establish and staff schools. The first major surge in the growth of the orders in the country was in the 1880s, with the second coming in the early 1900s.[65] Over the next 50 years, Catholic religious orders in Australia focused increasingly on education as Catholic schooling, like government schooling, sought to keep pace with the population growth. By 1950, there were 44 orders in the country involved in teaching: 27 of nuns, 8 of religious brothers, and 9 of priests.[66]

By the early 1960s, the Commonwealth Government, as has already been pointed out, had begun to provide some public funding for nongovernment schools. At the same time, there was a gradual replacement of the teaching orders by Catholic lay teachers. Within a 20-year span, matters had changed dramatically, with the proportion of lay to religious teachers being 90 percent to 10 percent, respectively. The gap increased further during the 1990s. Indeed, in 1996, in New South Wales, the most populous state in the nation, there were only 354 religious teachers in Catholic schools as opposed to 14,502 lay teachers.[67] Clearly, Australia was not proving to be an exception to the general decline in the number of the religious involved in Catholic schools throughout the English-speaking world.

Developments in New Zealand followed a similar pattern to that in Australia. Shortly after the first European settlers arrived in the 1790s, they were followed by Christian missionaries interested in the spiritual welfare both of the migrants and the indigenous Maori. They included Anglicans, Wesleyans, and French Catholic missionaries. The latter arrived mainly on the initiative of Irish immigrants who had migrated from Australia and who constituted the majority of the Catholic population.[68]

Most of the early European settlers regarded education as the responsibility of the churches, and for several decades, provision was organized on a denominational basis. Government grants to the main Christian churches for the building of schools were provided from 1847 to 1877. Soon, however, Catholic schools had to be self-financing and had to be staffed largely by members of the religious orders. This situation was brought about as a result of the passing of the Education Act of 1877, which made primary schooling compulsory for all children and set up a school system that would be free and secular. Most of the population accepted the arrangement, but some, most notably the Catholics, did not.

Over the next 100 years, the Catholic Church in New Zealand was very much an Irish church[69] as the number of Irish immigrants had soared in the 1860s, largely as a result of the discovery of gold in the Otago region. Parish schools were founded by the local diocesan clergy, and the religious orders also established their own schools. Between 1900 and 1950, the number of Catholic schools in New Zealand increased from 132 to 240, and enrolments increased from 10,687 to 30,504. This pattern of growth paralleled a similar growth in the Catholic population.[70] The period also witnessed an increase in the number of Catholic clergy in the country; between 1900 and 1950 the number of priests increased from 146 to 533, and the members of the religious orders increased from 691 to 2,094. Also, by the 1950s, the Irish born had become a much smaller proportion of the Catholic population, while an increasing proportion of children of Southern European Catholics began to be enrolled in the schools.

As in many other countries, a decline in the numbers joining the religious life also had begun to manifest itself. This put pressure on the church to reach a more favorable accommodation with the state in order to start appointing and paying large numbers of lay teachers. The eventual outcome was the 1975 "Integration Act," which was well received by the church. It laid out conditions under which a school could be admitted to the state system of education, while maintaining the right to give effect to its traditions and beliefs, including the teaching of religion. Once admitted, such costs as the teachers' salaries, school maintenance, and caretaker costs would be borne by the state.[71] This accommodation took place at the very time the religious orders' presence in the schools, including that of teaching brothers, began to seriously decline.

Regarding all of the countries considered so far in this section of the chapter, including New Zealand, the emphasis has been on the work of the teaching brothers in primary and secondary schools. It is important, however, to highlight that brothers throughout the English-speaking world were also, albeit to a much lesser extent, involved in other educational practices. For example, orders of brothers occasionally responded to local economic conditions and requests by providing specialist forms of education. When the Marist Brothers opened schools in Glasgow, Scotland, in the 1860s, they also conducted night classes to give secular and religious instruction to working males. O'Hagan notes that because there was a wide variety of ability between the adolescent and adult pupils, and because many were ashamed of exhibiting a lack of knowledge, the brothers had to be somewhat imaginative in their approach. This included the establishment of lending libraries under the auspices of the Parish Young Men's Society, "supplemented by brass band groups and drama societies."[72]

Another example in this regard is the second-level school opened at Abergowrie, in tropical northern Queensland, Australia, by the Irish Christian Brothers, in 1934.[73] Terence Maguire, the local bishop of Townsville and Australia's first native-born prelate, interpreted the emphasis at the time in Catholic social teaching on the decentralization of political power as implying that he should become involved in the development of rural society. He became convinced that he should promote a policy aimed at settling more farmers on more farms, make it possible for them to stay there, and diversify the kinds of farming being pursued in order to make it a less precarious way of life. He was particularly keen to see the establishment of a school where farmers' sons would get an education not only in the Catholic doctrine and principles, but also in the technical and scientific knowledge they would need to develop their farms, as well as in accountancy to help them conduct farming as a business. The Irish Christian Brothers responded by establishing a school at Abergowrie, which was conducted along such lines.

Brothers have also been involved in the teaching of deaf children.[74] The Abbe Michel de l'Epee is generally considered to have been the founder of deaf education, having opened a school for the deaf in France in 1760, where he pioneered his "instructional method of signs."[75] Developments based on his ideas and practices were brought to Canada by brothers of the French religious order, the Clercs de Saint Vaiteur, who, shortly after their arrival in 1848, opened a school for the deaf in Montreal. Around the same time the Irish Christian Brothers opened a school for the teaching of deaf boys at Cabra in County Dublin, Ireland.

The fact that the brothers conducted teacher training colleges for their own members will be considered in detail in Chapter Five. At this point, however, it needs to be noted that they also established a number of teacher training colleges for lay students. One such college was the De La Salle Teacher Training College at Hopwood Hall in the North of England, which was opened in 1947, to complement the only other male Catholic teacher training college in England at the time, namely, St. Mary's College, Strawberry Hill, in London, which was run by the Vincentian Fathers. The De La Salle order took on the operation of Hopwood Hall at the request of the bishops of the north of England and operated it until 1989.[76] The order also established seven teacher training colleges in the United States. Griffin has examined how these were established initially for members of the order only, but were later expanded to include provision for lay people.[77] The order also went on to develop in-service programs at the colleges for brothers, lay people, and nuns who were teachers.

Religious orders of brothers were also involved in providing education through liberal arts colleges and universities, some of which evolved from teacher training colleges. The De La Salle order was particularly prominent in this regard, establishing a wide network of such institutions worldwide. Currently, 20 of these are in South America, 20 in Mexico and Central America, 11 in the Philippines, nine in continental Europe, one in Pakistan, and one in non-English-speaking Africa at Abidjan-Riviera, along with Christ the Teacher Institute of Education in Kenya.[78] Within the English-speaking world, the order's most extensive provision has been in the United States, as part of the nation's overall Catholic universities and colleges' sector, which, by the beginning of the twenty-first century, had grown to around 240 in number. Historically, by far a greater number of such institutions has been run by priests and nuns, as well as by diocesan authorities and lay governing bodies.[79] Nevertheless, the brothers too have had a strong presence,[80] even with those orders who only established a single institution, as is the case with the Irish Christian Brothers, who established Iona College in New Rochelle, New York, in 1940.

The largest group of brothers' colleges and universities in the United States has been that comprising six De La Salle institutions. Among these, their Christian Brothers University, established at Memphis, Tennessee,[81] in 1871, functioned initially as a combined elementary school, high school, and college, granting both high school diplomas and bachelor's and master's degrees from 1871 to 1915, when the college division was suspended. Elementary classes were dropped in 1922, and the institution operated solely as a high school until 1940. It reestablished itself as a junior college in 1942 and began granting "associate of arts" degrees. Then, in 1953, it expanded into a four-year institution, initially offering degrees in business administration and electrical engineering. Over the next four decades, a whole range of bachelor's and master's degrees were added, while it also became a coeducational institution in 1970.

Manhattan College in Riverdale, New York, [82] founded in 1853, La Salle University in Philadelphia,[83] founded in 1863, Saint Mary's College in Moraga, California[84], also founded in 1863, Saint Mary's University of Minnesota in Winona, Minnesota,[85] founded in 1912, and Lewis University in Romeoville, Illinois,[86] founded in 1932, have similar histories in terms of starting out as multipurpose De La Salle institutions and progressing to become coeducational colleges and universities. Some also developed a reputation for certain specializations; Lewis University, for example, became known for its pioneering of aviation technology courses, and Manhattan College combined traditional liberal arts and sciences with professional and technical education in a single collegiate institution, while also having a major focus on the education of the disadvantaged. Furthermore, not all of them started out initially as De La Salle foundations. For example, the order did not assume direction of Lewis University until invited to do so in 1960, by Bishop Martin McNamara, bishop of Joliet. Saint Mary's College in California initially operated under archdiocesan direction until the archbishop of San Francisco, Joseph Alemany, persuaded the De La Salle superior general to send brothers in 1866 to assume direction of the college. Saint Mary's University of Minnesota was established by Bishop Patrick R. Heffron, the second bishop of Winona, and was run by diocesan clergy until it was purchased from the diocese by the De La Salle order in 1933. Manhattan College has had a different experience yet again, since its sponsoring board of trustees combined both secular independent members and De La Salle representatives.

A Broad Outline of the Origins of, and Developments within, Some of the Principal Religious Orders of Teaching Brothers

This final section of the chapter provides a broad outline of the origins of, and developments within, some of the principal religious orders of teaching brothers involved in education throughout the English-speaking world for the period under investigation, a number of which have been mentioned already. To provide an exposition on all religious orders of teaching brothers would necessitate a book in itself. This is not only because of the large number of them, but also because of the need to account for the intricacies of institutional histories and church politics. Here matters are restricted primarily to considering the three major religious orders of teaching brothers operating in the English-speaking world throughout the period, namely, the De La Salle Brothers, the Marist Brothers, and the Irish Christian Brothers. Some brief attention is also drawn to a range of orders with a much smaller membership.

The De La Salle Brothers is the popular term for the religious order of brothers more correctly known as the Institute of the Brothers of the Christian Schools. This order was established by a French priest, Jean Baptiste De La Salle, at Reims, in France, in 1680, and has been prominent in educational work of all kinds throughout the world since the eighteenth century. It was established in particular for the education of the children of artisans and the poor. Initially, the order was active, not so much in the establishment of schools, but in the provision of trained teachers for the existing Catholic schools in France. Its development of a codified approach to the curriculum and teaching in the *Conduct of the Schools* has already been noted in the first part of this chapter.

When the *Catholic Encyclopaedia* was published in 1913, it picked out two pedagogic innovations of the De La Salle Order for particular note. The first of these was the employment of the vernacular language in teaching reading.[87] This approach, so common at the present time that consideration of the possibility that other approaches might be undertaken rarely arise, was innovative when introduced by the De La Salle Order, since the practice in schools in France at the time was largely to teach reading by using Latin texts. The second innovation was the use of "the simultaneous method." This contrasted with "the common approach," which was that of one-on-one instruction within the groups of students allocated to individual teachers. The *Catholic Encyclopaedia* elaborated as follows:

> In the common schools the individual method was adhered to. Practicable enough when the number of pupils was very limited, the individual method gave rise, in classes that were numerous, to loss of time and disorder. Monitors became necessary, and these had often neither learning nor authority...To St. John Baptist De La Salle belongs the honour of having transformed the pedagogy of the elementary school. He required all his teachers to give the same lesson to all the pupils of a class, to question them constantly, to maintain discipline, and have silence observed.[88]

It was concluded that "a consequence of this new method of teaching was the dividing up of the children into distinct classes according to their attainments," and that later on there was "formation of sections into classes in which the children were too numerous or too unequal in mental development."[89]

During the French Revolution, the De La Salle Order was suppressed, but it was restored in 1802, and over the next ten years regrouping took place. Soon there were houses in Italy, Corsica, Belgium, the Island of Bourbon, and Cayenne. Within another 50 years, the order had a presence in Canada, the United States, Egypt, Germany, Singapore, Algiers, England, Ireland, Australia, Mauritius, India, the West Indies, the Cape Colony, and Australia.[90] Battersby notes that a sudden increase in the number of De La Salle Brothers in some of these countries took place in the early 1900s "due principally to an influx of brothers from France following the application in that country of the Waldeck-Rousseau laws of 1901, and of the Combes laws of 1904."[91] The order had over 10, 000 members in France at this time, and the result of the laws against religious congregations was that some 7,000 thousand of them were expelled and had to seek refuge abroad. Large groups went to South America, the United States, and Canada, while a small group went to Britain.

By the beginning of the twentieth century, De La Salle Brothers were offering education across much of the world in elementary schools, high schools, boarding schools, agricultural schools, technical and trade schools, and schools specializing in commercial subjects, as well as running teacher training institutions both for members of the order and Catholic lay students. Membership peaked during the early 1960s, when there were almost 16,000 members. Currently, about 7,000 brothers still exist worldwide. While this includes a presence in most English-speaking countries, the order is especially well represented in the francophone and Spanish-speaking parts of the world.

The next largest order of religious teaching brothers is the Marist Brothers, more correctly known as the Marist Brothers of the Schools. This order was founded in France, at La Valla, in 1817, by Marcellin Champagnat, a young French priest of the Society of Mary, otherwise known as the Marist Fathers (SM). The origin of the Marist Fathers was the Catholic revival that took place in the Archdiocese of Lyons after the French Revolution. A small group of young men preparing for ordination to be priests for the archdiocese decided to form a new religious order. They were influenced by the work of the Jesuits. However, they were also cognizant of the need "to do good quietly"; prior to the revolution, the Jesuits in Western Europe had been suppressed by the pope because he deemed them to have become too powerful within the church. The outcome was the establishment of the Marist Fathers, with the objective of facilitating the Catholic revival through conducting parish missions in France and doing missionary work overseas.

Champagnat was one of the early members of the Marist Fathers. He established the order of the Marist Brothers when he commenced training a group of young men as catechists and then went on to prepare them as teachers to educate poor boys according to the methods of the De La Salle Brothers. Eventually he formed them into a religious order based very much on the De La Salle "rules." Soon members were spreading across France in response to requests from parish priests to staff schools in their parishes. By 1840, when Champagnat died, there were 280 brothers working in education in various parts of the world, including in the Pacific Islands. The latter situation had come about due to the Vatican insistence that the Marist Fathers would only be "recognized" officially by the church if they accepted

Western Oceania as a field of overseas missionary work. Most of the existing religious orders were already committed to other areas of European expansion, and Oceania stood out as a major area in need of personnel to counter the work of Protestant missionaries. Due to their common origins, it was deemed only natural that the Marist Brothers would accompany the Marist Fathers. From here, they became established in Australia and New Zealand.

Currently, there are about 5,000 Marist Brothers in 77 countries. While this number of brothers is significantly less than it was in the 1950s and 1960s, there is still a strong presence in schools as teachers and administrators, and in retreat houses, as well as in teacher education and other areas of work. Brothers are spread, to use the order's own classification of areas in which its members work, across Africa and Madagascar, North America, Latin America, Asia, Europe, and Oceania and the Pacific.[92]

The third largest group of religious teaching brothers is the Irish Christian Brothers. This order is officially termed *Congregation Fratrum Christianorum*, but is commonly known among its members and those who attended their schools simply as the Christian Brothers. This sometimes leads to confusion with the De La Salle Brothers, who traditionally have often been given the same title in the local areas where they have worked. The Irish Christian Brothers order was established in the city of Waterford, Ireland, in 1802, by a wealthy merchant, Edmund Ignatius Rice, whose wife had died in childbirth ten years previously.[93] With the support of the local Catholic bishop, Dr. Hussey, he commenced his work by opening a school for poor boys in the city in the same year. In taking this direction, he was influenced by the work of the Presentation Sisters for the education of poor girls. Soon the order spread throughout Ireland, opening similar schools for poor boys in various major centers of population. The work extended to include not only primary, but also secondary and technical education, besides running orphanages and a school for the deaf. From Ireland, the order spread to Liverpool and other parts of England. By the second half of the nineteenth century, communities had been opened in Australia, Newfoundland, Gibraltar, New Zealand, and India, and early in the twentieth century the order had a presence in Rome and the United States. Later still, footholds were established in South Africa, South America, and Papua New Guinea.

Membership of the Irish Christian Brothers peaked in the early 1960s, with around 3,900 brothers. Like a great number of other orders, they have declined worldwide since then; in 2000, there were about 1,700 brothers, mainly located in the English-speaking world, especially in Ireland, Australia, and the United States. This decline made it impossible for the brothers to continue to take personal charge of the many schools and institutions that were established by the order. Also, while the order was far from extinction in 2000, there was much debate about rediscovering its original spirit and redefining who constituted the poor in the modern world. This resulted in new projects, including working with impoverished inner-city communities, the sick, and the marginalized in developing countries.

Among a range of smaller orders of teaching brothers is the Presentation Brothers, who also consider Edmund Rice to be their founder. They owe their origin to the decision of a few of the early Irish Christian Brothers to live strictly by the rule of the Presentation Sisters and place themselves under the jurisdiction of the local bishop. This happened in 1820, when the main body of the Irish Christian Brothers located themselves politically so that they were directly answerable to Rome. Eventually, in 1889, the Presentation Brothers also became directly answerable to Rome, although still as a separate religious order. They spread throughout Ireland and to the United States (1843), England (1876), and Canada (1910), establishing primary and secondary schools, industrial schools, and orphanages. Currently, around 100 Presentation Brothers live in Ireland, England, Canada, Ghana, St. Lucia, and Grenada.

Another small Irish order is that of the Patrician Brothers, whose official title is the Brothers of Saint Patrick. This order was founded by Dr. Daniel Delany, Bishop of Kildare and Leighlin, at Tullow, County Carlow, Ireland, in 1808. From here, schools were established in various parts of the country, and in Sydney and Madras. In 1893, the order became directly responsible to Rome rather than to local Catholic bishops. Today, Patrician Brothers are to be found in Ireland, the United States, India, Australia, Kenya, and Papua New Guinea. While their work is still primarily in teaching, some also work as chaplains in schools and other institutions, and as social workers and spiritual advisers in parishes.

The Marianists, officially known as the Society of Mary, is a much bigger order. They are somewhat unusual in that while they are dominated by brothers, they also have members who are priests; currently, there are about 500 priests and over 1,000 brothers. The order was founded by Joseph Chaminade, a priest who survived the persecution of Catholics during the French Revolution. At the present time, members are involved not only in primary, secondary, and university-level education, but also in community and parish work. They are to be found living in Canada, the United States, France, Italy,

Ireland, Spain, Chile, Kenya, Malawi, Zambia, Congo, Ivory Coast, and Tunisia.

Another order of religious teaching brothers is that of the Brothers of Christian Instruction, also known as the Ploermel Brothers. This order was founded in 1817, at Saint-Brieuc, Cotes-du-Nord, France, by Jean-Marie-Robert de la Mennais, and was modeled on the De La Salle Order. Initially, it was established to provide education for the poorer children in the Breton countryside. Eventually, it spread beyond the boundaries of France, largely to the French-speaking world, although a presence was also established in England, the United States, and some of the English-speaking African countries.

A similarly named order is that of the Brothers of Christian Instruction of St. Gabriel, popularly known as Gabrielite Brothers.[94] Its origin was the amalgamation, in 1835, of an order founded by St. Louis Grignon de Montfort in 1705, at La Rochelle, France, with another order founded by Monsignor Deshayes, Vicar-General of Rennes. From the beginning, the order was concerned with education, especially for the poor, for orphans, and for the physically challenged. It spread mainly throughout France and Germany, but also established a presence in Canada and the United States.

The order of St. John of God Brothers, officially known as the Brothers Hospitallers of Saint John of God, was founded in Spain by St. John of God, who was born in Portugal in 1495. It is primarily known for the care of the sick in countries around the world and for being officially entrusted with the medical care of the pope. However, the order also runs "special" schools for children with disabilities. Currently, in 49 countries throughout the world, St. John of God Brothers work with the poor, the sick, the handicapped, the elderly, and the dying in hospitals and health centers, in schools and in residential communities.

Another order is the Xaverian Brothers, founded in Bruges, Belgium, in 1839, by Theodore James Ryken. The order was named after St. Francis Xavier (1505–1562), the renowned missionary to the Far East and patron saint of the foreign missions. Initially, a school was opened in Bruges and a branch house was opened in Bury, Lancashire, England. Then, in 1854, brothers were sent to establish schools in Louisville, Kentucky, United States, on the invitation of the local bishop. Eventually, they spread to various areas in the United States, England and Belgium, conducting primary and secondary schools. In the first half of the twentieth century, the brothers also began opening schools and engaging in pastoral work in mission territories. Today they work in Belgium, Bolivia, Canada, Democratic

Republic of Congo, England, Haiti, Kenya, Lithuania, Uganda, and the United States.

Various other orders could be considered. These include the Holy Cross Brothers and the Sacred Heart Brothers, both of whom are involved primarily in schools in the United States, and the Brothers of Charity who, by contrast, are involved in 27 countries throughout the world. In another context, it would also be interesting to examine the work of a host of "local" religious orders, many of which were established by, and consequently were subject to the authority of, the bishops of individual diocese. Among such orders in Australia was that of the Brothers of the Sacred Heart[95] and the Brothers of St. John the Baptist. There are also fascinating accounts to be related like that of two Irish Christian Brothers who were invited to India by Dr. Patrick Joseph Carey, SJ., Vicar Apostolic of Bengal, in 1848, to establish a school and orphanage for poor boys and who ended up forming a distinct order called the Calcutta Brothers. The order continued to exist until 1890, when its members joined the Irish Christian Brothers.[96] And then there are the untold stories of small indigenous religious orders like the Brothers of St. Martin de Porres in the Sudan,[97] along with the failed attempts to establish a number of local orders of brothers in the United States.[98] Rather than elaborate on the fortunes of these and a wide range of other orders, however, the next chapter focuses on how brothers, including teaching brothers, were constructed by the church as being different both from the lay people and from the fellow religious.

CHAPTER 3

Brothers, Not Priests

The question is frequently asked of Brothers: How come you are only a Brother? Why did you stop there? Why didn't you go on to become a priest.[1]

So far, this book has focused very much on macroissues. It has been argued that the Catholic Church engaged in a major project from the beginning of the nineteenth century aimed at reestablishing its power and authority among the faithful, raising the status of Catholics socially so that the Church's own position in society would be elevated, and Christianizing people in the Catholic faith by setting up missions wherever the colonial powers established themselves. The provision of education was a major part of this project, and the teaching religious constituted the main teaching force in the schools that were established. Furthermore, alongside nuns and priests, brothers played a large part in the overall work of the teaching religious across the countries of the English-speaking world. A broad overview of the origins and spread of the main teaching orders of brothers operating in a variety of these countries, in missionary territories, and among emigrant communities, has also been provided.

Attention in this chapter is given to how teaching brothers were constructed by the church as being different from priests and nuns. The nature of this construction was often confusing for lay people, as the extract from a recruitment pamphlet produced by the Blessed Sacrament Brothers quoted at the opening of this chapter illustrates. The question posed in this extract was immediately addressed in the pamphlet with the refrain "the Brother *has* gone the whole way." This was reference to the view of religious brothers that they considered themselves equal to fellow religious within the divine hierarchy of vocations. They saw themselves as responding, just like priests and nuns, to a divine "call" to dedicate their lives to prayer and good works while living in community.

Priests, Brothers, and Nuns: Members of a Special Group Chosen by God

Central to the life of being a religious within the Catholic Church throughout the period under consideration in this book was living in a community so that all members could, as the rules of one religious order put it in the 1920s, "reduce within the bounds of Christian charity all those sentiments for relations with which flesh and blood would inspire them."[2] The particular rule went on to say that "it is not sufficient that the body quits the world, the heart also must break off all attachment thereto." Such rules were translated into a series of very strict practices aimed at detaching one even from one's family bonds. For example, various religious orders did not permit their members to keep memorabilia from, or make verbal references to, their lives before they joined the ranks. As Thompson reminds us, even contact and communication with families and friends were severely restricted, or prohibited.[3] In the case of many of the orders, this emphasis on "quitting the world" was taken so seriously that a member could not even visit a dying relative, or attend a parent's funeral, without gaining special permission, which was often not given.[4]

Thompson[5] goes on to argue that one of the origins of this stripping away of identity so that one would "die to the world" and be "born anew into Christ" was the Christian communal ideal that traced its roots back to scripture and the notion of a society in which there "does not exist among you Jew or Greek, slave or free, male or female; all are one in Christ Jesus" (Galatians 3.28). Wittberg takes a more social science perspective, viewing the situation as an example of how Catholicism responded to an inescapable consequence of all religions, namely, that "the members of any religion, or religion-based cultural system, will vary both in their ability and in their willingness to strive for, and attain, the ultimate sacred values of their faith."[6] She draws upon Weberian notions in her analysis, especially the argument that the sacred values that have been most cherished could not be attained by everyone, nor would everyone be desirous even of trying to attain them. Thus, she argues, there has been an "inevitable tendency towards status stratification between 'heroic', or 'virtuoso' religiosity, and 'mass' religiosity."[7] She concludes as follows:

> Religious virtuosity must be integrated into this larger ideological framework, and its links to the other symbolic elements must be specified. Is God more pleased with virtuoso than by mass spirituality? Will religious virtuosi achieve higher places in heaven? Are all members called to virtuoso spirituality, or are only a few so chosen? If the latter, who are those few and why are they selected? What are the signs of "true" religious virtuosi, and how can these persons be distinguished from fakers and hypocrites? Who is qualified to decide whether a particular form of virtuosi spirituality is genuinely pleasing to God?[8]

The remainder of this section of the chapter details in a general way how Catholicism responded, particularly throughout most of the period under consideration in this book, to such questions, by constructing the life of priests, brothers, and nuns as occupying a higher level spiritually than that of lay people. In considering the exposition, it should be kept in mind that such a construction also served the church well by legitimating its efforts aimed at recruiting new members to ensure not only the continuance of religious orders, but also their enlargement. An outcome was that for many decades throughout the period, the church continued to have a large, unpaid, and loyal workforce to service its expansionary activities.

Various scholars see the historical roots of religious life within the Catholic Church in "the pre-Christian occurrence and role of prophecy in Hebrew experience."[9] The general and popularly articulated position of the church, however, is based on the notion that it has required of all its adherents over the centuries that they respond to the call of God, through Jesus, "to discipleship, to the following of a way, to an accompanying of his ever-present personhood in our own life's journey."[10] The religious were seen as those who have been able to respond in a "special" way because of their "undivided hearts." In other words, the forsaking of marriage was viewed as allowing the religious to dedicate their lives to contemplation and prayer of such intensity that they could establish a powerful connection to God. The achievement of this connection was, in turn, seen as being a great asset in the effort to ensure one's own salvation. Furthermore, it was viewed as opening up for the religious the possibility of interceding with God on behalf of others. In time, the practice of working collectively to do "good works" developed in some religious orders. Again, this was seen not only as doing God's will on earth, but also as the taking of an additional step to try to ensure one's own salvation.

Living in community, with its associated symbols and practices, provided the binding force that kept the committed to their life of prayer and labor. Throughout most of the period under consideration, however, the situation was articulated in more spiritual terms in the various rules and constitutions of the religious orders. For example, the constitutions of the Canadian order, the Congregation of the Religious Hospitallers of St. Joseph, stated in the 1950s that the "general end" of the order was "to procure the glory of God by the sanctification of its members."[11] While the wording varied a little from order to order, the emphases were largely the same. [12] Two in particular stand out. The first was very much on the notion that by living the religious life members could, as the constitution of another order put it, "strive for the perfection of their state."[13] The constitution of some others spoke of the ultimate aim of the "rule" as being "the attending to our own perfection and salvation, under the influence of God's grace,"[14] and stated that members should constantly keep in mind the "primary obligation to seek perfection."[15] The notion here took on a number of meanings over the centuries. For some religious orders, what was being referred to was that their members could transform themselves through ascetic practices "and thus regain the purity of soul once possessed by unfallen humanity in Eden."[16] For others, it was a call to discipline the senses in ascetical practices. For yet others, it was a way of expressing a view that one could achieve "union with God in ecstatic mystical experiences" through spending hours in "rapt contemplation of the divine."[17]

The second emphasis in the core justification of the religious life was that it provided one of the best environments for living in accord with the vows of chastity, poverty, and obedience, and thus placed one squarely on the road to perfection. Chastity, as Wittberg has noted, has been a "basic constitutive behaviour of religious virtuosity in Roman Catholicism" ever since the establishment of religious orders. Indeed, as she points out, there has hardly ever been a religious order for which chastity was not an essential element.[18] She also argues, however, that over the centuries, there have been some changes in the reasons advanced for the sexual abstinence of the religious. It is helpful to view the variety of reasons as having oscillated between two extremes: at one end there has been a consideration of celibacy as being an extraordinary pure, or holy, state, while at the other end there has been a view that sexual intercourse can tend toward being evil. What has been constant throughout, however, has been a glorification of celibacy as representing a calling by God that is higher than marriage. Within the period that is the main focus of this book, such glorification was given its most comprehensive expression when Pope Pius XII issued his papal encyclical, *Sacra Virginitas*,[19] in 1954. This was a legitimation from the highest level of the long-standing practice of all the religious of taking the vow of chastity as a public expression of their commitment to their beliefs and way of life. It was also, as Sullivan has put it, a "rather Jansenist, negative, anti-sex stance."[20] Specifically in relation to brothers, as Bollen[21] has demonstrated, this meant that "if duty necessitated a short conversation with a female," great reserve and modesty were to be observed. Also, any female servants employed in the monastery to do domestic work "were to be of mature years and irreproachable character."[22] This was all code for saying that particularly attractive women should not be employed, and that brothers should, wherever possible, keep women at a distance and guard themselves against their charms.

The second vow taken by members of a religious order is that of poverty. The meanings attached to this vow have varied much more over the centuries than have the meanings attached to the vow of chastity. For most of the nineteenth and twentieth centuries, it meant that members were required to surrender their property to their religious order on entering the cloister and were not allowed to use, or lend, property without permission. In many orders, sets of associated practices, which were codified in minute detail, were outlined. They included such requirements as asking permission to use a pencil, or a piece of stationery. In the case of the brothers, Bollen points out, this meant that they had very few, if any, personal possessions beyond bare necessities; an annual clothing allowance, he notes, could mean that one was allocated just enough to buy "a pair of shoes, a pair of trousers, a couple of shirts, socks and a set of underwear."[23]

The reasons for taking the vow of poverty and living according to such practices have also varied greatly over time. They have included arguing that imitating the poverty of Christ can bring one closer to God, highlighting the potential of ascetical living in helping one achieve union with the Divine, and holding that renouncing possessions constitutes a barrier to coming in contact with worldly institutions and irreligious people. Another argument was that committing to foregoing a materialistic outlook maximizes one's potential to help the downtrodden and the marginalized.

The third vow taken by all the religious, that of obedience, has also varied in meaning over time. In the case of many orders of brothers during the period under consideration, however, the reality was as outlined by Bollen, namely, "willing compliance with the superior's directions and with rulings of the provincial and provincial chapters."[24] He goes on as follows on the dominant view among the religious:

> Its alternative was the Protestant evil of "private judgment." Disaster, schism, and disunion would easily arise if once simple Obedience to Superiors and Rules be tampered with, for Obedience is the very basis of the Religious Life.[25]

Specifically in the case of the Irish Christian Brothers in Australia, Bollen portrays a situation where no books were to be read except in the library of the monastery, there was to be no study or reading of nonreligious works after evening prayers, smoking was allowed only with permission from the superior-general, and "light alcoholic beverages were permitted to perpetually professed brothers, but spirits only with written consent from the provincial."[26] While there were slightly different interpretations of the vow in other orders, there was consensus among all of them that it had an essential role to play in maintaining their unity and direction.

The reality of what living in a community bound by the vows of chastity, poverty, and obedience meant in the middle of the twentieth century, has been put bluntly as follows:

> No wine, no women, no song or dance; no money, no fancy foods, or new clothes; no freedom to leave the monastic grounds when I chose; no newspapers, no radio or television, no record player or tape recorder; no car, not even a bicycle I could call my own; no contact with old friends outside the monastery, no contact with women at all.[27]

By living such an austere life, so the argument went, the religious would be seen as a symbol to the world that spiritual values were more important than material ones.[28] At the same time, it was known that the task would not be easy. Because of this, the superiors of religious houses were charged with the special responsibility of seeing that there was to be no straying by their subordinates from the straight and narrow. As the constitution of one order put it:

> The Superior should consider seriously that, by reason of her office, she will have to render an account to God of their perseverance in

> their vocation and of the spiritual and temporal welfare of the Sisters entrusted to her care.[29]

This largely meant that there should be constant monitoring of the religious to ensure they remained faithful to their vows by resisting all temptations to their commitment to "renouncing marital love, self-determination and the satisfaction of wealth and power."[30]

Because most orders decreed that their members were bound by "the exact observance"[31] of the aims and rules of their constitutions, the religious were obliged to read these regularly. Here their lives were depicted as being heroic sacrifices, and their work was portrayed as being extraordinarily difficult, yet borne with a cheerful spirit because it brought them closer than lay people to God. Passages in the rules and constitutions of religious orders could be called upon for neat summaries expressing the ends of what was referred to as the "noble calling" of those in religious life. These usually read along the following lines:

> [The aim of the Order is] the greater glory of God, that the members of it may not only apply themselves to attain their own salvation, but also employ themselves with all their power in promoting the spiritual improvement of their neighbour, by affording Religious and Secular education to children, and all such persons as may present themselves for instruction, in the truths of our Holy Religion.[32]

There were also references to the "special object" of an order being "the salvation of souls" and "the spirit" of an order being "mercy towards those who are afflicted with ignorance, suffering, and other like miseries."[33]

Thus, the religious were frequently reminded that the church considered them to be superior individuals who had, as it was put in the constitution of one order, a "high calling"[34] from God. In this way, they were engaged in habitually confirming for themselves that their way of life was a most lofty one. Their superiors also returned regularly to this theme and brought it to the attention of their members. For example, as late as 1968, at an international meeting of the Irish Christian Brothers who, as the previous chapter has outlined, had schools throughout the English-speaking world, the order's major superior reminded every member that he had a "special vocation"[35] and also that "the totality of his consecration to the Church's service and the uniqueness of the manner in which he responds to God's love" distinguished him "from the lay faithful."[36]

Clarifying the Nature of Religious Orders of Brothers by Differentiating between Orders of Priests, Brothers, and Nuns

In considerations so far, the terms "nuns," "priests," and "brothers" have been used as if they are clear-cut categories representing three clearly defined groupings of those leading the religious life within the Catholic Church. The reality, however, is much more complicated. The nature and extent of the complication is particularly confusing for many who are more familiar with other Christian churches. For one thing, they often expect all members of Catholic religious orders to be living a monastic life; but that is not the case. This is quite in contrast with the Eastern Church, where monasticism had its beginnings. Here, religious orders are not differentiated as they are in the West, and most Eastern Orthodox religious individuals are monastics.

Then, there are those who assume that in Western Christianity, living the life of a religious within an order of priests, brothers, or nuns, is the monopoly of Catholicism. Following the Reformation, monasticism did disappear in Protestant countries since it was contrary to the Lutheran doctrine of salvation through faith alone. Wittberg has summarized the argument for rejection as follows:

> The idea of a "depository" into which religious virtuosi channeled grace and from which the masses could draw indulgences—a popular metaphor in late medieval preaching—was antithetical to the Protestant emphasis on personal responsibility for one's salvation...In place of a dual system of virtuoso and mass spirituality, many Protestant denominations substituted a "this-worldly asceticism" by which *all* Christians were expected to work out their salvation...all were called equally to holiness.[37]

Nevertheless, the influence of the Oxford Movement in England in the nineteenth century brought about the reestablishment of religious orders among Anglicans.[38] A "most self-conscious ideology" concerning the religious life was also developed by the nineteenth-century Anglican hierarchy, "which promoted the establishment of religious communities in order to keep devout and unmarried Anglican women occupied" and to "forestall their defection to Methodism, or Catholicism."[39] In addition, a few other Protestant groups established religious orders, as did groups of ecumenical Christians at Taize in France.[40] Nevertheless, Catholic religious orders have continued to be by far the most visible among the Christian churches. Arguably, they are also the most complicated when it comes to trying to understand their relationship to one another and to church governance as a whole. The remainder of this section now illuminates the matter through an exposition on some of the main distinctions that can be drawn between, and within, religious orders of priests, brothers, and nuns. This then sets the broader scene for the specific considerations in later chapters on religious orders of teaching brothers.

The first major situation in need of clarification is that not all priests are members of religious orders. Rather, they can be divided into two principal groups, namely, diocesan priests and religious order priests. Traditionally, diocesan priests have only taken vows of chastity and obedience. Their main involvement has been in parish work, particularly administering the sacraments of the church and visiting the old and the infirm. Only a very small number have been involved in schools, at least on a full-time teaching basis. It was normal, however, for diocesan priests to visit schools regularly to supplement the teaching of religion conducted by the nuns and brothers. In some countries, each diocese had a boarding school too, generally known as a junior seminary, which was under the authority of the local bishop and staffed by diocesan priests. While the junior seminaries usually followed the secondary school curriculum of other Catholic schools in the state, or country, those who attended these schools were supposed to have some inkling that they might eventually attend a diocesan seminary and train to become diocesan priests themselves, and they were regularly encouraged to foster thoughts in that regard.

The great majority of schools staffed by priests were those conducted by individuals who lived together in communities as members of religious orders. Such priests are deemed by the church to have the same powers as diocesan priests in that they can celebrate Mass, remit sins, preach, and administer the sacraments. What distinguishes them from the rest of the laity and the clergy is their claim that they try to imitate Jesus of Nazareth by binding themselves publicly, or privately, through vows of poverty, chastity, and obedience, to lead a dedicated life. Additionally, as has already been pointed out in the previous section of this chapter, they may profess to obey certain guidelines for living and they are quite often devoted to some specific form of service.

The term "religious order" is itself also not without complication when considering how to classify different "types" of priests. There are actually two types of Catholic religious orders: those officially termed "orders," whose members take solemn vows, and those termed "congregations," whose members take simple vows. This distinction needs elaboration since it applies to nuns and brothers as well, even though the convention adopted throughout this book is to speak of them all as belonging to "orders." Strictly speaking, orders are of three types. First, there are the monastic orders of priests, of which the largest is the Benedictines. In some of these orders, their communities are enclosed, with the monks rarely leaving their monastery and devoting their lives to prayer and contemplation of "the Divine." The Cistercian Monks are among the most notable in this regard. Then, there are those orders of priests classified as Mendicant Orders of Friars. These include the Franciscan priests and the Dominican priests.[41] All of these make solemn vows and pray the Divine Office[42] in choir. In general, they all have their origin in the Middle Ages. Third, there are those religious orders of priests termed "Clerks Regular." These are societies of priests who take vows and are joined together for the purpose of priestly ministry; the Society of Jesus (the Jesuits) is a well-known example. Congregations, on the other hand, are societies of priests whose members are bound by vows and live in community to perform certain kinds of services. Included here are such organizations of priests as the Passionists, Redemptorists, and Vincentians.

Much the same distinction between orders and congregations exists in the case of those generally called "nuns." According to Canon Law, the common use of the term is inaccurate for most of those referred to as nuns, as officially they are termed "religious sisters." On this, Armstrong[43] has pointed out that, traditionally, Canon Law has defined nuns as belonging to an enclosed "order" of women remaining in convents throughout their lives and devoting their time to prayer and spiritual contemplation. Religious sisters, on the other hand, take simple vows of poverty, chastity, and obedience, and devote themselves to "prayer and good works." Sturrock's definition is helpful in elaborating on the distinction:

> The word "Nun" is the canonical term for female religious belonging to a strictly enclosed contemplative "order." The word "sister" is given to any religious who has taken vows and belongs to a "congregation." The "community" to which she belongs is usually a local group and part of the wider congregation.[44]

Traditionally, two characteristics have been fundamental to religious life: a shared sense of mission and the personal commitment to work collaboratively toward it.[45] As Smyth has stated, it was a changing sense of what constituted "serving God," and the perceived need for education and works of charity, that led to challenges to the official view that all nuns should remain within their convents and refrain from engaging in work in the community.[46] Peckham-Magray details the distinction that eventuated. She states that two canonically valid forms of religious organization for women evolved within the Catholic Church. First, there was the religious order. Women in these communities took solemn vows, were committed to strict enclosure within their convents, and received the title of "nun." Second, there was a newer form of organization known as the congregation. Women in congregations took simple, less binding, vows, worked outside the convent, and went by the title of "sister."[47] At the same time, the popular practice that developed, and that is adhered to throughout the remainder of this book, was to use both "nuns" and "religious orders" as generic terms and not to bother with the finer ecclesiastical distinctions in terminology.

Within most female religious orders, a distinction that reflected class divisions within the wider society was also made. For many years in those European countries where the religious orders originated, only those who paid a dowry were permitted to become "choir sisters" and train to become teachers or nurses. Those from poorer homes became "lay sisters." A lay sister was defined as a member of a religious order who was not bound to the recitation of the Divine Office and was occupied in manual work.[48] While the many convents that spread throughout the English-speaking world during the nineteenth and twentieth centuries were primarily the stronghold of the middle classes, they also attracted women of the lower classes. Typically from farming, or poor urban, backgrounds, these women were allowed to enter, but often only as "lay" sisters who took nonbinding vows, as opposed to the choir sisters who took solemn, lifelong vows. The general structure that developed was one in which lay sisters carried out the domestic work in the convents, particularly cooking and cleaning, so that choir sisters could be free to pray the Divine Office, engage in intellectual pursuits, and do the apostolic work of the congregation, which was usually either teaching or nursing. Through these practices, the class structure of the nineteenth century was reproduced in the convent and established a pattern that continued well into the twentieth century.

Trimingham Jack has written at length on lay sisters. She argues that the relationship between the choir sisters and lay sisters may be thought of as both hierarchical and symbiotic: "It was hierarchical in that the lay sisters were considered inferior to the choir nuns, it was symbiotic to the extent that each category was partly defined by the other."[49] She draws attention to the fact that in the theological explanation for the tiered system, lay sisters were referred to as having a vocation marked by simplicity and humble hidden service like that of Jesus of Nazareth, but argues that such glorification was, in reality, practiced as it allowed the choir sisters to feel comfortable about the lower status of their lay-sister peers by temporarily promoting it above their own. She draws an analogy with the romantic concept of the "noble savage," which was applied by Europeans to Australian Aborigines in the eighteenth and nineteenth centuries even as they were destroying that very culture. She concludes by saying that attempts to glorify the position of any group in a lower social position than ourselves "is a way of attributing to its members a status we are not prepared or able to offer them in a formal or ongoing way."[50]

The separation between choir sisters and lay sisters did not have a counterpart in the case of diocesan priests. However, it was very much in evidence among many of the male religious orders of priests since they had brothers of the order living with them under the same roof. This situation had its origins in a separation that arose in relation to males in Western monasticism in the Middle Ages. In the beginning, the members of religious communities were called "brothers" without distinction, and the great majority of them did not receive priestly ordination because they did not claim to have a vocation to the ministry. A priest could join these communities, but could not claim privilege just because he had holy orders.[51] When priests were needed, one of the brothers was ordained to meet the community's sacramental needs. Eventually, however, the practice developed whereby the more educated became priests and the others became brothers, even though there were many exceptions wherein those who were educated to a sufficient level to be ordained chose not to take that route.

The situation, then, was that, for the period of main interest in this book, brothers who were members of religious orders of priests were the counterpart of the lay sisters, as their work consisted of domestic duties. They usually assisted in the training institutions for young brothers, in boarding schools, and in welfare institutions in a number of roles: cooking, cleaning, and repairing and maintaining buildings, grounds, and equipment. Because of this orientation in their work, they played a very significant role among the missionary orders of priests, particularly when taking on the task of building mission stations. The life of a brother in this situation was often one of being on the move, cutting, building, and maintaining roads, as well erecting churches, schools, and houses.[52]

Brothers who were members of religious orders of priests differed from lay sisters in a number of ways. For one thing, they often sat with the priests at meals and partook in recreation with them. In some instances, they acted rather like teacher assistants, especially by involving themselves in coaching school sports teams. Also, their allocation to the lesser ranks had nothing to do with not having an equivalent of a choir sister's dowry on entering the order, a matter on which they were no different from priests who were members of the order. Rather, these religious brothers were individuals whose membership of the order was welcomed, but who usually were deemed to have insufficient intellectual ability for studies leading to ordination as priests.

As recently as February 22, 1995, Pope John Paul II summarized, as follows, the church's view on the contribution of religious brothers over several generations, those who, as he put it, led the "consecrated life" of the "male religious who do not receive Holy Orders":

> The Church's recent history confirms the important role played by the religious who belong to these institutes, especially in educational or charitable works. It can be said that in many places it is they who have given the young a Christian education, founding schools of every kind and for all levels. Again, it is they who have created and administered institutions offering social assistance to the sick and the physically and mentally handicapped, for whom they have also provided the necessary buildings and equipment. Thus their witness to the Christian faith, their dedication and their sacrifice should be admired and praised, while it is to be hoped that the aid of benefactors—in the best Christian tradition—and subsidies provided by modern social legislation may increasingly enable them to care for the poor... The "great esteem" expressed by the Council shows that the church's authority highly appreciates the gift offered by "brothers" to Christian society through the ages, and their collaboration in evangelization and in the pastoral and social care of peoples.[53]

Those being referred to here, like the religious orders of nuns and priests, lived in community with fellow members and took vows of poverty, chastity, and obedience. In addition, they were not ordained and, consequently, were not empowered to administer the Seven Sacraments of the Church.

Some religious congregations that only included brothers among their members had a small number of "domestic brothers" living in community with teaching brothers until the abolition of the distinction following the Second Vatican Council (1962–1965). Like lay sisters and brothers in religious orders of priests, domestic brothers were individuals whose membership was welcomed, but who were deemed not to have the level of intelligence required for enrolment in a program of teacher preparation, or other professional activities. Their principal duties were to prepare meals for the community, to keep the house clean, to "take care of provisions, furniture and utensils," "to superintend farm-work or trades, and occasionally to train boys for such avocations."[54] Just as with lay sisters, engagement in these activities was seen to be important as it allowed the colleagues of the domestic brothers to concentrate on their professional duties, including teaching, without being distracted by domestic chores. On this, the "Rule" of the Irish Christian Brothers decreed as follows:

> They [lay brothers] shall also be full of charity for the Brothers and shall serve them with joy and respect, conscious that it is Jesus Christ whom they serve in the person of their Brothers. They shall endeavour, as far as they can, to be useful to them, to procure them what they need, and to afford them every relief, especially in sickness.[55]

Unlike the situation with nuns, however, safeguards were in place to ensure that the lay brothers did not become marginalized within a congregation. Included among the safeguards was an expectation that they would take their meals with the teaching brothers and join them at recreation.

It is also important to be aware of the official relationship that the Catholic Hierarchy had with religious orders whose work was primarily teaching. For those not familiar with the bureaucratic structures of the church, the assumption often is that the bishops, who regularly speak and act with a powerful authority, held sway over all of the orders. It is certainly true that when it came to the decision as to whether or not an order could establish an initial foundation, usually a school, within a particular diocese, the local bishop had the final say. On this, Arthur gives the example of the decision of the English Jesuits to establish a secondary school in Manchester, encouraged by a decree on secondary education by the Fourth Synod of Westminster in 1873.[56] He goes on:

> The local bishop objected to the proposed school and campaigned to have the Jesuits made subject to Episcopal control in matters of educational provision. He appealed to Rome and Pope Leo XIII accepted that the local bishop could decide on such matters himself; consequently, the Jesuit school was never built.[57]

This papal decision, Arthur concluded, marked an important step in the expansion of episcopal power over schooling and over the educational endeavors of the religious orders. While he was referring only to the situation in Britain, the power to which he referred applied throughout the English-speaking world.[58]

Notwithstanding, the situation as portrayed so far, it is also important to take cognizance of Grace's[59] point that the bishops' "array of awesome authority" never achieved total hegemonic domination. Much of the literature on the Irish Christian Brothers, for example, makes it clear that, until the 1960s, the order was characterized by a culture very negatively disposed toward the bishops, a situation with origins stretching back to the early years of the order when it successfully resisted attempts by members of the hierarchy to bring it under their jurisdiction.[60] To understand how such a situation could have prevailed, it is necessary to know that two broad divisions existed within religious orders, including religious orders of brothers, namely, pontifical orders and diocesan orders. Pontifical orders operated almost exclusively under the governing authority of their own superiors, with minimum reference to the diocesan bishop. This often meant governance through a superior-general at the international level, a provincial superior at the level of the region, or province, and a local superior at the monastery, or convent, level.[61] As a result, the various pontifical religious orders tended not to consult, or negotiate, with each other, or with the diocesan authorities, in planning their work.

Internal governance of pontifical orders followed a general pattern.[62] At the apex of the governance hierarchy of pontifical orders of brothers, as has already been pointed out, was the superior-general. This person was usually supported by a general council, which consisted of himself, his vicar (the person who took the place of the superior-general in his absence from office), and consulters, all of whom were elected. Each province across the world had, in turn, its own provincial and a provincial council. These were also elected, and they functioned in a mode similar to that of the general council. Within each province were local communities, with a house council and a superior appointed by the provincial council. At definite intervals of time, usually six years, each province was required to undertake a provincial chapter meeting, at which elected representatives within the province, along with the provincial council, considered the life and functions of the congregation within the province, reviewed its statutes, and elected a new provincial council. A general chapter was then held, where representatives from each province brought forward their suggestions on changes to the existing statutes and rules of the congregation. When the general chapter completed its deliberations, it forwarded its amendments to the Sacred Congregation for Religious in the Vatican for ratification.

The principal orders of teaching brothers, namely, the De La Salle Brothers, the Marist Brothers, and the Irish Christian Brothers have, from their inception, been pontifical orders. While they were free from the authority of bishops, they were still answerable to Rome, and this sometimes could mean interference. For example, by the late 1930s, there was great uneasiness within the ranks of the Irish Christian Brothers.[63] The superior-general's office was deemed to have too much power, since by now the rules of the order permitted appointment for life. There was also a belief that general chapter meetings were manipulated by appointing brothers as superiors to major communities who were in sympathy with those in authority. Matters were not helped by the cancellation, due to the Second World War, of the general chapter that was meant to be held in Dublin in 1940. The extent of suspicion and disquiet was such that the Australian brothers considered seceding from the order. Rome intervened by suspending the internal governance of the Irish Christian Brothers and appointing a Jesuit priest, Fr. John Hannon, to the de facto role of superior-general. Then, in 1947, with cries for reform being as strong as ever, Rome imposed a new superior-general on the order. Even though he was a member of the order, he was not elected. Indeed, it was not until 1960 that normal elections were held once again for the appointment of a new superior-general. From then on, again due to intervention from Rome, election was held once every six years.

Many of the smaller orders of brothers, were, for many years, diocesan orders. Under the diocesan model, when an order established its first "house," it became known as the diocese's "mother house." This, in turn, often led to branch houses being formed. Sometimes these branch houses themselves became independent houses in their own right, whose members then took the initiative to form their own branch houses yet again. The standard justification for the maintenance of such a model of governance was that it provided more flexibility to diocesan orders to respond to local demands than was available to pontifical orders. For example, if there was a desire to establish a school, a diocesan order could do so within a short period of time without having to submit proposals and plans through a hierarchical framework of governance. On the other hand, because of their lack of an international dimension, members of diocesan orders were often not as exposed to ideas and trends developing elsewhere as were members of pontifical orders. Also, they did not have the same level of resources at their disposal to organize major campaigns aimed at recruiting members to their ranks as had pontifical orders. It is to this matter of recruitment of religious brothers, both to pontifical and diocesan orders, that the next chapter now turns.

CHAPTER 4

Recruitment

If you have a vocation, our Lord is offering you a life of happiness greater than you ever dreamed of, happiness that will never fail. The pleasure the world promises you will never content your heart.[1]

The above extract from a recruitment brochure produced in the 1940s is typical of the message the teaching religious disseminated among young people in an attempt to woo them to join their ranks. In such material, as well as in the message communicated orally from the pulpit and through Catholic schools, a particular notion was promoted regarding how prospective members would know if they were being invited by God to join a religious order. Essentially, this was a notion that, for whatever reason, God only spoke directly to individuals in very exceptional situations, as the Bible says he did to Saint Paul on the road to Damascus. All others had to be prepared in order to be alert to less direct signs that they were being "called." To this end, it was common to encourage Catholics from a young age to contemplate notions of being altruistic for religious reasons and to consider the possibility that when such notions entered their minds, the origin might be God attempting to influence the path of their lives. The church engaged in this practice through four main avenues, namely, through the regular work of the clergy, through the circulation of printed material relating specifically to vocations, through the schools, and through special recruiting agents. Each of these avenues will now be considered in turn, particularly in relation to recruitment to religious orders of teaching brothers.

Recruitment through the Regular Work of the Clergy

Throughout much of the period under consideration, young people attending mass on Sundays were regularly told it was possible they had a vocation to become a religious and that they should consider this seriously. What was even more common in this setting, however, was for the local priest to concentrate on the parents, exalting them to encourage their children to consider joining the religious life. They were also told from the highest level that any success they had in this regard would be a great honor. Pope Pius XII expressed this very clearly in 1954 when he posed to all Catholics the following rhetorical question:

> How could the Church have fulfilled her mission of education and charity during these last few years, especially in the immediate past, without the aid given, with so much zeal, by hundreds of thousands... How otherwise could the Church fulfill her mission today?[2]

He went on to urge "fathers and mothers to willingly offer to the service of God those of their children who are called to it" and, as he put it, to "consider what a great honour it is" when they embraced the religious life.[3] Many were happy to respond, albeit for a variety of reasons. For some, it was clearly out of a firm belief that this was part of their religious duty. Other parents, as Lowden[4] points out for the English middle-class context, facilitated the recruitment exercise through the delight they expressed when a son or daughter indicated a desire to join a religious order, taking pride in the honor it would bring to the family within the Catholic community. Others yet again were influenced during special visits to their homes by representatives of religious orders of brothers and priests who impressed upon them that if their sons joined a juniorate, they would be assured of a finer education than they could otherwise afford.

The process of praising the life of the religious during church services was partly to confirm in the minds of those who were already priests, brothers, and nuns that their choice was the most noble one available, but more especially to keep the minds of parents focused on playing their part in the recruitment process. For example, Archbishop Duhig of Brisbane in Australia was echoing a common refrain in 1933, when he told a gathering of lay Catholics that any role they might take up could only be secondary to that of the religious.[5] In "seeking out vocations," to use the term used at the time, the parish clergy adopted the same emphasis in their sermons. Furthermore, they never let up. They were instructed in the strongest possible terms by the bishops that they should seize every opportunity to speak in public and in private on the importance of vocations and that in the task "too much zeal is better than too little."[6] Regarding their more private conversations, they were told to introduce the subject every now and then in their talks in the home with parents.[7] What was to be impressed was that the parents' duty was not entirely fulfilled in bringing up their children as pious Catholics since they were also bound to foster vocations to the religious life.[8] The mother was to be particularly targeted in this regard since, as it was put, it is a home permeated by "the influence of a pious and deeply religious mother that produces the sacerdotal spirit, the substance that is necessary."[9]

The possibility that an adolescent might be too young to make an informed decision regarding joining a religious order of brothers was not entertained. On the contrary, the New York–based branch of the De La Salle Brothers argues as follows:

> The best age for choosing one's vocation is in youth, when the heart is pure, when the will is free, and when one's life is not spoiled by bad habits; that is, about the age of fourteen years up to eighteen. And the best time to follow a religious vocation is immediately, without hesitation or delay.[10]

Priests throughout the English-speaking world were told that they should be able to identify particular boys in this age group in their parishes with "the character and dispositions" suited to the religious life since they had known them from infancy and "instructed them in the truths of faith,"[11] and that they should approach them directly to encourage them to be priests, or religious brothers. They were also told that they might find a family opposed to their efforts since the expectation might be that the boy would be called upon to carry on his father's business, or because the parents wanted to keep him at home due to their affection for him. Such opposition was to be resisted, it was held, since "the person who is predestined to direct a boy's first steps" toward the religious life "may be one of the priests of his parish."[12] A particular recommendation to priests was that they could well succeed in "winning the boys for Christ" by providing "examples of self-sacrificing zeal taken from the lives of the saints."[13]

Recruitment through Printed Material Relating Specifically to Vocations

Catholic Sunday newspapers also played a leading role in the recruitment process. Australian Catholic newspapers, for example, regularly reported in heroic terms on groups of young religious heading off for mission stations in New Guinea, the Solomon Islands, and India, among other places. In a similar vein, the literature on marriage that priests made available to engaged couples stressed that the religious life was a privileged gift, while the great majority would have to settle for the good but "ordinary" state of marriage. Such an attitude was also regularly expressed publicly in terms that echoed those of Cardinal Gilroy, when, in 1963, he encouraged Australian parents to pray that God would give their children "the inestimable privilege of a call to religious life."[14]

Many religious orders distributed relatively inexpensive magazines that were sold through schools and homes, and sometimes even directly to families. These works gave a lot of attention to eulogizing the life of the religious—particularly those working overseas as missionaries—through positive accounts of their demeanor and their activities, often accompanied by photographs that showed them in good health and happy, usually in tropical settings. Magazines aimed especially at primary and secondary school pupils were also produced. The Irish Christian Brothers, for example, distributed their own boys' monthly magazine, *Our Boys*. While it included what were considered to be wholesome stories of adventure and excitement, it also contained formal advertisements encouraging pupils to consider the religious way of life and inviting them to write to the order for further information. Br. Michael Keating from County Kerry, in Ireland, recalls that he saw such an advertisement in *Our Boys* when in his first year in secondary school in 1939. He stated:

> I decided to write away. One of the questions I was asked to fill out was "Why would you like to be a Brother?" I asked my sister Kathleen, what I should write down. She advised me to say, "To save my own soul and the souls of others." And so I was accepted for the Juniorate in Baldoyle, Co. Dublin, to arrive at the end of August 1940.[15]

Patrick C. Power, in his narration on his life as an Irish Christian Brother, also states that he had been reading such advertisements in the same magazine for over three years and eventually, in 1942, at 14 years of age, he wrote expressing an interest in becoming a member. Very soon afterward he was on his way to Dublin to become a "postulant,"[16] someone in the first stage of membership.

It was also common for accounts in Catholic newspapers and magazines to hold up the founder of the order as an exemplar of heroism, as someone who had turned his, or her, back on the pleasures of the world in order to serve God and serve those in need. Michael Keating's younger brother, Jerome, who went on to become superior-general of the Irish Christian Brothers, "confided to his mother that, after hearing about the life of Edmund Rice, the founder of the Irish Christian

Brothers, he too had decided to join the order."[17] Heroic accounts of founders were provided in the recruitment literature produced by the different religious orders for distribution in schools and made available in the porches of churches, from where it found its way into Catholic homes. The literature produced by the Jesuit Brothers, for example, lauded the life of their founder St. Ignatius of Loyola,[18] the Hospitaller Brothers of St. John of God sketched out the life of their founder, St. John of God, as their great inspiration,[19] the Vincentian Brothers, stressed the importance of following the example of their founder, St. Vincent de Paul, "the great Apostle of Charity,"[20] and the Blessed Sacrament Brothers stressed the importance they attached to basing their lives on that of their founder, St. P. Jullian Eyonard.[21]

The recruitment literature was usually in leaflet form. In aiming to entice young people to consider becoming religious, it highlighted the notion that the church valued the way of life of nuns, brothers, and priests more than that of lay people. This was often stated in extracts like the following:

> God has an invitation for all men. The majority are called to the married state, where by the grace of the Sacrament of Matrimony, they may become good husbands and fathers of Christian families. For others, the invitation may be to a perfect life, that of the Counsels, to a life devoted to the service of God, consecrated by the vows of religion, whether as a priest, brother, or nun.[22]

Occasionally, the position was foregrounded in almost poetic form, as in the following extract from a recruitment brochure that builds to a climax in attempting to impress the "spiritual greatness" of joining the religious life:

> How stirring it is sharing Christ's yoke and burden! How great it is mounting guard with our King over the souls of men! Your whole day, your whole school life, your whole powers, will be enlisted in the service of this one sublime idea.[23]

At other times, verse was used, often appealing to guilt if one responded negatively and the reward of supernatural life if one responded positively. The following words recommended by the New York branch of the De La Salle Brothers in the 1930s,[24] for use by vocations' organizers, was along such lines:

> So many others I might ask,
> Yet, I am calling thee;

> And wilt thou hesitate My child,
> To come and follow Me?
> And when life's pilgrimage is done,
> With thee I'll keep My tryst;
> In heaven's court though shalt be called
> The chosen friend of Christ.

At other times yet again, extracts could be mantra-like in form, where the religious life was held up as being "the grandest call of all,"[25] because its blessings ensured that, as the following extract states:

> One falls more rarely
> One rises more speedily
> One walks more cautiously
> One rests more securely
> One dies more confidently
> One is purified more speedily
> One is rewarded more abundantly.[26]

Such a form of presentation heightened the attraction of the unique quality of religious life that would be revealed on joining the order. To this was sometimes harnessed the device of speaking directly to the reader, as in the following extract:

> Does it appeal to you [the life of the religious]? Until recently, you have never thought of becoming a Brother. But you can see the great possibilities of such a life and you would like more detailed information.[27]

Such stylistic devices are likely to have been used to attempt to heighten thoughts about considering joining a religious order through provoking personal inner conversation on the matter.

A number of religious orders of brothers also found it necessary to impress that the life of a brother was equal in status within the church to that of a priest. The Passionist Brothers stressed that their members, like priests, were "consecrated to God by the vows of poverty, chastity and obedience," that a brother was "not a servant dressed in religious habit," and that "beneath the Cross, priests and brothers stand side-by-side striving together for the salvation of souls."[28] The Blessed Sacrament Brothers struck a more negative note in making the same point, stating that they rejected a notion of "brothers as being only half religious in comparison to those who were priests" and clarifying that they were equal, but different, with the brother's vocation being "entirely distinct from that of the priest."[29]

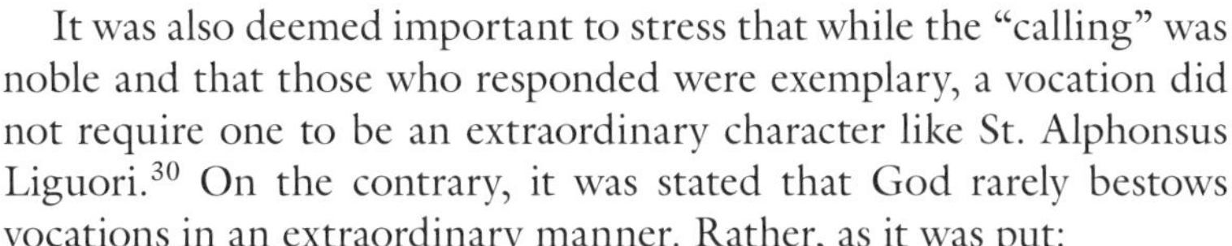

It was also deemed important to stress that while the "calling" was noble and that those who responded were exemplary, a vocation did not require one to be an extraordinary character like St. Alphonsus Liguori.[30] On the contrary, it was stated that God rarely bestows vocations in an extraordinary manner. Rather, as it was put:

> He contends himself with acting in secret on the minds and hearts of those whom He has chosen, or He makes use of secondary causes to transmit His calls and put His designs into execution. A sermon, a conversation, a random word, an escape from an accident, even hero-worship of a popular priest; these things become the auxiliaries of Divine providence.[31]

The literature also regularly spelt out the qualities required of the "normal" person contemplating becoming a brother as being those of:

> Sufficient health
> Genuine piety
> Good common sense
> Purity
> A heart capable of being trained in generosity
> A will capable of being trained to discipline
> A character capable of being trained to community life.[32]

None of these attributes, of course, would have struck most readers as being extraordinary, given the stress placed on them as qualities to be aspired to by all Catholics within the very authoritarian structures of the church of the day.

The recruitment literature also appealed to a wide range of sentiment. In particular, there were appeals to heroism by calling others to join existing brothers in their "wonderful work," with particular emphasis being placed on its caring dimension. The St. John of God Brothers drew attention to their involvement in "general hospitals, clinics, schools for blind children and facilities for the mentally and physically handicapped," whenever and wherever "there is suffering to be cared for."[33] In a similar vein, the Vincentian Brothers stated that "in assisting poor and unfortunate people in saving their souls," they were also helping to "alleviate their physical suffering."[34] Appeal was also made to the idealistic sentiments of potential recruits of late-teenage and early-adult years by emphasizing that sacrifice would have to be made. Thus, the Vincentian Brothers emphasized that their members "willingly leave their homeland to work in conditions—often unenviable—to win souls for Christ."[35]

At the same time, care was taken by those who produced the recruitment literature to balance the "self-offering" appeal of the religious life with more "human" attractions, lest they be seen as advocating a commitment to a life of misery. For example, it was usual to impress that plenty of healthy wholesome food would be available. Significant emphasis was also placed on the community aspect of life, indicating that one's life would not be lonely as peer support would be available at all times, albeit in group situations, rather than through the establishment of individual friendships. Thus, the various booklets disseminated contained photographs of happy smiling groups at recreation, sitting together at prayer, playing team games, or indulging in board games. Also, these photographs regularly contained a mix of ages, with elderly members creating an image of the cloister as a place of security for their younger peers. Such visual representations were accompanied by texts that spoke of community life being attractive because everybody shared the same ideals.

Nor was it a life portrayed as being without drama. As has been argued elsewhere,[36] the image of living a calm regulated life was balanced by hints at the prospect of excitement on the mission fields. Such excitement "was held out as being within reach of those attracted to working in exotic locations through accounts in mission magazines of churches, hospitals and schools being built deep in the jungle, or on the shores of palm-fringed tropical beaches."[37] For example, images of the exotic could be conjured up by the literature produced by the Vincentian Brothers, which contained photographs of brothers in Fiji sitting in dugout canoes alongside Melanesians with smiling faces.[38] The St. John of God Brothers detailed their work in "Africa, South East Asia, Korea, Japan, Israel, South America and The Reunion Islands."[39] Similarly, the material produced by the Jesuit Brothers spoke not only of work in cities, but also "for the mountain people to the West…and for the jungle regions to the East" presented maps of India, and included photographs of brothers getting their vaccinations to go to work in tropical lands.[40]

The central point impressed on young people, however, was that one's eternal salvation was endangered if one did not respond to possible indications that one was being called by God to be a religious brother. This was expressed in a manner designed to promote strong feelings of guilt and even fear regarding the salvation of one's eternal soul. One influential booklet on vocations stated that "he who refuses to obey the Call of God"[41] exposes himself to spiritual danger. It went on to say:

> Such a one slips more easily into spiritual mediocrity and even into unbelief. The young man who refuses to obey this invitation from God will surely live to regret it.[42]

The alternative, as the recruiting literature of the Passionist Brothers put it, was to place oneself "on the highroad to Heaven" by joining an order: "You can save your soul in the world, but as a Passionist Brother you will have a far greater certainty of salvation."[43]

Recruitment through the Schools

Brothers had it regularly impressed upon them that in showing fidelity to their way of life, they were not only increasing their chances of saving their own souls, but were also demonstrating to the general public what being a religious represented and thus playing a part in providing their students with a model of a life they might wish to adopt for themselves. Not only were they expected to assist in recruitment through example, they were also expected to actively encourage their students to enter religious life, as it was put. This emanated from the highest level; in 1954, for example, Pope Pius XII urged teachers to do what they could "to provide every help for the youth entrusted to their care," who felt "called by divine grace to aspire to the priesthood, or to embrace the religious life" in order that they might be able "to reach so noble a goal."[44]

The importance of offering such encouragement to students to join a religious order had for long been enshrined in the rules and constitutions of orders. Usually, it was along the lines of the following:

> Occasions should be frequently made to inculcate the possibility of the highest virtue in every walk and station of life, and to depict the grandeur of consecrating oneself completely to God in the religious state especially.[45]

Often, as Orsi arguesin his oral histories on "the material world of Catholic childhood" in the United States in the early to mid-1900s, particular pupils whose attitudes and demeanor seemed to indicate that they would be suitable candidates were quickly marked out by their teachers and by their priests;: "Everybody I talked to that grew up in the 1930s, 40s, 50s, and even into the 60s, could remember someone who was recognized as the embodiment of the religious and moral ideal. A lot of attention was focused on these kids."[46] Morris, in a similar vein, speaking in relation to his school days in Australia in the 1930s, has stated that, having expressed to his class teacher, Br. Fintan, that he felt "a desire to enter the religious state," he found himself "more and more the object of Br. Fintan's attention"[47] in the weeks that followed.

Hastings, reflecting on his education by the Jesuits in England, has recalled in like fashion, commenting that the religious "were always watching amongst us for potential recruits for the order."[48] Similarly, Leishman has reminisced on the way in which various brothers and priests in his school in New Zealand focused on him from time to time, telling him that he would be "ideal for what we need."[49] Along with appealing to his sense of duty, the religious also sought to activate a sense of heroism in him by reminding him that "Brotherhood is a wonderful thing."[50]

In many instances, the outcome of such practices, as Sheehan has stated, was pupils "conditioned by the constant emphasis on vocation . . . a sign of having been chosen to play a special role in understanding and teaching."[51] Indeed, particular instructions were given to various orders on how to go about the pupil "conditioning" in the schools in the interest of recruiting new members. The Marist Brothers, for example, were instructed to cultivate their own powers to discern "the signs of religious vocation to our Institute" and "to direct likely subjects to our Juniorates, or Novitiates, at the opportune moment."[52] In this way, they were told, they could play their part in "increasing the number of workers in the Apostolic field."[53] Henare has recalled that during his secondary schooling in New Zealand, he and his classmates were spoken to regularly about becoming a priest or a brother: "Every day we were praying for vocations to the Marist Brothers, or the priesthood."[54] The Irish Christian Brothers, regardless of the country in which they worked, also urged their members to "seek to lead generous and pious youths to devote their lives to God's service as priests in the work of the Ministry, or as religious in the cause of Catholic education."[55]

Brothers in charge of senior classes were given even more explicit instructions, being told that they should avail themselves of school libraries, short annual retreats, school sodalities, "zealous instruction on the advantages of the religious state," and the maintenance of a religious atmosphere in the schools, to "foster vocations to the religious life."[56] The rule of certain orders went on as follows on the importance of such activity:

> Nowhere is it reasonable to expect so many Postulants for our Congregation as in our own Schools, in which so many opportunities are afforded for inclining to the religious state the holy dispositions which many of the pupils have inherited from pious parents. Few are the schools in the Congregation in which, amongst the most virtuously inclined of the pupils, eligible subjects may not be found. But many pass to secular avocations, notwithstanding strong inclinations towards the religious state, having failed to disclose their secret longings owing to that bashfulness not unusual in boyhood, but which the confidential enquiry of a kind teacher, whom they loved and trusted, would have enabled them to overcome.[57]

Great importance was also attached to the role of the formal "secular" curriculum in recruitment. Latin, the international language of the church, was considered to be particularly important in this regard, especially in the recruitment of boys, partly because it involved the "mystery" that inspired awe among Catholic congregations.[58] Other "secular" subjects were also considered important. Thus, when the New Zealand government sought to make the secondary school curriculum more "relevant" in the 1940s, the Catholic Church expressed opposition to the proposal to downgrade history at the expense of a new subject, social studies.[59] The fear was that this new subject would uphold a materialist concept of life, and it would not be possible to teach history from a Catholic viewpoint, thus seriously affecting the drive to impart among pupils a desire to join a religious order.

Individual brothers, as has been argued already, were regularly reminded through their rules and constitutions that in their recruitment work they were acting directly as Christ's instrument. In some cases, this was stated in rather heroic terms:

> When done purely for God's glory, how meritorious is the action of him who has become the instrument of conveying God's call to those whom He has chosen...What an inestimable service he renders to the Church in cultivating and developing vocations which give holy Priests to the Sanctuary and pious members to the Congregation. These are the most precious fruits of the teaching of the Christian Brothers' Schools, and the highest testimony of its efficacy.[60]

A further motivating force was the contention that success in this work would reap recruiters a supernatural reward. What was impressed on brothers was that in helping to replenish the ranks of their orders, they were also storing up for themselves extra bonuses to be realized in eternity.

Finally, it is important to highlight that not all the religious, including brothers, who were members of teaching orders, were recruited directly through secondary schools. Indeed, many had been in the workforce for a number of years after leaving primary school, secondary school, or university, before joining. Furthermore, the major influence on many who joined directly from school was not the local priest, their parents, or their classroom teacher, but one of the special recruiting agents who traveled around to schools to give talks on the religious life and disseminate literature aimed at enticing young people to join their ranks.

Recruitment through Special Recruiting Agents

For many years, particularly, in the United States, Australia, and New Zealand, the harnessing of the classroom by religious orders of brothers to encourage students to contemplate joining their respective orders was supplemented by their superiors making visits back to Europe every few years, particularly Ireland and England, in search of recruits from within the ranks of those who had joined religious houses already, from those still in school, and from those in the workforce. By the end of the nineteenth century, however, many orders in all of these countries had also appointed special recruiting agents who visited Catholic schools on the home front, conducting recruitment sessions. These individuals were themselves brothers who had spent a considerable amount of time "in the service of the Church," to use the terminology of the day.[61]

Different orders appointed special recruiting agents at different periods in time, depending on their rate of expansion. In the case of the Irish Christian Brothers in Australia, it was deemed necessary to establish the special position of "postulator" in 1906. This position was filled by a brother specially chosen to visit schools, give instruction on the religious life, and seek members for the order. Connole gives the following account of the work of Brother Ignatius Hickey, postulator in the 1920s and early 1930s:

> Brother Ignatius came into the classroom and the Brother came to him to know if he would speak to the boys at once. He asked the Brother to go on with the class-work while he went among the boys . . . Brother

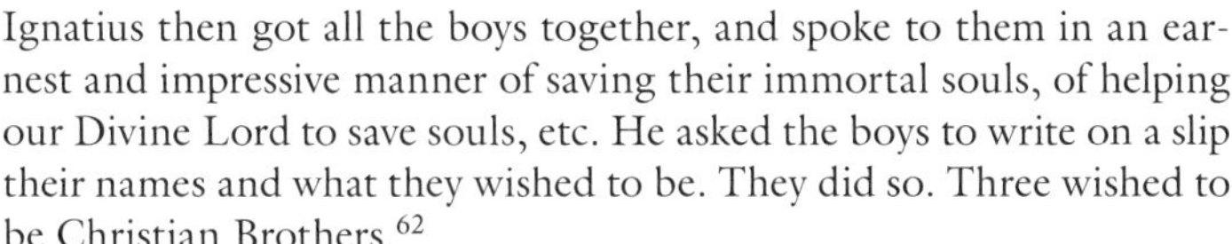

> Ignatius then got all the boys together, and spoke to them in an earnest and impressive manner of saving their immortal souls, of helping our Divine Lord to save souls, etc. He asked the boys to write on a slip their names and what they wished to be. They did so. Three wished to be Christian Brothers.[62]

Connole also recalls the work of Brother Justus Smith, who was postulator from 1938 to 1954:

> For sixteen years he travelled the length and breadth of Australia and he was a welcome figure, especially in outback communities where seldom or never do they see a visiting Brother. Brother Justus was always casting about for new ways and means to further his great mission. It must be close to the truth to say that he had read everything written on vocations. He would travel thousands of miles in country trains to the West of Queensland to interview the parents of boys who were boarders in one of our colleges and who had given their names to him as prospective postulants.[63]

Morris, speaking specifically about his attendance at a school of the Christian Brothers in Australia in the 1930s, states that a few days before the postulator arrived, the regular teaching brothers engaged "by way of conditioning preparation"[64] in a variety of activities, including a visit to the brothers' monastery to see the chapel.

Various accounts of the presence of recruiting agents in brothers' schools are also to be found in autobiographical works from across the English-speaking world. Redrup[65] describes how one of these individuals was introduced to a class of boys in an Australian Marist school in the 1930s:

> "Boys," announced Brother Avellino, "this is Brother Hubert who is the Principal of our Juniorate at Mittagong. He's come here today to speak to you about the Marist order and its place in the world. Please make him welcome!"

Geraghty[66] recalls along similar lines the visit of the person he termed the "vocations collector" to his primary school in Sydney in the 1950s:

> Brother Andrew (Spitballs) used to visit each classroom, addressing the boys, asking each to fill out a printed form to indicate whether he was even vaguely interested in becoming a religious [brother]. When I indicated interest by a single tick in the "yes" box, I found myself in

> a serious one-to-one conference with Brother Andrew, being encouraged to say my prayers to the holy founder of his order, and to reflect (at the age of eleven) so as to discern the will of God. Suddenly things had become serious. He told me to discuss my vocation with my parents and to request a character reference from my parish priest. I was on my way. The next stop would be the minor juniorate of the Marist Brothers at Bowral where there happened to be room for me.

The decision to attend a juniorate was usually taken after a private interview with the recruiting agent, where the aim was, as the New Zealand ex-priest John Clarke put it, to "nurture and encourage the possibility of a vocation."[67]

Juniorates were secondary schools run by individual religious orders that enrolled those who declared an interest in entering religious life with their particular order. In some ways they were not very different from regular Catholic boarding schools, although usually the teachers were specially selected both for what was seen as their excellent teaching abilities and their fervent commitment to the religious way of life and to the religious order to which they belonged. In his account of the visit of Brother Hubert to his school, Redrup[68] goes on to describe the approach used in order to win the attention of those boys present:

> In a narrative style of the utmost simplicity our visitor proceeded to tell us the story of a meagerly-educated French country priest who had been so distressed by the level of ignorance he encountered in the children of his first mountain-parish near Lyons, following 25 years of revolutionary and Napoleonic upheaval, that he resolved to remedy the matter; within his parish at least. The small group of young peasants that Father Marcellin Champagnat brought together and trained as teachers to this end had become the Marist brotherhood; a worldwide religious teaching order, now several-thousand strong.

Furthermore, he recalls the impression that this made on him:

> As Brother Hubert told the story, his Juniorate seemed to me to combine the best features of all the English Boarding Schools I'd been reading about for years past in *Magnet*, *Gem*, *Champion*, *Nelson Lee*, *Boys' Own* and *Chums*. There were playing fields for every conceivable sport, a dam for swimming in and illimitable surrounding bushland in which to adventure...I'm sure the gentle Brother must have spoken of the more serious and spiritual aspects of training for a Marist Brothers' life and of the subsequent vows of Poverty, Chastity and Obedience that would serve to separate new disciples utterly from "the world" that

> I'd hardly begun to be aware of; but I suspect that I absorbed little of this side of his message. What I did carry away from the address given us by this most assuming of "big-wigs" was the notion that God determined whether a boy should become a Marist Brother by granting him the privilege of a "vocation"; and that any fortunate St. Patrick's boy who ever came to feel that God had granted him a "vocation" should speak with Brother Avellino. Brother Hubert's talk proved fateful. In that classroom, on that day, I decided that I loved the Marist brotherhood and that God wanted me to become a Marist Brother.[69]

He concluded by saying: "In a very real sense I was fairly launched on my lifetime's first romance; a romance that settled the shape of the balance of my boyhood."[70]

Boudreau and Stanton indicate that the pattern in recruitment practices varied little regardless of country concerned. They offer the following testimony from a young adolescent boy who joined the Salesian Brothers in New York in the 1950s following a weekend visit to the seminary:

> The vocation director was careful to point out all the features of the seminary. It had a working farm complete with an apple orchard providing the best cider I have ever tasted. The centrepiece of the school building was a large gym where we watched the seminarians happily playing basketball or dodge ball. We saw the swimming pool. Wow, I thought, I'd be living in a place with a swimming pool![71]

Quite often the presentations of the recruiting agents were aimed also at appealing to the youthful sentiments of their audiences and were accompanied by maps, photographs, and slide shows designed to excite their adventurous minds. O'Malley recounts a visit from the postulator of the Irish Christian Brothers to his school in Ireland in the late 1950s; "He had set up a makeshift screen—a white bed sheet draped over a blackboard—and had a slide projector in readiness."[72] The slide show that followed moved from a picture of the juniorate, "a dull grey building," to a group of happy boys sitting at a long dinner table and "having what looked like a party of buns and lemonade, and beaming freckle-faced at the camera," to boys swimming and playing games (both indoors and outdoors), and finished with a group of very young brothers in clerical habit and clerical white collar, with the postulator remarking: "A nice happy bunch. No sad faces here."[73]

The recruitment strategies reached a fairly sophisticated level by the 1960s with the use of film. The remainder of the chapter illustrates this point by presenting the results of an analysis undertaken of a recruitment film produced in Australia.[74] It is also illustrative of the "loosening up" that took place in the church in the final years of the Second Vatican Council, a time when a less authoritarian, yet no less pious and heroic, image was being portrayed of the life of a brother, as the order, like many other religious orders, tried to adapt to the fresh winds of change emanating from the Vatican.

The film in question was commissioned in 1965 by the New South Wales Province of the Irish Christian Brothers in Australia. Using the voices of actors within the Australian Broadcasting Corporation, the product entitled "Profession in Christ" became the centrepiece of the postulators' presentations in schools and parish halls throughout much of eastern Australia over the next decade, while copies with slight variations (and different titles) were also produced for use in Western Australia and Papua New Guinea. The film depicts the lifestyle of a group of brothers from the time of being "received" into the order. The subject matter comprises a range of activities that characterize the life of a typical brother. The mode of communication is a color film constructed in documentary style, with a disembodied narrator providing running commentary on the visual track. The film is presented as a narrated story in which, apart from one episode, the characters themselves do not speak. Four main episodes can be identified: the vow-taking ceremony, vacation activities, school/work practices, and "other" aspects of a brother's life.

The narrator plays a key role in developing relations between the film and its audience. The voice-over track is characterized by continual shifts between two distinct narrative styles. One style is formal and is most readily identifiable in terms of the field of religion. This style is used most often in the depiction of the church and ceremonial scenes accompanied by prayers. The voice is soft-spoken and solemn, with little variation in pitch, intensity, or tone. It is accompanied by visual images of church rituals, distinctive costumes, and ceremonial actions to display the particular conventions of the Christian Brothers. The tenor of this narrative voice is descriptive, factual, and authoritative, signaling the formality of the events and the nature of the social roles and relationships of those involved. For example, the opening "scene" of the film includes shots of religious art accompanied by the reading of a prayer over background music, followed by scenes from the consecration ceremony with the voice-over statement, "Christmas morning, the day Christian Brothers make their vows."

As the title screen and credits appear, the voice-over segues into the reciting of the words of the vows being taken, without explanation or interruption. The reciting continues over a montage of images of the novices, the congregation, and the bishop. This style of language invites the audience to identify with, and take up, the subject position of a novice (the first stage in formally joining a religious order), in effect, to join the vow-taking ritual. The narrator is clearly not a novice himself. Indeed, the tone and formality are suggestive of a higher institutional authority. This further serves to interpolate the viewer into a prescribed role in a community of shared values.

The second style of narrative voice is more friendly and welcoming. In this style, while the narrator laughs and jokes only infrequently, he is at all times quite friendly in attitude. This informal style is introduced in the second major episode of the film, which is devoted to the vacation and leisure practices of the newly initiated brothers. Here the narrative voice is similar to that of a travelogue, inviting the audience to enjoy the Australian culture and lifestyle from the perspective of a Christian Brother on holiday with his peers. The voice in this scenario is similar in volume and tone to the religious style, but with greater variation in pitch, and is less formal and less authoritative. It is underscored by energetic, lively music.

The informal mode of address suggests a more equal power relation between speaker and audience. The narrator states, for example, that "the fresh salty air is good to get that chalk dust feeling out of your bones." In this case, the voice-over provides a descriptive account of scenes that include motifs of Australianness such as "eskies" (family ice-boxes used for picnics), the beach, surfboards, TV, a dartboard, "combi" vans and Holden station wagons, together with statements like "a little sun, then into the surf." There is an assumption that the audience is familiar with this scenario and thereby can identify closely with the characters in the film. Here, the power relations between the producer of the text and its viewers are on a more equal footing.

Lemke[75] states that every context of situation has two aspects, namely, an interactional context and a thematic context. The thematic context of the film under analysis is that of community and identity. In this regard, two identifiable communities are portrayed: the familiar, ordinary Australian community, and the unfamiliar, extraordinary Christian Brothers' community. The interactional context of the film that appears alongside this depicts activities that locate the brothers in these ostensibly distinct communities and then gradually introduces connections between them. In particular, the lifestyle of the Christian Brother is carefully interwoven with that of other, ordinary Australians and the broader Australian community. This is established by the text incorporating familiar words and imagery to evoke feelings of national identity. It is likely, for example, that the audience would immediately identify closely with the beach-loving, sporting young Christian Brothers we see having fun with their mates. They are shown to be typical Australian males in many respects.

The shifts in narrative style between formal/religious and informal/everyday, are also subtle and frequent, integrating the formal and perhaps unfamiliar aspects of the Christian Brothers' lives into the more easily recognizable and "laid-back" Australian way of life. For example, the vacations episode includes a scene in which the brothers are studying marine biology. The narrator states that "the wonders of nature recall the psalmist's prayer," and then slips seamlessly into reciting the prayer himself. In this way, the closeness between the two lifestyles depicted in the film are emphasized, thus making the position of the target subject less different from one's existing subjectivity, and therefore attainable.

The newly consecrated brothers shown in the opening scenes provide an image of the preferred reader, an Australian male in his early 20s, even though "there were, beside the Australians, some from New Zealand and New Guinea." Brothers are also quite exceptional, taking up a "vocation of the highest order." By reinforcing in words and images the high values of the teaching religious, audiences are hailed to inhabit this subject position. The scenes of ceremonial rituals and the recital of vows and prayers convey the exclusivity of the Christian Brothers' community. In the initial scenes, "generous young men made their vows—chastity, poverty and obedience" to become fully fledged Christian Brothers. They engage in an exclusive ceremony, clearly part of a special community. We are told of "a feeling of community in the air that day. Joy and peace to men of good will." It also becomes apparent that one can belong to both communities, that of the everyday and that of the Christian Brothers, when, in the following scene, the newly consecrated brothers "load up for four weeks' vacation," just like other ordinary young Australian males, though in this case of the highest caliber.

Within the film, the major player is established as a typical young Australian male who displays the special virtues and characteristics of a Christian Brother novice. His Australian identity is signaled by his leisure activities, including surfing, swimming, tennis, boating and fishing, as well as watching TV and playing darts. He also plays music, yet knows it "isn't the popular thing to do when others are trying to rest." His clothes are conservative, but casual, while on vacation and when engaging in outdoor work. He wears a bathing costume, a floppy cricket or army style hat, and an open-necked shirt with rolled-up sleeves. He is carefree, smiling, and capable. The general setting of the film is also distinctively Australian, marked by geographical elements such as the beach, the outback, and the bush. This imagery of Australian cultural identity promotes an idyllic version of a lifestyle with which viewers are already familiar, and to which they probably subscribe.

The narrator introduces the final episode with the statement: "A brother's world is not entirely one of books and boys." This suggests that we are about to see some typical everyday nonreligious activities of a brother's life. In fact, it is in this episode that the religious discourse is most prominent, as the text conveys visually and verbally that the lifestyle practices of the brothers are always aimed at giving service in the name of the Lord. Disrupting the expectation of the ordinary/everyday discourse gives the extraordinary/religious discourse more impact. Having portrayed in previous episodes the nature and significance of various activities in the life of the typical brother, the text now completes the construction of a character whose life is built around prayer and service. The notion of service is "made real" in shots of the brothers at prayer, in "the spirit of contemplation" at their annual retreat, and during the profession of vows. They are in the "service of humanity as a whole" as they engage in gardening and farming work, kitchen chores, and recreational activities such as chess, pool, and table tennis, all in "the family spirit." Membership of this community is sealed by the shot of a brother receiving a blessed medal. In lauding the values of the professed Christian Brother, the text signals that this is indeed an ideal subject position for audiences to occupy.

To conclude, this chapter set out to impress the extent to which the church was very much aware of the need to reproduce its spiritual workforce of brothers, along with that of priests and nuns, if it was to continue to offer Catholic education by drawing upon teachers it considered to be its most loyal members. The chapter also outlined how the church engaged in this reproduction through four main avenues, namely, through the regular work of the clergy, through the circulation of printed material relating specifically to vocations, through the schools, and through special recruiting agents. The analysis, however, has not been exhaustive. Rather, it should provoke cogitation on issues worthy of further study. For example, it raises questions about the extent to which the nature of "vocational guidance" in Catholic schools, including those run by brothers, differed from that in state schools and from those of other religions insofar as the message that was given was that working within the parameters of religious life was superior to working within the career structures in the secular world. In addition, it is important in considerations like this not to lose sight of Armstrong's point that one of the reasons people decide to embark on the life of the religious is that "they are looking for something that the world cannot offer."[76] And, as the next chapter illustrates, those who joined a religious order with such motives, as with all new recruits, very quickly discovered that their new life was indeed very different from that which they had experienced living at home with their families, and one that was very much cut off from the secular world.

CHAPTER 5

Learning the Rule

All acts of subordination, calumny or detraction against the Superiors, murmuring against their ordinations, groundless complaints, stubborness and all disrespectful conversations and behaviour are criminal in the sight of God, and directly militate against the fourth commandment.[1]

Lines like those quoted above, read aloud at the beginning of each term in many Catholic schools around the world during the period under consideration, convey the extent to which boys were expected to show respect and obedience to the teaching religious. Furthermore, boys who went on to join a religious order found that, far from being relaxed, this expectation intensified. The consequence was that one of the most distinguishing characteristics of the life of a teaching brother, as with all fellow religious, was that it was conducted within a very authoritarian framework. Those who chose the life, however, were not expected to fit in immediately. Rather, they went through a number of stages of what was popularly known as "religious formation." For many who joined the orders, this commenced while in attendance at a juniorate. Others who did not attend a juniorate experienced a lesser, yet still influential, form of preparation at the same age because of the nature of the organization of, and the pedagogical approaches adopted in, "regular" Catholic schools, particularly if they happened to be boarders. Both groups then came together to proceed through an intensified regime of "formation" as "postulants" and "novices," before becoming fully-fledged members of a religious order. In most cases, the brothers were also prepared as teachers during this initial religious formation phase, although there were situations where this did not happen until later. Also, having graduated from being a novice, a brother continued throughout his life to engage in various practices designed to regularly renew his commitment to his order and its way of life. The length of each stage in this formation experience varied somewhat over time, and also from one religious order to another. Accordingly, the following account does not necessarily apply to the period under consideration in this book, nor does it apply to all orders. It does, however, constitute a framework for providing a general overview on the processes involved.

The Juniorate

The role of the "ordinary" Catholic day school in the recruitment of individuals for religious orders has already been considered. Those who received all of their secondary schooling within such a setting were also inducted to some extent into the way of life of the religious as the school day was punctuated with regular prayer, as was life in the cloister. While this was so in day schools, it was even more so in boarding schools. The preferred mode of inducting young aspirant brothers into the religious life, however, was through attendance at a juniorate. This type of school, as indicated in the previous chapter, was run by individual religious orders and enrolled only those who declared an interest in entering religious life with them.

Some students who decided to enter a juniorate did so when they were as young as fourteen years of age. Older ones, depending on age and prior education, entered an appropriate grade and usually remained until they completed their secondary schooling. Most of the costs involved were met by the religious orders who ran them. Parents, however, were sometimes asked to make a contribution. Often this was done by providing suitable clothing, a matter referred to by Blake in an account of two young teenagers in the southwest of Ireland heading off to join the Irish Christian Brothers' juniorate in Dublin in the early 1940s:

> Each carried a new trunk in which their mothers had carefully packed their outfits for the new life ahead. Each was attired in a black suit, white shirt, black tie and shiny black shoes, the formal dress of aspirants to the religious life.[2]

Blake concluded by stating that the two young adolescents would not see their homes again for at least five years, although their family members, if they could afford to make the journey, were allowed to visit them a few times each year.

Juniorates had a somewhat greater emphasis on discipline, and all aspects of life were saturated with a religious ethos than was the case in "regular" Catholic schools. The general daily pattern was along the following lines: Students rose at about 5.45 A. M. and commenced an hour's study at 6.00 A. M. They then went to the chapel for Mass at 7.00 A. M., ate their breakfast at 8.00 A. M., and commenced a normal school day at 8.30 A. M. Lunch was at midday, followed by more classes. The school day finished with an hour's organized sport in the afternoon; occasionally this was substituted with manual work and construction jobs in cases where there was a farm associated with the juniorate. This was followed by a set series of prayers, the rosary at 5.30 P. M. and then tea.

The evening timetable consisted of study from 6.45 P. M. to 8.45 P. M., 15 minutes break, then short prayers and a hymn at 9.00 P. M., further study from 9.00 P. M. to 10.00 P. M., and then bed. Weekends were also highly organized, with timetabled study periods, games periods, long walks, and time for doing various chores, including washing clothes and polishing shoes. Once again, an emphasis on prayer was maintained, with large proportions of time being taken up through attending Mass in the morning, saying the rosary in the afternoon, and attending religious ceremonies, including Benediction, in the chapel at night.

Dunne makes a positive comment on his experience at a Christian Brothers' juniorate in Ireland in the late 1950s as follows:

> There was no corporal punishment and bullying was not tolerated. We were treated fundamentally as adults who had taken on immense responsibilities...The teachers were all Brothers, and were among the best the Congregation had. It was all profoundly civilized, carefully disciplined and impressively caring. Animal spirits were catered for, not only in almost daily organised games, but also in regular "manual labour," emphasized as part of an ancient monastic tradition. And there was an open-air, unheated swimming pool, used for much of the year and part of the character-building Spartan regime. It was, indeed, very much as I had imagined boarding school from the stories of Greyfriars, with its emphasis on games, codes of honour and study.[3]

Power and O'Malley, on the other hand, in relating their experiences in the same juniorate in the 1940s and the 1960s respectively, paint pretty grim pictures of an authoritarian approach and of loneliness and unhappiness.[4] In view of the great dearth of documented reminiscences,[5] however, it is almost impossible to arrive at any conclusion of what the experience was generally, although Cardinal Heenan of England had no hesitation when looking back in 1971 on his life in a juniorate, albeit one for those aspiring to be priests rather than brothers, in stating that it was "academically wasteful and boring."[6]

In some juniorates, students were immediately introduced to the "great silence" required of the fully-fledged members of the religious orders. Redrup recalls his introduction to the practice shortly after he became a pupil at the Australian Marist Brothers' juniorate in the 1930s:

> "I judge you've not been told about the Great Silence, John," the Brother finally began, "so let me explain. From the end of each evening meal until the end of breakfast next morning, all of us maintain complete silence. This is what we call the Great Silence. To break it, other than in circumstances of absolute necessity, is a very grave fault."[7]

He also gives the following graphic account of how the juniorate had a monthly ritual that paved the way for the public self-chastisement practices that would come to be a feature of life of those who would persevere beyond this stage of preparation:

> Our monthly behaviour card were distributed by the Principal on the first Saturday of every month, during his regular Saturday-evening homily...Our monthly demerits were accumulated from a weekly Faults list that was pinned to the main notice board in the Intermediate Classroom every Saturday evening. The list, whose pinning-up was always the week's most stressful occasion, recorded the names of those Juniors who had offended under each heading during the previous week.[8]

Amongst the faults listed were "breaking silence," "disobedience," "irreverence," "poor demeanor," and "inadequate effort."[9]

In the juniorate, boys were provided with some introduction to the history and traditions of the religious orders with which they were associated. Also, while they did not engage in teaching practice, their minds were regularly oriented toward the notion of teaching as a vocation and as "a calling from God." Furthermore, each was regularly reminded that he would have to decide at the end of his secondary schooling whether or not to proceed to become a postulant, the first official stage in religious life. He was told to pray for divine enlightenment to help him make his decision, while at the same time it was emphasized that it was a grave sin not to heed "the divine voice" that told him if he had a "religious vocation." Also, while boys were regularly informed that they did not have to make a commitment until

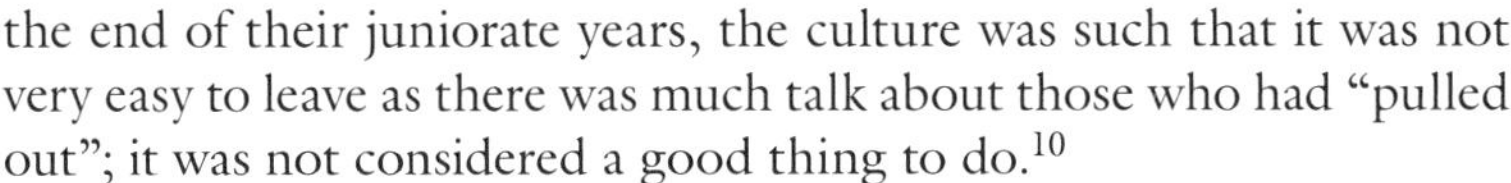

the end of their juniorate years, the culture was such that it was not very easy to leave as there was much talk about those who had "pulled out"; it was not considered a good thing to do.[10]

Postulant and Novice

The formation process for life as a brother based on an observance of the vows of poverty, chastity, and obedience intensified in earnest when some of those who graduated from the juniorates linked with both "ordinary" school leavers and those who had been working for a number of years in the "secular" world, to enter the first stage of formally joining a religious order by becoming a "postulant." This stage represented a break with the past. It involved embarking on "a particularly intense form of professional socialization" that attended to all aspects of the lives of recruits, "including their affective maturity and sexual thoughts, feelings and behaviours."[11] For nuns, the period of 18 months or more spent as a postulantwas usually significantly longer than that spent by brothers. On their first day, the aspiring nuns partook in a religious ceremony at which they received a distinctive dress and veil. In some religious orders, they then underwent a crash course in very basic primary school teacher training for four-to-six weeks, including lectures on how to teach mathematics, reading, and spelling. This was followed by a number of months in various schools, working with teachers in the classroom. Often, each postulant was then sent out to a regional convent for 12 months and put in charge of a primary school class, with an experienced nun acting as a monitor.

In the case of some of the orders of brothers, the period as a postulant differed significantly from that of nuns in that it could be for as short as six weeks, during which the aspirants continued to wear "secular" dress. They lived with the "novices," namely, those who had progressed to the next stage, and they came under all the novitiate rules, including a decree that letters had to be handed unsealed to the superior, while mail received was to be handed to the addressee with the envelope already opened. This six-week postulancy usually ended with an eight-day "retreat," or time of intense prayer, after which they became novices.

Throughout the Catholic world, postulants were assisted in their striving to be good by being required to listen at mealtime to the spiritual writings that were read out to all in the community by a community member. In this way, they learned about what was termed "the spirit of the order," about the life of the founder, and about the heroic deeds of the early members who established monasteries, schools, and other educational institutions. Also, they were molded into a state of single-mindedness, with no reading for pleasure and with an absence of the radio when it started to become popular in the general society.

At the end of the postulancy, members who had stayed the course were initiated into being novices. This was a time of intense spiritual preparation and of training in the religious way of life. During the first year, there was no mention of teaching, apart from reading the lives of well-known former members and of their work for God through the educational roles that they fulfilled. The second year, however, often also incorporated a teacher preparation year, the nature of which will be considered in the next chapter. In the case of most orders, this meant primary school teacher preparation, even for those who, at a later stage, went on to teach in secondary schools.

This period in the novitiate was, for many, characterized by a dramatic change in their lives. It was at this point that the importance of the religious life wherein being "dead to the world, dead to the flesh, dead to our old selves," as it was generally put, took center stage. Put simply, the notion seems to have been that it was a life that provided the greatest opportunity to approximate perfection in this world. The task of striving for it required that one lay aside one's sensitivity and need for love and affection. In this way, one's personality could be "broken down" as it were, and be reformed through age-long methods in an attempt to achieve the asexual "pure form" of the next life. The Irish Christian Brothers, for example, stressed that members should "strive after the perfection of their state," and that "perfection consists in the intimate and complete union of the soul with God through charity."[12] By striving for this state, so the argument seemed to go, one brought oneself nearer to the state one would be in if one managed to get into heaven after death, thus greatly increasing one's chances of achieving eternal salvation.

The position held was that while the perfection required of "ordinary Christians" was "confined to the observance of the Commandments of God and of the Church," the perfection demanded of the religious demanded, in addition, "the practice of poverty, chastity and obedience."[13] Of these, the vow of obedience was, to some extent, seen to be the overarching requirement, since engaging in the associated practices created the environment that also assisted in living according to the vows of poverty and chastity. It was with such a view in mind that the rule of the Marist Brothers emphasized that obedience was an essential aspect of the spirit of the congregation, "a virtue whose proper practice sanctified the individual and made for order and stability in the community."[14]

As with the vows of poverty and chastity, a series of rules that, as the Directory of the Irish Christian Brothers put it, contained "abundant interior and exterior aids,"[15] was outlined, which served as "so many steps" in helping them to live up to their vow of obedience. Critical debate between the brothers was discouraged, as was the promotion of critical debate among the students they taught in class. Equally, they were not allowed to engage in reading for pleasure. Certainly, they were supposed to study ardently. However, they were also told that they should avoid "an inordinate love of study which may injure piety and health."[16] The situation was clarified for the Irish Christian Brothers as follows:

> There are certain dangers attending study which can and must be guarded against. *Knowledge puffeth up*, and unless counterbalanced by humility, leads to destruction. Plausible excuses often betray the earnest student to indulge in light literature; the necessity of a good style and richness of thought are special baits. If such reading leads to the loss of devotion, what a price has been paid for an unnecessary advantage.[17]

Subscription to this view meant that brothers were forbidden to read books, or publications, other than those made available in the community library, they had to obtain special permission from their superior for any reading not connected with their studies, and they were not allowed "to study or read secular books" in their dormitories, or rooms, without permission.

The Marist Brothers' rule also made it clear that "in what concerns food or clothing, if they need anything whatever, they shall never take it of themselves, but should make their wants known to Brother Director, and then be content with whatever he may give or order them."[18] This was meant to help brothers to live up to their vow of poverty. They were meant to become completely detached from possessions and obtain permission for everything they needed. On this, the rule of the De La Salle Brothers stated:

> All Brothers shall not have anything of their own, but all things shall be in common use in each of the houses . . . the brothers shall not have anything for their personal use, except a New Testament, an Imitation of Christ, a Rosary, a Crucifix, and a small pocket-book given them during the Novitiate.[19]

Furthermore, they were forbidden to receive or borrow anything from anybody, including their relatives. In particular, they were not to "have any money privately."[20]

The third vow binding all brothers was the vow of chastity. This was the vow given most prominence by the orders. It expressly led to rules forbidding any unnecessary contact, or familiarity, with the opposite sex. The rule of the Marist Brothers stated:

> Persons of the other sex shall not be admitted to the interior of the House, unless accompanied by someone in authority; they shall be admitted to the parlour only, the door of which, if not transparent, shall be left open during the interview.[21]

Brothers were also regularly reminded that they should guard against developing friendships with lay members of either sex: "They shall have no intercourse with lay people unless through necessity; and in the visits they are obliged to pay or receive, they must be brief, and maintain themselves in that reserve, prudence, and gravity, which their profession requires."[22]

Particular emphasis was placed on the need for brothers to be reserved and dignified when teaching their pupils. The rule of the Marist Brothers expounded on this:

> They shall avoid taking them by the hand, touching the face...They should keep attentive watch over the affections of their own hearts, in order to preserve them free from all particular affection or inclination for certain pupils; for such affections are amongst the most dangerous snares of the devil, and are often followed by the most fatal consequences.[23]

They were also informed that they should always observe strict modesty when dressing and undressing: "They shall, in all things, observe the strictest modesty. They shall dress and undress with all becoming decency, and shall never leave the dormitory or their bedroom without being suitably dressed."[24]

Brothers were also trained in other practices that were meant to construct them as asexual beings devoid of individual personalities. The particular rules of the Marist Order are worth quoting at length to illustrate this:

> They must guard against all immoderate demonstrations of joy, which announce levity of mind and thoughtlessness; also against a sad, sullen, unsettled or unhappy air, which is generally a sign that the soul is under the dominion of some passion.
>
> When standing, they should keep the body erect, without constraint or affectation, not leaning to one side, but equally on both feet, which generally should be nearly joined.

> They must not keep their hand in their pockets not inside the breast of their habit, but should let them hang naturally, or have their arms folded.
>
> When seated, they should keep the body upright, the feet nearly joined, avoid crossing the legs, throwing themselves back on their chair, or leaning back against the desk, changing their position every moment, or making any extensions of the legs or of the arms which denotes weariness or sloth.
>
> When speaking, their tone of voice should be moderate but sustained; that is to say, neither too high or too low, too slow or too fast; nor should it be harsh or effeminate.[25]

The extreme disciplining of the body required by these rules was meant to produce almost robotic-like individuals who would not only be but would also appear to others, both religious and secular, to be the personification of modesty, virtue, and humility.

A brother was also trained to be suspicious of himself if he ever found he was inclined toward establishing a friendship with a peer. As the rules of the Marist Brothers put it:

> [Brothers] shall guard against all personal friendships; because such friendships are not only hurtful to common charity, but even those which are innocent in the beginning, often degenerate into sensual and criminal friendship.[26]

In a similar vein, the rule of the Irish Christian Brothers decreed that "members had to avoid touching one another, even in jest,"[27] and even when they went on walks they could never be together in pairs.

The ideas of centuries that underpinned such rules were presented in condensed form in Pope Pius XII's encyclical *Sacra Virginitas* of March 25, 1954. Here the logic of the virginal state was spelled out as being "a kind of spiritual marriage in which the soul is wedded to Christ" and thus "surpasses marriage in excellence."[28] Elsewhere, the pope had already stated that chastity and virginity, "which imply also the inner renunciation of all sensual affection," were not meant to "estrange souls from this world." Rather, the notion was that they should "awaken and develop the energies needed for wider and higher offices beyond the limits of individual families."[29]

In *Sacra Virginitas*, the pope went on to commend "constant vigilance" in safeguarding the chastity of the religious, and he offered two strategies to achieve this. First, he argued, the religious would need to be particularly watchful over the movements of their passions and senses and so control them "by voluntary discipline" and by "bodily mortification."[30] Second, he pointed out the importance of avoiding occasions to sin, stating the importance of removing far from oneself "anything that can even slightly tarnish the beautiful virtue of purity."[31] Such advice served to legitimate practices that had long been utilized by the religious themselves. The Irish Christian Brothers, for example, were instructed as follows:

> Practice the means whereby the attacks of the enemy are forestalled; namely, distrust of self, custody of the senses, extending to the avoidance of reading dangerous books or papers, care in avoiding sensual friendships, promptness in repelling temptations, openness of conscience.[32]

Also, as has already been pointed out, once aspirants joined any religious order, great stress was placed on renouncing their sexual role and function to attain the neutral personhood that was seen as being central to the struggle to attain perfection. In the case of some orders, this meant impressing on new recruits that their sexual urges were to be disciplined. Geraghty outlines as follows the associated view to which he was introduced as a member of a novitiate in Australia in the 1950s:

> I was engaged in a program to develop moral perfection which, I was assured, was perfectly attainable. All I needed was discipline, energy, self-control and determination. I needed to suppress my basic human and sexual urges in order to cooperate with my ecclesiastical superiors in their God-given vocation of training me for glory.[33]

He goes on to say that in the seminary, "modesty was paramount,"[34] and films based on love stories were vetoed.[35]

Some religious orders of brothers also required that their members take additional vows to those of obedience, poverty, and chastity. The Marist Brothers, for example, had to take a "vow of stability," according to which they had to regularly remind themselves that their work as educationalists, while important, was secondary to their prayer life and their desire to seek personal perfection, and also that in their educational work their involvement in religious education took priority over their work in teaching secular subjects.[36] The De La Salle Brothers and the Irish Christian Brothers also took this vow and, in addition, took a "vow of gratuitous instruction."

Overall, the process of "religious formation" can be characterized as being one of bringing the inductee to a state of self-abnegation. The emphasis was very much on developing a communal identity rather than a personal one. Members ate together and prayed together, with the process being overseen by a novice master. This was usually a very rigid individual whose job it was to test and discern the vocation of the novices.[37] Boudreau and Stanton offer the following testimony from a former Salesian brother in New York on one way in which this role was carried out:

> One of the major parts of the monitoring process was what I remember as a bi-weekly or monthly private meeting with the Master of Novices…it was his job to pry into the personal and spiritual lives of each novice to make judgments about the suitability for the Salesian life. Every novice knew that sincerity was very important in these meetings but that something said might lead to a secret departure.[38]

The central function of the novice master was "to break the spirit; this was not regarded as cruelty since conformity was all."[39] He instructed the novices in the rules of the order and trained them to accept unquestioningly all aspects of their totally regulated life.

Novices also had to engage in practices that were meant to help each other reach spiritual and moral perfection. In the case of some of the orders of brothers, this meant being encouraged to tell the master of novices of any misdemeanors of their peers, the argument being that this was "to help them to help each other." Novices were also urged to speak regularly to the novice master and relate thoughts, or deeds, that were against the rule. This was not a substitute for the Sacrament of Confession, but rather a relating of transgressions such as making noise in the corridor, or feeling grumpy. Power has outlined as follows how, in his experience, this practice operated:

> We novices held our Chapter of Faults in the assembly hall. You knelt down and said this, for example: "My very dear Brothers, I accuse myself of the following faults and beg your forgiveness if I gave bad example to anyone. I broke the silence three times; I was angry on the football field twice and rushed through the dormitory corridor once." After this, the novice master said something like, "Act better in the future, Brother, say three Hail Mary's. You may now return to your seat."[40]

This, of course, was not just a practice restricted to novices. Rather, it was in the novitiate that brothers were inducted into routinely engaging in the "chapter of faults." In other words, this was when it became routine as one of a series of self-abnegation exercises in which they engaged for the rest of their lives as the religious.

Continuing Renewal of Commitment throughout the Lifespan

The end of the novitiate years led to the "stage of first profession" to the religious way of life, the essence of which was living in the community of a religious order and leading a life of poverty, chastity, and obedience. To maintain the stability of the order, commitment to this way of life was expressed publicly through the taking of vows. "First profession" was sometimes termed "temporary profession" and was, in a sense, a rite of passage until the final profession, which in Canon Law implied a perpetual commitment.[41] In the case of some religious orders of brothers, this meant that vows were taken and were renewed on a yearly basis, while in the case of others it meant taking them for three years. During these periods, the individual was free to reconsider his situation until the time of the final vows, which might be anything up to nine years after the initial taking of temporary vows. All of this time was spent as an "ordinary" religious, living the standard life of a member of the community and of a teacher in a Catholic school.

The taking of the first vows, the "first profession," was preceded by Mass. A special ceremony then followed. The rule of the De La Salle Brothers[42] laid down that it should proceed as follows:

> The ceremony for making the Vows shall begin with the *Veni Creator*, followed by the Versicle and the Collect; then each Aspirant shall pronounce his Vows, kneeling on the altar step, holding a lighted candle, after which he shall go to the brother Superior General or his representative, and kneeling, give him the formula of Vows, kiss his hand as a sign of obedience, and receive the accolade...The Brothers who have pronounced Vows shall sign in the Special Register.

Some orders also incorporated into the ceremony a component that was entitled "the reception of the habit," this being the distinctive dress worn by brothers at work and in the monastery, as opposed to the regular clerical black suits that were worn in public. O'Malley, under the pseudonym of "Brendan," recalls his own "reception of the habit" as follows:

> *I renounce the world and its pomps for the love of Our Lord Jesus Christ.*
>
> Brendan removed his jacket and handed it to the Brother beside him. Kneeling in his clerical black trousers and white collarless shirt, he joined his hands and waited for a moment before continuing.
>
> *I have chosen to wear the livery of my Lord Jesus Christ.*

> The Superior general, venerable looking in rimless glasses, held forward the folded habit. Brendan kissed it reverently, stood up and stepped to one side of the chapel sanctuary, making way for the next in line.[43]

O'Malley's exposition concludes with the statement that "the colours of the flowers and candles, the smell of new cloth and incense, the raw fervent voices of the choir, the pealing of the organ and the happiness welling up within him" brought a lump in the throat of the newly professed brother.

The reception of the habit during the ceremony served to reinforce the message that there was no room for individuality within the life of the religious. Everybody wore the same type of dress, and now those who took first vows had this legitimated during their religious ceremony. Indeed, the rules of the different orders of brothers ensured such homogeneity by laying out the dress code in great detail.[44] At the same time, there were differences between orders. For example, a characteristic of the Marist Brothers and the De La Salle Brothers was that, unlike brothers in most other male religious orders, they did not wear a Roman collar in class. Rather, as the Marist rule stated:

> Article 612: They shall wear a white rabat, about five and a half inches long, five inches broad, with a slit of an inch and five-eights from the middle of the bottom.[45]

The point, however, is that within each order, all wore the same type of clothes and there was even a requirement that the umbrellas they used should all be alike.[46] Thus, there was no room for individual dress choice and bodily self-expression.

Following the reception of the habit, all who remained members of a religious order of brothers were exposed to both "rituals of intensification" and "rituals of revitalization,"[47] devised to keep them "dead to the world." Rituals of intensification included a range of daily practices. Every day followed the same pattern, with only slight variation. It was very much along the lines outlined already regarding life in the novitiate. Power sketches in some detail the pattern that prevailed in the case of the Irish Christian Brothers during his time in the order.[48] Along with a clear timetable for work, meals, recreation, and sleep, "times of silence" were also set aside each day within congregations, during which brothers were expected to avoid making noise when walking and when opening and shutting doors. Great emphasis was also placed on regular daily prayer as being the "most proper and efficacious means of avoiding sin and correcting their defects, and doing all things well."[49] Indeed, the Marist Brothers' rules stated that members should not rest satisfied with morning meditation, but should "endeavour to continue it through the different actions of the day, by the remembrance of the presence of God and the practice of ejaculatory prayer."[50]

Brothers were also required, on a daily basis, to seek what were termed "subjects for mortification" in their own character. The purpose of this was explained as follows in the rule of the Marist Brothers:

> To combat his predominant passion, to overcome his inconstancy, to curb the sallies of his temper, to endure a lively and fervid imagination, a fund of impatience difficult to repress, so many seasons of unaccountable sadness and depression, so many fears and scruples, a crowd of perplexities, often so very fatiguing—all these combats, all these trials, are rich treasures of abnegation and penance, and, consequently, of merit for a Brother who knows how to turn them to good account.[51]

In other words, there was a commitment, to use a Foucaultian notion, to producing "docile" bodies and minds.[52] Pontifical orders such as the De La Salle Brothers, the Marist Brothers, and the Irish Christian Brothers, also moved their teachers from school to school, sometimes once a year, and often with no more than a day's notice. While this was sometimes deemed necessary to meet the teaching needs of the order, it also served to ensure a brother did not become too attached not only to fellow community members, but also to his location of residence.

There was no attempt by the orders to disguise such practices, with the Marist Brothers clearly stating that the purpose was "to maintain order and regularity."[53] To the latter end, various surveillance practices also operated to ensure that the activities were carried out with the regularity intended. The most prominent of these was going to Confession. Brothers also partook in the "chapter of faults" on a weekly basis, with each brother being required "to declare his faults in an audible and distinct voice so as to be heard by all present."[54] The process opened with "self-accusation." It was followed by "fraternal correction," when peers reminded the brother of the faults omitted in his self-accusation, or pointed out some of his failings to him. Offering correction was not designed for the sake of providing the "correctors" with perverse pleasure. On the contrary, it was decreed that "it should be given in few words, with a great spirit of charity, and so as not to hurt the feelings of any one."[55] It was also decreed that "he who gives it ought to have in view only the advantage of the Institute and the good of the person admonished."[56] Similarly, it was decreed that "he who receives the admonition shall humble himself, thank him who gives it, and refrain from excusing himself, even when the imputation is incorrect."[57]

There was more; members were also trained to become self-observant. Each internalized the systems of surveillance and became his own overseer. In particular, there was the daily "examination of conscience." On this, the rule of the Irish Christian Brothers decreed that three times a day a brother should consider "the state of his conscience as it relates especially to a particular vice or virtue, or to one of his exercises or duties, in order that he may perceive his infidelities and may labour seriously to correct all his faults and to perfect his virtues."[58] Following each engagement in this practice, a brother was also obliged to resolve to apply himself faithfully to overcome whatever fault he had identified. Thus, the docile continually checked to make sure they were not doing things that could threaten the smooth organization and management of the community and the order, and also reaffirmed regularly their own commitment to both and to what they saw as their higher calling from God.

Surveillance was also conducted through the annual visit to each community of a specially appointed brother termed "the visitor." The main function of this individual was to inspect the community in order to advise on its good functioning and that of associated schools. The visitor also had the duty to discipline individuals for various misdemeanors, including smoking in private and not sufficiently preparing one's school work. More unpleasant for him was when he had to persuade brothers to leave the order, perhaps because of difficulties they had in maintaining fidelity to their vow of chastity, or in maintaining the daily regimen of prayer and work.

So far, the emphasis in this account has been on various "rituals of intensification." Brothers, however, also engaged in "rituals of revitalization." For one thing, great stress was placed on ensuring that all took an annual vacation, albeit along with other members of the community. While it was deemed essential to produce individuals with the same degree of religious fervor as those living the enclosed monastic life, it was recognized that because teaching brothers had to work in the classroom like their lay teacher colleagues, there was a real danger that they could end up mentally and physically exhausted unless there was some relaxation in their annual routine. Therefore, it was common for each community of brothers to rent a house in a quiet countryside, or a seaside setting, where they rose a little later each day and engaged in more physical exercise than normal, while still following a fairly strict routine of regular prayer and spiritual reflection.

During the school vacation, a period of time, often up to a week, was also set aside for a community "retreat." This involved the members of each community immersing themselves in prayer, religious reflection, and spiritual exercises, and reading religious works, including the lives of the founders of religious orders and the history of the orders themselves. Through such activity, engaged in annually until they became old and infirm, brothers renewed their motivation and values annually, and became recharged emotionally such that their commitment to their way of life was regularly revitalized.

This chapter has outlined how young recruits were inducted, through a number of stages, into the life of a fully-fledged brother. As they proceeded through each stage they increasingly internalized the authoritarian framework that characterized the life of the religious. This framework was to govern their lives right up to the point of death. When brothers ceased full-time teaching, they tended to remain on in a community if they were in good health. Here, they continued to live according to all the rhythms of life of their younger brethren. While they no longer had full-time teaching loads, they often substituted for absent colleagues. Other duties included working with small groups of what at the time were termed "slow learners," particularly in providing additional tuition. Eventually, when they became infirm, they were looked after in special retirement homes where they prepared spiritually for departure from the world.

Even in dying there was great order. What was promoted, as Keenan has put it, was an "awareness of dying" as a 'merciful release from this "vale of tears" in "an ever-present reality within the normative framework of religious life."[59] The general sociological frame within which this needs to be considered, he argues, is as follows:

> While biologically one expires alone, one dies within a social context of significance. The "natural" fact of death becomes a "social fact" as group norms about appropriate ways of dying and commemorating come to exercise, in Durkheimian terms, the characteristics of "exteriority" and "constraints" in relation to individual physical and psychological experiences of death and dying.[60]

Among the patterned ways of dealing with death, as laid out in the constitutions of the Marist Brothers in 1923, was the following:

> Chapter XVII
>
> Art. 94—When a Brother is in his agony, all the Brothers of the House, if they are not in school, shall assemble beside his bed to recite the prayers for the dying, in union with the Priest...to assist the sick Brother to die well.[61]

Such practices were certainly designed to provide support for the dying brother; religious orders were death-affirming societies. Furthermore, as with the practice of writing up the life of every brother after he had died and publishing it in a necrology, which was distributed to all monasteries of the order around the world, they contributed to a tightening, rather than a weakening, of community bonds. As Keenan concludes, by their deaths, as it were, Marists were reborn as a society.[62] This, indeed, was also the situation with regard to all of the major orders of teaching brothers at the time.

CHAPTER 6

An Education Rigid and Unbending

The world was seen as essentially evil; Catholic youth were susceptible to the wickedness of the world and needed to be reminded of the other world. Catholic schools were vital in the battle against evil; they could provide the necessary vigilance and control over youth. Character training was important; it would initially occur in the home, but the school would continue the battle to ward off evil influences.[1]

This opening quotation captures the prevailing Catholic perspective on human nature during much of the period under consideration. It was also the dominant perspective influencing the approach to Catholic education, including that overseen by teaching brothers. This is not to overlook the fact that in many countries Catholics were educated within a Catholic school system structured along lines reflecting that of the corresponding state system, with a primary school level and a secondary school level existing as two distinct phases. To maintain credibility among the general public, Catholic primary schools normally adopted the various syllabi prescribed for state schools, with their emphasis on reading, writing, and arithmetic. Generally, as with their state-run counterparts, Catholic secondary schools also prepared students for national, or state-wide, public examinations in order to obtain the credentials that were the gateway to public service and other white-collar positions and, in turn, to social mobility.

Those familiar with the structure of Catholic school systems, but not with the distinctive ethos alluded to at the opening of this chapter, might be prompted to ask what was distinctive about Catholic education, including the education provided by brothers. One answer to this question centers on the private nature of Catholic schooling in some countries, most notably the United States, for all of the period under consideration, and Australia and New Zealand for portions of it. This characteristic, however, does not hold true for a number of other countries where state assistance, often substantial, was available in return for meeting particular conditions. These conditions related to the need to employ a certain number of "qualified" teachers and to be open to regular inspection of school buildings and facilities by state-appointed inspectors.

Regardless of the country concerned, however, Catholic schooling, including that provided by religious brothers, was distinguished by the process of education. It is helpful to consider this process as having had three main and interrelated, characteristics. The most obvious of these was the emphasis placed on the teaching of Catholic religious knowledge and practices, both within school and in extracurricular sessions. The nature of the religious formation of Catholic religious brothers, as with that of nuns and priests, also influenced the nature of the teaching approaches adopted by them. In particular, it was necessary to adopt a set of practices aimed at maintaining the regimen of the cloister within the schools, thus minimizing the possibility of opportunities arising that might entice a brother to leave the religious life. Finally, a range of other practices also operated to ensure that Catholic schools were permeated by a religious atmosphere that was all-pervasive.

The Teaching of Religious Knowledge and Religious Practices in Brothers' Schools

Praetz has characterized the view of the Catholic school as being primarily that of inculcator of moral virtues, "fortifying the will through the exclusion of negative influences and strengthening motives for good conduct through positive training and instruction."[2] This view was also made crystal clear to members of religious teaching orders in their rules and constitutions, particularly in sections outlined along the following lines: "It is necessary that children should be thoroughly instructed in the truths and precepts of the Catholic Faith, so that they may adhere to it through all difficulties and temptations, and show forth Christian teaching in their lives."[3] Pronouncements by senior members of the Catholic Hierarchy over the decades also served to remind brothers that their principal task was to work hard to prepare students to strive for eternal salvation. In Ireland, Cardinal Paul Cullen, judged to have been "one of the two or three most influential ecclesiastics of the entire nineteenth century"[4] across the

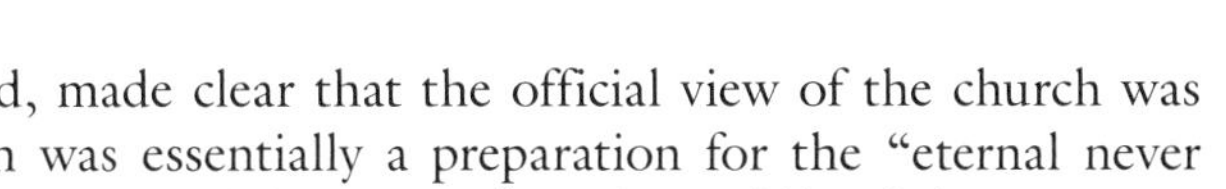

Catholic world, made clear that the official view of the church was that education was essentially a preparation for the "eternal never ending existence beyond the grave."[5] In the middle of the next century, in 1949, the bishops in Australia took the same stance, stating:

> The Catholic view is perfectly clear. Every child born into this world is a child of Adam, inheriting the nature which Adam, as it were, bequeathed to the human race. Adam's sin—the sin of direct disobedience to the command of the Almighty God—was to have disastrous effects. Evil as the results of his sin were, however, they did not completely corrupt human nature. They disfigured it—but not beyond hope of repair.[6]

Thus, they argued, the task of education is "to restore the sons of Adam to their high position as children of God, citizens of the kingdom of God, by the harmonious development of their physical, social, intellectual, moral, aesthetic and spiritual powers."[7] In the United States, John O'Hara, cardinal-archbishop of Philadelphia, pronounced along similar lines in the 1960s.[8]

The general approach to the teaching of religious knowledge that developed out of such a perspective has been summarized by Rodriguez regarding his Catholic education in the United States in the 1950s:

> In school, religious instruction stressed that man was a sinner [and] portrayed God as a judge. I was carefully taught the demands He placed upon me. In the third grade I could distinguish between venial and mortal sin. I knew—and was terrified to know—that there was one unforgivable sin (against the Holy Ghost): the sin of despair. I knew the crucial distinction between perfect and imperfect contrition. I could distinguish between sins of commission from sins of omission. And I learned how important it was to be in a state of grace at the moment of death.[9]

While the pupils' minds were formed in this way through many of the practices that operated in Catholic schools, they received the intended message in its most concentrated form during formal religious knowledge classes. Various titles were assigned to these classes at different times and in different places. They included "religious instruction," "catechetics," "religious education," and "Christian doctrine."

An early approach to the teaching of religious knowledge, following the popularization of print knowledge, emerged around the time of the Council of Trent (1545–1563) and is sometimes referred to as "traditional catechesis."[10] The church's view was that it had been provided with a body of truth and that the most suitable way to pass it on to its members was through a catechism. This new approach replaced earlier forms of oral instruction as the prime source of Catholic teaching. In the early 1800s, a catechism consisted of a methodical summary of the teachings of the church, with the emphasis being doctrinal and moralistic. By the middle of the century, Catholic schools were using a variety of catechisms, the most common one popularly known as the "Penny Catechism." They were usually small books with a list of several hundred short questions and accompanying answers. Students were required to commit the answers to memory and to recite them orally when requested to do so. The questions were laid out on the following lines:

> Who made the world?
> God made the world.
> Who is God?[11]
> God is the Creator of heaven and earth and of all things and the supreme Lord of all.

This approach, as the academic and poet Brendan Kennelly has put it regarding his own primary school education in Ireland in the 1940s, introduced him to the notion that "everything was answerable."[12] Rodriguez has commented in similar fashion regarding his schooling in the United States in the 1950s, stating that "the Baltimore Cathecism taught me to trust the authority of the Church."[13] Campion has outlined how the same approach was adopted in Australia, arguing that the "directness and sureness," as well as the simplicity of the prose used, "imparted a special brand of confidence."[14] However, he has also contended that the catechism could be deceptive, and at times "it must have puzzled and perhaps stretched the minds of the young learners"[15] with entries such as the following:

> Which are the principal mysteries of religion?
> There are two principal mysteries of religion: First, the Unity and Trinity of God; Secondly, the Incarnation, Death and Resurrection of Our Saviour.

His point is that the sophisticated concepts contained within these propositions were dealt with in primary schools solely through learning by rote and committing to memory, without discussion, or explanation. Drawing attention to the same point, Praetz has argued that there was no willingness on the part of the religious to change their practices because, as a synopsis of faith, "the catechism had formed part of the religious training of the teachers both at school and at the novitiate" and "its use simplified the work of teachers and inspectors."[16]

To accompany catechisms, various syllabi were prepared to guide teachers on how religion should be taught. For example, the *Syllabus of Religious Instruction in Schools* prepared for the Melbourne Archdiocese in Australia, was issued in separate editions in 1917 and 1933. In 1950, a similar document was prepared for distribution to all Catholic schools in the state of Victoria.[17] This latter syllabus covered schooling from kindergarten grades to matriculation level and provided notes on suggested timetables, on how to manage a number of classes of several grade levels simultaneously, and on how to organize student projects. It then dealt with each grade level individually, providing short specific instructions under various headings.

Other practices also operated in Catholic schools, including those run by brothers, to reinforce the religious formation of pupils through the formal teaching of "religious knowledge" classes. The Irish Christian Brothers, for example, decreed that on entering the classroom in the morning the brother was to kneel and recite privately the 'Prayer Before School."[18] Each pupil, on arrival, was to do likewise, kneel before the statue of Our Lady, and recite the "Morning Offering to the Sacred Heart." The rule also decreed that, throughout the day, every hour when the school clock rang, the students should all stand up to say the "Hail Mary," "always waiting to make the Sign of the Cross along with the Brother at the commencement and conclusion of the prayer."[19] Great significance was also attached to the annual school religious retreat. Generally lasting about three days, it involved students immersing themselves in prayer, religious reflection, spiritual exercises, and the reading of religious works. Students' religious zeal was also intensified at this time through studying the lives of the founders of religious orders and the history of the orders themselves.

Work by brothers to intensify the religious zeal of their pupils also took place through preparation for, and participation in, Gregorian chant competitions between schools. Other drama-laden practices included preparing for the services of the Holy Week and Easter, holding elaborate processions on the feast days of various saints, being prepared for the sacraments of Confirmation and Holy Communion, and attending special "High Masses" at various times during the school year when often up to 16 priests might be present on the altar. The situation was, as Rodriquez has put it, one where:

> The religious calendar governed my school year. In early September there was a nine-o-clock mass on the Friday of the first week of school to pray for academic success…In June there was a mass of graduation for the eight-graders.[20]

He concluded by saying that "between those events, school often stopped or flowered as routine bowed to the sacred," with certain days being set aside as special "feast days," or days celebrating the life of particular saints, as well as "holy days" commemorating special occasions in the history of the church.[21]

The sacrament of Confession came in for special emphasis. Pupils were encouraged in the schools to confess regularly, and they were trained in the preparation ritual. This involved a systematic examination of conscience, in which they reviewed their behavior with regard to God, other individuals, and themselves. Because of the practice of frequent attendance at Confession, and through the encouragement of regular self-denial, pupils were constantly reminded that a fresh beginning was always possible as long as they were truly sorry for their sins and sincere in their desire to mend their ways.

Pupils' religious zeal was further intensified through the pride instilled on being admitted to one of the various pious associations organized through brothers' schools. These included the Apostleship of Prayer, the Sacred Heart Association, the Confraternity of the Divine Child, and the Missionary Association of the Holy Childhood.[22] Largely, membership involved committing to saying daily prayers for particular pious causes of the church and distributing leaflets outlining these prayers among their peers and the Catholic public more widely. Sometimes, it also involved organizing concerts and bazaars to raise money for those religious working in missionary lands.

A more select group was invited to join special prayers and devotional groups termed "sodalities." These have been characterized as follows:

> The sodalities, in the hands of the Church, were special training grounds within the general training of the school; they aimed at cultivating higher ideals and stressed the obligation of self-improvement and of using one's influence for good, thereby turning to account the latent capacities of leadership, stimulating them and directing them to the common good. Essentially, the sodalities were for a small nucleus, an elite; they were to act as cells exercising an influence for good upon the larger organism.[23]

School journals regularly published photographs of enrolled pupils, accompanied by laudatory accounts of their activities. However, a small number of sodalities like the Legion of Mary, whose organizational structure has been outlined as follows, shunned such publicity:

> The Legion was conducted along the lines of a Roman legion, with brass banners of the imperial eagle standing puissant over the sign, Legio Marie... Members of the Legion were bound to convert non-believers to Christianity. They were expected to descend, always in pairs, into dens of anti-Catholicism to try to convince unbelievers of the truth of the Church.[24]

Members of the Legion of Mary were required to be very secretive about their activities. While they kept minutes of their meetings, these were not freely available. Members were also instructed on the need to preserve absolute secrecy in regard to any issues debated at meetings.

The Influence of the Brothers' Religious Formation and Their Distinctive Way of Life on Their Approach to Teaching

The nature of the religious formation of brothers and their distinctive way of life also influenced their approach to teaching throughout most of the period under consideration. In particular, many of their pedagogical practices seem to have been shaped by a need to replicate within the school setting the regimen that prevailed within the cloister. Thus, the training of brothers in the certitude of Catholic doctrine goes some way toward explaining why questioning was not a feature of education in their schools. The existence of an extensive range of literary evidence attesting to the prevalence of this lack of questioning and a discouragement of critical debate in the classroom is particularly rich regarding the situation in Ireland. The poet Thomas Kinsella, who attended O'Connell's Schools in Dublin, for example, has argued that while the teaching process was efficient, "inspiration was not necessarily inherent in the system... it was a matter of running into exceptional people,"[25] while fellow artists Thomas Murphy,[26] Charles Harper,[27] and Robert Ballagh[28] have also indicated that there was a lack of encouragement for the development of a questioning attitude, particularly toward religious beliefs.

Angus has concluded along the same lines in relation to the Irish Christian Brothers' schools in Australia, stating that rote learning was promoted and that intellectual concerns were "reduced to a functional, mechanistic production of credentials."[29] The cultural context that shaped this situation has been characterized as follows:

> A Brother had to fend for himself against the isolating effects of religious life and the incessant demands of a boarding school. He was equipped for his main task, but neither equipped nor much encouraged to explore the Church's treasure house of learning let alone profane culture. "We are Christian brothers not Jesuits—the *bon mot* of an influential novice master affirmed a common, severely practical outlook which had, perhaps, a social class slant."[30]

Also, as Rodriquez has reminded us in relation to his primary school education in the United States, anti-intellectualism was not just something confined to religion classes:

> During those years when I was memorizing the questions and answers of the Baltimore catechism, I was also impressing on my memory the spelling of hundreds of words, grammar rules, division and multiplication tables... Stressing memorization, my teachers implied that education is largely a matter of acquiring knowledge already discovered.[31]

He concluded by saying of his teachers that "in religion class especially, they would grow impatient with the relentlessly questioning student."

Braniff has drawn attention to a culture of anti-intellectualism among the Marist Brothers in Australia. He illustrates this with a quotation from a former pupil reflecting on his experience in a Marist school in the 1920s:

> Brother Brendan was kindly enough, but negative. He discouraged me from attempting a University Exhibition. One would be shocked at their lack of training... At that time there was prejudice against scholarship on the part of some of the brothers, their viewpoint being that scholars were dodging manual work and that study was dangerous to humility.[32]

Donovan has made a similar observation regarding the De La Salle Brothers in New Zealand and Australia for the same decade, noting that there was discouragement of university-level studies for brothers themselves for fear that they would be consumed with pride in their achievements.[33] Also, in those cases where permission was given to brothers to undertake university studies it was usually forthcoming only after their final vows were made. Among the reasons given for this were a fear that young brothers might be exposed to undesirable influences, the costs involved, and the belief that they were already fully occupied with their teaching and religious duties.[34]

The argument so far is that it was necessary for brothers to adopt a pedagogical approach that supported the anti-intellectualism that had been fostered among them during their period of religious formation lest they come to question their own commitment to the religious life. For the same reason, brothers were required to keep parents very much at a distance. This action was justified on the grounds that, because of their "religious calling," as it was termed, only teachers who were members of religious orders knew what was best for pupils in their education. Such a position was regularly impressed on parents in pronouncements from the Catholic Hierarchy. In Australia, Bishop Murray of Maitland referred in 1868 to the devotion of the religious teachers to the cause of education for no private or personal gain,[35] Archbishop Vaughan made a claim in 1879 that parents knew the advantage of bringing their children into direct contact with teachers who were "living examples of highest sacrifice,"[36] and Bishop O'Reilly spoke in 1890 of the school class as the religious teacher's family circle, the schoolroom as his or her home, and the relationship between the teacher and the class as having a religious sanction and bearing "the impress of a heavenly seal."[37] Such pronouncements reflected the dominant pattern of thought among both the religious and the laity that prevailed across the English-speaking Catholic world until well into the latter half of the twentieth century. Overall, what was communicated was that the lay state was very much an inferior one. This was based partially on the position that in opting for it, one was placing oneself in a situation where much greater freedom was given to human desires, many of which were viewed as being intrinsically evil and as working in opposition to a striving for perfection in this life in order to maximize one's opportunity to gain eternal salvation.

In general, then, it was considered necessary for brothers to keep lay people at a distance, not just to preserve their own notion of themselves as superior beings in the eyes of the Lord, but also lest they be exposed to temptation that might lead to a breaking of one's sacred vows. Thus, a rule of the Irish Christian Brothers required members to "abstain from frequent and unnecessary conversations with seculars."[38] Because of rules like this, and the fact that they were forbidden to talk to lay people about their life in the monastery, brothers were unable to make use of their own life experiences, or happenings in the neighborhood, to facilitate conceptual development and develop inquiring and creative capacities among pupils. When it was deemed appropriate to meet the parents of pupils, brothers were required to conduct the meeting in a very formal atmosphere in a hall, or room, set aside specially for the purpose, and any conversation that was to take place was to be in as few words as possible.[39] These requirements were partly indicative of a fear that those in religious life might, as a result of contact with parents, be prodded into serious contemplation of the attractions of forming personal relationships with those of the opposite sex and be enticed, as a result, to leave their respective religious congregations. Such thinking appears to have underpinned the concern expressed by the De La Salle Brothers in England when, in 1946, they asked the authorities of their schools, "as a matter of urgency," to do away with the practice of employing females, "which had developed here and there as a result of the war-time situation."[40]

Brothers were also required to be on their guard lest they found themselves forming personal relationships with lay teachers employed in their schools. This situation hindered the sharing of educational experiences between both groups. Brothers were not encouraged to engage in regular dialogue with their lay colleagues about the development of curriculum and pedagogy. Also, there was no entertainment among the various orders of brothers of the view that married life, or living as a single person outside of religious life, might enhance one's qualities as a teacher and a school manager. Indeed, it was emphasized that the religious should only consider employing lay teachers as a last resort. From their early days in Ireland, this presented no difficulties for the Irish Christian Brothers because they were able to rely largely on their own resources, supplementing their teaching force with trained monitors rather than with paid lay teachers.[41] Such an arrangement, however, was not always possible when they established schools overseas. For example, in the 1880s, when Brother Ambrose Treacy was directing the expansion of the Irish Christian Brothers in Australia, he employed trained lay teachers to assist with more specialized work.[42] His correspondence, however, had a tone of condescension about it; he was convinced that the presence of brothers in classrooms was essential for the proper implementation of their educational system that stemmed from their monasticism, and he feared that lay teachers would not understand the ethos of a Christian Brothers' school.[43]

The Irish Christian Brothers' view of the lay teacher persisted well into the twentieth century. It found expression in their "rules," where it was stated that brothers were required to avoid "engaging in political conversations with assistant teachers."[44] By "assistant teachers" was clearly meant lay teachers. What was being made plain through this terminology was that a lay teacher was to be employed in a school only when no brother could be made available to fill an essential teaching position. The brothers also promoted the view that lay teachers could not possibly approach teaching with the same degree of responsibility as could members of the order, and that they would ignore their duties unless they were constantly monitored. Thus, individual brothers were told that they would need to ensure "the same conscientious discharge of duty from the lay teachers, who ought not to be allowed to bring newspapers into the classroom, much less to read them therein."[45] They were also told to so arrange their own classes as to have the other pupils in the room under observation. "This would ensure," it was concluded, that "to a certain extent, they will never lose sight of the children who are in groups or classes around the maps or blackboards, or reciting lessons, or in charge of Assistant Teachers."[46]

Kehoe analyzed the testimony of lay teachers working for various religious orders in Australia between 1872 and 1972, and concluded that the adoption of a demeaning view of their role for much of this period meant that they often had to use the students' toilets, could not eat and converse with brothers at lunch time, and were not privy to discussions concerning school matters.[47] In countries where brothers' schools were in receipt of state finance and thus open to inspection, members of the orders were instructed by their superiors to permit the state's inspectors to enter their schools, be present when they were examining a class, and "gladly receive any suggestions"[48] that might be offered. In general, however, the attitude was that such personnel were to be welcomed as guests purely because this safeguarded their receipt of official grants, rather than because there was a possibility they might contribute to improving the pedagogical work of the school.

Following the Second World War, as the provision of Catholic education in many countries began to expand faster than the expansion of the religious orders, the employment of greater numbers of lay teachers became necessary. This was accompanied by some religious orders declaring that their lay counterparts should enjoy good working conditions and be happy in their schools. Even so, the approach was that of benevolent employers toward their employees, rather than one informed by a view that they were partners with the lay teachers in the provision of Catholic education. During the late 1940s and throughout the 1950s, a series of studies in various parts of the United States found that "lay teachers, men and women, in elementary and secondary schools, felt that they were being treated kindly, but not professionally."[49] They were not involved in the shaping of school policy, participation at faculty meetings was confined to procedural questions, and administrators were quite open in stating that while they considered lay teachers did an adequate job, they would replace them with the religious if they became available.[50]

By the late 1950s, change was on the horizon. Catholic education continued to grow throughout the English-speaking world. The attitude of the church in the various countries concerned required school places for every Catholic child. This often meant that no limit was placed on enrolments. The situation was compounded when, in the late 1960s and early 1970s, the number of people entering the religious orders decreased, while others began to move out of classroom teaching and administration into new forms of work. The inability of religious orders to meet the additional demand for teaching staff meant that increasing the recruitment and employment of lay teachers, often trained in government institutions, became the only real alternative. The change in the mixture of staff led to the appointment of lay principals and the withdrawal of orders from individual schools.

It was around this time that the church in general, and religious orders of brothers in particular, also changed their attitude to coeducation. From the middle of the nineteenth century, coeducation had been growing slowly in European countries, especially in state systems. In the United States, it grew more rapidly, except in the Catholic sector where, as in the Catholic education sector in Europe, there was great resistance.[51] Reflecting on this, Thomas Shields of the Catholic University of America, in his entry on coeducation in *The Catholic Encyclopedia*, first published in the United States in 1908, rejected the claim of improved discipline on the grounds that "while the boys probably part with some of their roughness it is by no means certain that the delicacy of feeling and the refinement of manner that are expected in girls, gain much by the association."[52] He also argued that while "each sex has its own mental constitution and its special capacities,"[53] this does not mean that "unlike natures shall be molded into a superficial resemblance to each other."[54] It is true, of course, that Catholics were not the only advocates of this position and not the only opponents of coeducation in secondary schools at the time. What distinguished Catholic resistance, however, was "the nearly complete absence of dissenting views,"[55] especially when it came to insisting on single-sex education to support the domestication of women within the family relationship.

The argument emanating from Rome that educating the sexes together would lead to promiscuity became intertwined in the teaching of Pope Pius XI with an argument in favor of single-sex education on the grounds that males and females needed to be prepared to fulfill separate roles within society. This received strong expression in his encyclical of December 1929, *Divini Illius Magistri*:[56] What is not contained in the encyclical statement, yet which must have been uppermost in the minds of senior church prelates at the time, was that such a position also helped to minimize the temptations to those already in religious life to leave all behind and rejoin the world of the laity.

Another way in which opportunities that might entice a brother to leave the religious life were minimized was by isolating the religious from the laity, as well as from the female religious, in their teacher preparation. In the 1930s, a senior De La Salle brother in Australia described the situation bluntly. The occasion was the opening of the order's own teacher training college and state recognition of the qualifications of its graduates. What pleased the brother about these developments was that they meant there would be no need to run "the risk of sending our Brothers to be trained in the college for teachers in Armidale, where young ladies are trained side by side with young men."[57]

Throughout much of the nineteenth century, the training of brothers as teachers in most of the orders was largely on an apprenticeship model, with some theory being presented within the local community house, which was often located alongside the brothers' school. The theory usually consisted of some reading on philosophy and educational psychology. In the case of the Irish Christian Brothers, the early approach was one whereby, following a year of induction into the rules and practices of the community, along with spiritual formation, there was a year of teacher preparation with a period of supervised teaching. On appointment to a school, the young "apprentice brother" was given a supervising teacher, who would assist him and sometimes supervise his classroom lessons and his studies in what were known as "the grades." These grades consisted of a program devised in 1887 by the Brothers' Education Committee, which had a number of stages of study in subjects ranging from drawing to Greek. Similar grade programs were later developed for Irish Christian Brothers in other parts of the world. The usual arrangement was that "failure to make progress in the Grades, examined twice-yearly, meant a deferral of the annual vows by which a young brother reached his final profession."[58]

In his work on the preparation of Irish Christian Brothers as teachers in Australia, Connole details the establishment of the juniorate and scholasticate at Strathfield in Sydney in 1922, and notes that the latter "leaned to the practical rather than the academic side of teacher training." [59] The central character in the enterprise was known as "the master of method," a position also common in the similar approaches to teacher preparation used by the De La Salle and Marist Brothers. Overall, what took place was a combination of academic study and instruction in teaching methods, coupled with practice teaching in a nearby Brothers' school. It was during the scholasticate year that brothers at Strathfield also commenced their studies for the grades, which by this stage were outlined at seven levels, each being "divided roughly into Religion (Doctrine, Bible and Philosophy), Education and Psychology, English, Mathematics, Latin and/or Modern Languages, the Natural Sciences and History."[60] Such preparation, Bollen has concluded, was deemed sufficient: "Competence beyond matriculation standard in teaching subjects could be gained on the job with help from older men and required work on the Grades."[61] Thus, until the 1950s, university education, while not unknown, was not a common experience for brothers.

The situation did not vary greatly among other orders of brothers, regardless of the country in which they were located. Collins[62] and Braniff[63] have identified a similar pattern in the teacher preparation of Marist Brothers in New Zealand and Australia, respectively, including their isolation from lay people and from the female religious. Some deviation from the norm prevailed in relation to the preparation of members of certain religious orders as teachers in the United States. Here, as Murphy[64] has documented, a particular difficulty arose in the early 1900s because of the great effort that went into protecting the chastity of the religious. By now there was huge pressure on Catholic education to meet secular requirements if Catholic students were to be accepted for service in public agencies and their school credits were to be accepted at other institutions of learning. In particular, trained teachers equal to those in the public schools "but tempered with Catholic truth,"[65] were sought.

The solution was to establish a faculty of education at the Catholic University of America. The problem, however, was how to keep the male religious separated from the females. Thomas Shields, Dean of the Faculty, responded initially by utilizing the campus while the men were away. Hence, the first program for females was a summer session. Shields then went on to build a campus for females separate from, but near the main Catholic University campus, "with provision for separate religious houses for those communities whose rule demanded it."[66] In this way, he helped to allay the fears of the superiors of the religious on two counts; the vow of chastity of their members was safeguarded by maintaining their segregation, while their commitment to the total way of life of their respective religious orders was maintained by having a community house on campus.

At the same time, not all religious orders in the United States availed themselves of this opportunity. Here, as in other parts of the English-speaking world, Catholic teacher preparation for many religious orders, including religious orders of brothers, was a combination of on-the-job training and summer school instruction.[67] Because members of religious orders were prepared as teachers not only in a single-sex environment, but also in isolation from lay people, the range of pedagogical practices to which they were exposed was limited to those favored by the order in question and its "master of method." Also, they were rarely placed in situations that would have encouraged them to reflect on the adequacy and appropriateness of those practices for various situations. Thus, there was very little experimentation in approaches to teaching in brothers' schools.

Other Aspects of the All-Pervasive Religious Atmosphere of Brothers' Schools

So far, this chapter has foregrounded the emphasis placed in brothers' schools on the teaching of Catholic religious knowledge and practices, both within school and in extracurricular sessions. The extent to which the nature of the religious formation of brothers influenced their teaching approach has also been considered. However, a range of other practices also operated to ensure that their schools were permeated by a religious atmosphere that was all-pervasive. On this, it is helpful to draw attention to Bryk, Lee, and Holland's *Catholic Education and the Common Good*,[68] one of the most significant works of scholarship on Catholic education in recent years. In their excellent exposition on the historical background to Catholic education in the United States, they have pointed out that for the great majority of pupils in Catholic schools throughout the nineteenth century, an education, as for those in the public school sector, largely meant primary schooling only.[69] From the beginning of the twentieth century, however, Catholic secondary schooling began to expand. In doing so, a general trend among the schools' managers was to reject the new American public school model, which espoused a more life-studies and vocationally oriented curriculum than had hitherto been the case. What was desired, as expressed by the National Catholic Educational Association (NCEA), was that a largely academic curriculum should be maintained, with a study of classical humanism being advocated for all secondary school students.[70] The argument, according to Bryk, Lee, and Holland, was that because the classics embodied the languages of Western civilization, "their study had moral and aesthetic value" and "they provided intellectual discipline and encouraged inventiveness."[71]

Broadly speaking, Catholic secondary schools throughout the rest of the English-speaking world were shaped by similar views.[72] These views were, in turn, legitimated by Pope Pius XI in 1929, in *Divini Illius Magistri*, his papal encyclical on education, where he cautioned against the errors of Deweyian-style pragmatism in the curriculum, argued that the church was a conserver of humanity's cultural heritage, and emphasized the importance of the teaching of Latin.[73] Nevertheless, one needs to be cautious in assuming that the models of Catholic schooling in all places throughout the overall period under consideration in this book were only those of a basic primary school education devoted to the teaching of reading, writing, arithmetic, and religion, and the provision of a predominantly academic-based secondary school curriculum. Opposition by the church upto the early decades of the twentieth century toward the De La Salle Brothers teaching Latin illustrates this clearly.

Given what has already been said about the commitment of the church throughout much of the period under consideration to the teaching of the classics, it may come as a surprise to some that De La Salle brothers were, for many years, forbidden to teach Latin, or have it taught in their schools. Rule 28 of the order, which dictated this policy, originated with the founder, who felt it was necessary for a number of reasons.[74] For one thing, he did not want any of the brothers to become enamored by Latin, a language intimately associated with the priesthood, lest they be tempted to seek ordination and leave the order. Equally, as has already been pointed out in Chapter Two, he broke new ground in France in promoting the vernacular as the language of instruction in schools and in moving away from the teaching of reading largely by using Latin texts. Thus, it seemed logical to ban the teaching of Latin lest it perpetuate former practices. Furthermore, when he established the order, the teaching of Latin was deemed an essential component of the curriculum for the wealthy. By forbidding the brothers to teach the language, the De La Salle sought to head off any temptation to abandon schools for the poor in favor of those for the rich.

Rule 28 lived on well beyond the period for which it was introduced and the circumstances for which it was meant to have application. This caused very few problems in France and in other non-English-speaking countries, where the De La Salle Brothers concentrated on teaching vocational subjects to the lower classes in primary and junior secondary schools. The leaders of the order in those countries seemed to have no difficulty in being labeled "the ignorant brothers" by critics who believed that a "proper" education was one based on the liberal arts.[75] In the United States, however, superiors of some of the schools run by the order were persuaded by the end of the nineteenth century to include Latin because of the desire of parents that their children receive an education that would give them access to the professions.[76]

Soon, the Jesuits were complaining that the De La Salle Brothers were ignoring their rule.[77] This led to an investigation by the Vatican authorities, but no action was taken. The issue was not resolved, however, as the initiative had also raised ire within the higher levels of the De La Salle order itself, especially among the dominant French conservative group of leaders. Their opposition was aired at the general chapter of 1894, and led to the American brothers being ordered to cease teaching Latin. Protests by American bishops, keen that the classics be taught in order to enhance the social status of a greater number of Catholic schools, and thus the status of the church itself within American society, were to no avail. Indeed, on January 11, 1900, Pope Leo XIII confirmed a decree of the Sacred Congregation of Propaganda, ordering the suppression of Latin in De La Salle schools and colleges throughout the United States.

The outcome for the order in the United States was that it struggled to survive and maintain credibility. De La Salle brothers in Australia were faced with a similar situation after the opening of a school at Armidale, in New South Wales, in 1906. The local bishop, Dr. O'Connor, requested that they teach Latin, particularly so that prospective students for the priesthood would receive the requisite secondary school preparation in the subject, and also so that others would be appropriately prepared for university entrance, which, in the case of certain degrees, required a particular level of competence in the language. As the brothers in the school felt they could not break their order's rule on the matter, O'Connor petitioned the Sacred Congregation for the Propagation of the Faith in Rome, in 1915, to enlist its support. The order, while unwilling to abolish the rule, did agree that Latin could be taught to the students, but in a building removed from the school. It also insisted that the teacher could not be a De La Salle brother.

The issue refused to go away, with Catholic bishops in the United States continuing to lobby to have the rule banning the teaching of Latin removed from the rules and constitutions of the order. The outcome was discussion once more at the highest level, this time at the thirty-fourth De La Salle general chapter, in 1923. By now, Rome had been persuaded that succeeding generations of superiors within the order had lost sight of the spirit of the rule and the historical context in which it had been drawn up. In due course, the superior-general received a letter from the Vatican expressing the wish of Pope Pius XI that brothers be allowed to teach Latin in their schools. The chapter acquiesced to the pope's wishes, thus bringing about a resolution to the problem.

The experience of the De La Salle Brothers in relation to the teaching of Latin in the United States and Australia is a good example to illustrate that while there was a great deal of uniformity in the experience of Catholic education, including in the education provided by brothers, throughout the period under consideration, it was not total. It also serves to illustrate that internal politics were played out within the church on education, as on other matters. In particular, it highlights that issues of territoriality existed between orders in terms of some feeling they had rights over certain aspects of the curriculum, and also that certain orders clearly saw themselves as superior to others in terms of who they taught and what should be taught.

At the same time, it is true to say that throughout the world, all brothers' schools, as with Catholic schools more generally, tended to eliminate content that mentioned the church unfavorably, that treated a particular topic in what was, in the church's view, an immoral manner, or that portrayed a way of life that was repugnant to the church.[78] Dealing with this matter in relation to the situation in the United States, Perko has argued that for the Catholic student, almost every action of the school day was tied, at least remotely, to the ultimate end of salvation or damnation. What was created, as he has put it, was "an environment in which all human activity was seen as having a religious dimension."[79] The sociologist Fichter made the same point in his study of a US parochial school:

> As we watch the teachers and pupils of the parochial school go through the daily routine of study, learning and play, we find that religion enters most of the routine. The distinctive feature of St. Luke's school is the religious, or supernatural "atmosphere," which is basically a process of motivation.[80]

Perko concluded that this dimension provided a strong organizing principle for the educational experience.[81]

Regarding Australia, there are indications of the various ways in which the authorities in the Archdiocese of Melbourne acted to safeguard children from what it saw as improper curriculum practices. They include representation being made to relevant government officials about what was seen as anti-Catholic and immoral content prescribed as examination topics. Also, material was sent to schools to ensure that the Catholic viewpoint was offered to counteract the religious, or moral, position taken in certain prescribed textbooks,[82] while teachers who were members of religious orders were instructed to ensure vigilant supervision over the books that were brought into the schools "lest through indiscriminate reading, danger can be occasioned to faith or morals."[83]

The official position of the Catholic Church was that in all countries in which Catholic schools operated, a major emphasis should be placed not only on religious instruction, but also on ensuring that the climate of schools would be one in which religion would be all-pervasive. A particular way in which this was meant to happen was through the promotion of Catholic viewpoints when teaching the various subjects on the curriculum. On this, Pope Pius IX declared that all branches of learning should "expand in closest alliance with religion,"[84] Pope Leo XIII spoke of "every discipline being thoroughly permeated and ruled by religion,"[85] and Pope Pius XI advocated that "all the teaching, the whole organization of the school . . . its teachers, syllabus and text books in every branch"[86] should be regulated by the Christian spirit. Thus, it is not surprising that many of those who attended brothers' schools during the period under consideration have recalled that they seemed to be constantly doing projects with an element of God, or a picture of God, in them. Taking up this point, Massam points out that the church promoted the teaching of history because its authority rested on the interpretation of tradition as much as on scripture.[87] Also, it is important not to lose sight of what was not taught in brothers' schools. In particular, schools, as with the Catholic population in general, were subject to the requirements of the *Index Librorum Prohibitorum* ("List of Prohibited Books"). The first version of this "Index" appeared in 1559, while the twentieth and final one appeared in 1948, before it was finally abolished in 1966. It consisted of a list of books Catholics were forbidden to read because they were deemed immoral, or contained theological errors.[88]

Sex education also tended not to be a feature of Catholic schools, including brothers' schools. In 1944, Bishop Thomas Toolan of

Mobile, Alabama, called sex education "a pagan doctrine."[89] Five years later, in 1949, the New York Catholic Conference objected vehemently to the screening of two sex education films called "Human Growth" and "Human Reproduction" in the New York public school system,[90] with Bishop Joseph Flanelly calling one of the films immoral and bad.[91] This was in line with the Vatican directives of the 1930s[92] and reiterated in the 1950s. Ireland is another country in which the church's open opposition to sex education was very strong. This manifested itself clearly during the period of the 1948–1951 government. Dr. Noel Browne, the minister for health, intended to make radical changes in the area of public health. The bishops were particularly worried about the lack of a legal guarantee that instruction to be given to expectant mothers would be in line with the teaching of the church on the use of artificial contraception and abortion. [93] The strength of their opposition eventually led to a change of government and the passing of a health bill to its liking, including on educational issues.

Throughout the English-speaking world it was not possible for the church to protect its interests in education through interfering in the political process to the extent that was possible in Ireland. What was possible, however, was to ensure that there was constant surveillance of pupils in order to ensure they followed those rules and regulations of the church deemed to be essential for salvation. At the most obvious level, "religious inspectors" regularly visited schools. These personnel were priests specially appointed by the bishops to visit all Catholic schools, both primary and secondary, in their respective dioceses to ensure that appropriate programs of religious instruction were being followed. Also, each year the inspector examined the pupils in Catholic primary schools in every diocese in religious knowledge by means of an oral examination, while pupils in Catholic secondary schools had both an oral and a written examination. Much more powerful, however, was the constant supervision carried out by the classroom teachers to ensure that their pupils did not stray from the "straight and narrow." Again, the underlying notion, expressed through the doctrine of original sin, was that the world is essentially a bad place and that children are naturally inclined toward evil. Thus, great stress was placed on the notion that proper adult surveillance was necessary to ensure that the child was steered along the path of goodness and righteousness.

A major way in which adult guidance was provided for pupils to steer them away from sin was by ensuring they were constantly occupied. On this, the rules of the Irish Christian Brothers stated that "the pupils should be constantly employed; as soon as one exercise is finished, they should begin the next without any unnecessary delay."[94] Similarly, it was stated that "outside the classroom, too, in the playground and such places, each Brother shall carefully watch over the pupils, so as to shield them from moral and physical danger."[95] Pupils also came under surveillance through practices that brought them to regulate their own behavior through guilt. This situation has been summarized elsewhere as follows:

> Statues of religious figures stood guard over them at various vantage points around the school, while scattered along classroom walls and corridors were images of Jesus and the Blessed Virgin, whose faces were depicted in such a manner that their gaze seemed to be constantly on pupils even when the teacher's attention was elsewhere. Cards carrying the same images in miniature form were used as prizes and encouragement awards in Catholic schools, and were kept by pupils in their prayer books, or were displayed in their bedrooms. All of this served to reinforce in pupils' minds that their misdeeds would not go unnoticed in the divine log which was being constantly updated and which would be wheeled out when they had to account for their actions on the "final day of judgment."[96]

On this, it was concluded that it was constantly impressed on pupils that each one of them had a "guardian angel" "whose job it was to watch over them physically, morally and spiritually; they were reminded also that this perfect being could report their misdemeanours to heaven for recording."[97]

Catholic schools, as Chapter Three of this book has already argued, also regularly reminded pupils that within the church's hierarchy of vocations, to be a nun, religious brother, or priest, was to occupy a role higher than that of the lay person. At the same time, they accepted that, despite the effort which they expended on encouraging boys and girls to "enter religious life," the majority would choose not to do so. Therefore, they also promoted a model of what it meant to be a Catholic male and a Catholic female living as lay people. The personal qualities emphasized for boys were self-discipline, hard work, and ambition. While these matched the dominant stereotypes to a great extent and were promoted to enable boys to either maintain their superior class position, or break through barriers of class and privilege, they were also promoted because the elevation of Catholics, especially within the professions, meant the elevation of the church within the society.

Brothers' schools were also particularly keen that their pupils would advance through the social ranks in order to enhance the status of their particular orders within the general hierarchy of religious orders in the church. This caused tension with some orders of priests, particularly those committed to the education of those in the middle and upper echelons of society. The attempts by the Jesuits in the United States to restrict the work of brothers of the De La Salle order to teaching the poor has already been pointed out, while there was also a tendency to caricature the humble origins of the Irish Christian Brothers and their pupils along the line of James Joyce's portrayal of "Paddy Stink and Mickey Mud," and the advice from Daedalus to "stick to the Jesuits...those are the fellows who can get you a position."[98] As far back as 1703, in his *Rules of Christian Decorum and Civility*, De La Salle had sought to overcome such an outlook by indicating how boys from the lower classes could become models of gentlemanly behavior and by describing "the good manners and the virtues that made an upright man."[99] In 1859, the Irish Christian Brothers adopted the same approach when they published *Christian Politeness* for senior pupils. This handbook, in which etiquette and the values of modesty and decorum were emphasized as being of paramount importance, was an adaptation of De La Salle's earlier work. It was revised in 1912, as *Christian Politeness and Counsels for Youth*,[100] and remained in print until it was replaced by *Courtesy for Boys and Girls* in 1962.[101] The importance of attending to the message of these handbooks for the social advancement of self, of the Irish Christian Brothers, and of the church, was summarized in another text by the order, *Fortifying Youth or Religion in Intellect and Will*, in the statement that "the real business of the teacher is not to keep his pupils going, but to give them the springs of self-improvement. His aim is to render himself superfluous."[102]

Fortifying Youth or Religion in Intellect and Will, which was circulated among Irish Christian Brothers' schools around the world and was influential up until the end of the 1950s, also emphasized that a characteristic of an educated Catholic male was that he was someone who was prepared and willing to defend his faith publically. It contained an extensive summary of Catholic doctrine and listed a series of quotations to arm students with "an effective weapon against the enemies of the Church."[103] The assumption was that Catholicism was intellectually superior to both Protestantism and contemporary non-Catholic philosophy. A Jesuit reviewer described it as "a splendid summary of what an educated Catholic boy should know and practice."[104]

Catholic boys were also expected to be "hard men" since they would have to struggle to advance in life, maintain their social standing, and be stalwarts of the church. Brothers' schools acquired a reputation for ferocious discipline within the classroom, a matter that is taken up in some detail in Chapter Eight. In Australia, many Catholic boys' schools, like government schools and those of other religious denominations, also promoted the army cadets, through which boys were able to demonstrate patriotism and were encouraged to be willing to fight and die for their country, if necessary. Connole points out that, from about 1912, the Irish Christian Brothers in Melbourne, Sydney, and Queensland underwent a course of military training and took out certificates enabling them to drill the junior cadets in the schools.[105] It became a very popular movement in the 1940s and 1950s, with schools in Queensland, encouraged by the local bishop, Dr. Duhig, also establishing air training cadet corps.[106] This emphasis within the range of extracurricular activities in the schools of the Irish Christian Brothers was consistent with the church's view of the desired Australian Catholic male being one who, while giving his first allegiance to his church, should also show allegiance to his country, while not forgetting the Irish origins of the majority of the nation's Catholic population.

Catholic boys' schools, including brothers' schools, also implicitly inculcated the hegemony of men over women.[107] They reinforced the view that a married woman's place was in the home and promoted the notion that a successful Catholic male should be accompanied in public by a wife who was a passive onlooker rather than a participant and an equal. Here it is useful to recall Connell's[108] point that one crucial way adolescent boys learn masculinity from their peers and mentors is by distancing themselves from women and differentiating themselves as sharply as possible from traits and behaviors deemed effeminate. This process, while observable in many countries in both government schools and those of other religious denominations, was carried it out with exceptional thoroughness during the period in question in Catholic boys' schools. For example, it was very rare to find female teachers in brothers' schools, while many of the domestic and other menial functions, especially those associated with catering for boarders, were carried out by lay brothers. Hence, as Brice has put it, brothers' schools were *totally* male worlds—women were excluded, unquestioningly the *other*.[109] What was conveyed, he argues, was the notion that "growing up into manhood entailed distancing oneself from womanhood and femininity, and accepting that men were superior, women subordinate."[110]

Keeping the sexes apart at the senior levels of Catholic primary school, as well as in secondary school, also acted to complement the model of the family put before Catholics. Boys, like girls, were offered the image of "the holy family" as one upon which they should base their own lives. Yet, they also had to develop an image of the ideal wife before they could be permitted to associate freely with women. The dominant feminine image was that of the Virgin Mary, symbol of a traditional concept of appropriate womanhood.[111] She was often venerated, particularly in boys' schools, in courageous terms, "with all the love of an affectionate son, and with all the devoutness of a chivalrous knight."[112] This veneration was reinforced through membership of single-sex sodalities like the Legion of Mary (already considered in Chapter One and Chapter Five) meeting after school.

Overall, then, various practices operated to develop Catholic boys' emotional commitment to the family. Thus, as Hamilton puts it, the masculinity that was encouraged differed from the hegemonic Anglo-Saxon one in some important ways:

> It was aggressive and passive, militant and sentimental, public and private. On the football field the students were encouraged to fight for their faith, while as members of sodalities compose sentimental verse.[113]

The reference to sport in the above quotation serves as a reminder that most Catholic boys' schools also adopted the English belief in team sports for moral training and proving manhood.[114] The view was that these sports were synonymous with assertiveness, aggression, courage, and toughness. Yet, there seems to have been somewhat less emphasis on the English public school notion of character building through sport and a greater emphasis on the importance of games for keeping boys out of mischief to reduce the possibility of committing "sins of the flesh." Also, as Chandler has pointed out specifically in relation to contact between Catholic and Protestant schools in England in the second half of the twentieth century, the Catholic schools had the opportunity to use sporting encounters "as a means of displaying the success of their 'belief system' and religious affiliation" every time they defeated "the old enemy."[115]

As with other aspects of Catholic schooling, the successes of boys' teams on the playing field, particularly against non-Catholic schools, contributed to the church's grand plan of using the educational system to elevate the social status of Catholics in society. These successes were widely reported in order to demonstrate that not only were Catholics a separate segment of the society at large, but also that they could mix with the best of the rest. The games' ethos in boys' schools in what was, or had been, part of the British Empire had evolved through the playing of competitive sport aimed at producing aggressive competitive loyal Christian team players appropriate for building the empire. To this, one can add that in brothers' schools, champions were nurtured in the interest of promoting not just a muscular Christianity, but also a muscular Catholicism to assist in building a Catholic "Empire."

At the same time, there were differences in the sports promoted in the schools of different orders of brothers. Within middle-class schools established when the British Empire was at its height, brothers' schools tended to play the imperial games of cricket and rugby union and compete for ascendancy on the sports field with their Protestant counterparts. The schools for the lower orders, on the other hand, tended to favor the more working-class games of soccer[116] and rugby league. One of the well-known examples of a soccer team formed by an order of religious teaching brothers is that of Glasgow Celtic. This was not established as a school team. Rather, it was set up by the Marist Brothers in Glasgow to promote community building among the working-class Catholics of the city, with the intention that it would also generate income toward the provision of free meals for poor school children.

In Ireland there arose a somewhat unusual situation after independence from Britain, with the great majority of the schools of the Irish Christian Brothers promoting the "national" games of hurling and Gaelic football in a show of solidarity with the nationalist movement,[117] and a smaller number of schools, catering to the better-off, still competing in rugby union and cricket competitions with the Protestant schools, which maintained a largely imperial ethos. By contrast, Catholic schools and colleges in the United States do not seem to have made distinctions along social class lines in the sports they promoted, most notably American football, basketball, and athletics. They did, however, promote the view that sport could facilitate one's social advancement.[118] In addition, they emphasized asserting the distinctiveness of one's religion and the cultural origins of many of their students, illustrated most notably in terming the football team at Notre Dame University "The Fighting Irish," a title it proudly parades to this day.

Up until the middle of the 1960s, as has already been pointed out in Chapter Two, the Catholic Church, the largest Christian body in the world, saw itself as being engaged in a battle against the forces of evil in this world to ensure that all would be united in the heavenly court. To this end, it operated with military-like precision due to the way its many institutions were organized. As Kelty has put it:

> There was a uniform governance of disparate structures, such as monasteries, universities, hospitals, as well as religious orders, exercised through the congregations of the Roman Curia. . . . A huge "army" of priests and the men and women of the various religious orders operated this vast enterprise known to the world at large as the Roman Catholic Church. At the head of the Church's corporate life there was the supreme pontiff, the Vicar of Christ, the Pope.[119]

Catholic education under this regime had a strong, straightforward, and often taken-for-granted aim, namely, to serve the development of faith.

This chapter has been concerned with the way in which the process of education in Catholic schools, including that overseen by religious brothers, operated with such an aim in mind. It has detailed the emphasis placed on the teaching of Catholic religious knowledge and practices, both within school and in extracurricular sessions. It has also considered how the nature of the religious formation of Catholic religious brothers, as with that of nuns and priests, influenced the nature of the teaching approach adopted by them. Furthermore, a range of other practices that operated to ensure that Catholic schools were permeated by a religious atmosphere that was all-pervasive, have been outlined. The worldview of which these features of the process of education in brothers' schools were component parts was, of course, equally shaped by the Catholic home, by attendance at Sunday Mass, and by the many spiritual and recreational organizations run by the church. Also, it was a view that came under very little interrogation from within the church during the period under consideration. This situation, as the next chapter details, was to dramatically change with the unexpected announcement of the convening of a Second Vatican Council in 1962, by Pope John XXIII.

CHAPTER 7

Responding to the Second Vatican Council

The strategy of suppression or intransigence which had been ruthlessly followed for over half a century since the condemnation of modernism was beginning to break down. The Vatican Council's emphasis on collegiality and participation by all the "people of God" can be seen as indicating a shift within a changing world to an "organic" management structure with far more emphasis on lateral consultation than vertical command... There was a movement away from a legalistic following of institutional rules and regulations to a concern with how Christians were to live fully human and liberated lives.[1]

This quotation captures well the great change that took place within the Catholic Church in the early 1960s. By the late 1950s, it seemed as if nothing short of a great shock would be required to shift it out of its authoritarian, hierarchical, and dogmatic approach in its dealings with both the laity and those in religious life. The shock came, however, when Pope John XXIII announced the convening of the Second Vatican Council (Vatican 2), which, between 1962 and 1965, brought together 2,500 bishops from around the world to deliberate. The result "was nothing short of revolutionary, profoundly affecting virtually every aspect of Catholic life."[2] This chapter commences with an overview on how the changes brought about by this momentous initiative in the history of the church, while radical, were preceded by developments over the previous 70 years, which indicated that the church was on a path of starting to open up to the modern world. It goes on to outline a set of educationally relevant principles that emerged from the council. This is followed by a consideration of specific education declarations. Finally, attention is given to how the religious, including teaching brothers, were redefined by the council, and the implications this had for education.

The Historical Background to The Second Vatican Council

Toward the end of the nineteenth century, the Catholic Church began to soften a little in its opposition to Modernism. At last, there were indications there was going to be some movement away from a policy that had remained relatively unchanged since the Council of Trent (1545–1563). While many of those advocating change might not have been totally enthusiastic, there was a realization that the church needed to respond to contemporary social problems by suggesting positive courses of action.[3] Soon, it was common to hear mention of "Catholic action."

The notion of Catholic action had its origins in the Catholic social movement that began on the continent of Europe in the late nineteenth century and whose ideas were worked out by continental theologians. These ideas were summed up and ratified by Pope Leo XIII when he issued his encyclical *Rerum Novarum*,[4] in 1891, which left a wide range of social and economic policies open to Catholics, while ruling out some extreme courses.[5] The ideal that was held up was that of class harmony toward which Christians should aim. Various activities aimed at achieving this ideal, which was promoted as the Christian answer to the doctrine of class war, were initiated in Europe. Out of these developed a network of organizations with a social purpose. These included cooperatives, friendly societies, farmers' organizations, youth movements, adult education movements, and trade unions.[6] The motivation behind this growth was partly to save Catholic workers and farmers from becoming socialists and partly to involve the church in addressing what were seen as the social evils of the time.

The intensity and extent of associated developments were weak among Catholics in southern and Eastern Europe, robust in Germany, Switzerland, Austria, France, and parts of Italy, and very strong in Belgium and the Netherlands. In all of these countries, however, Catholic action led to the growth of study circles, specialist journals, and congresses, aimed at providing an elaboration on the ideas underpinning *Rerum Novarum*. Essentially, while this encyclical left a wide range of social and economic policies open to Catholics, it ruled out some extreme courses: "As against socialism, it asserted man's rights to private property. As against individualism, it asserted the State's right to intervene against bad working conditions."[7] The movement that it spawned led to much intellectual activity in the church over the next 40 years aimed at elaborating the fundamental doctrine, formulating action plans, and then applying them to the particular circumstances of various countries.[8]

The ideals laid out in *Rerum Novarum* were restated by Pope Pius XI in his encyclical of 1931, entitled *Quadragesimo Anno.*[9] The latter was more precise than its predecessor in laying out how the church's social theories could be put into practice. The proposal was that members of each industry, or profession, should be organized in "vocational groups," or "corporations," in which employers and workers would cooperate to further their common interests, do good, and seek to make the world a more just place. The pope also argued that the adoption of such a course would be in accordance with the "principle of subsidiarity," whose essence was stated as follows: "It is an injustice and at the same time a great evil and disturbance of higher order to assign to a greater and higher association what lesser and subordinate organizations can do."[10] This was an argument that the state had taken on too many functions and that these should be cut back since its rightful place "is not to do everything itself, but to direct, watch, urge and restrain subsidiary organizations."[11] Such corporate thinking had a long tradition in Europe, especially in France and in Austria, and not only among Catholics. The pope, however, in embracing it during the middle of the Great Depression, gave hope to those who, while disillusioned by capitalism, sought a direction other than that provided by communism and fascism

By now, Catholic social teaching was also being accompanied by new developments in theology. Cornwell has pointed out that in the 1930s, a group of French theologians, most notably the Jesuit Henri de Lubac had begun exploring what the central concerns of the church should be by returning to the writings of the early Christians.[12] Pope Pius XII's encyclical, *Divino Afflante Spiritu* (1943), opened the doors of official church thinking just a little more, through making it permissible for Catholic scholars to adopt what, for them, were the radical approaches of historical and literary criticism in their study of the scriptures. For church clerics who were also academics, this movement brought them closer to their colleagues in non-Catholic universities than had heretofore been the case. Concurrently, changes were taking place with regard to the liturgy.[13] For example, since the 1920s, the "liturgical movement" had been active in the United States. It was characterized by congregations in attendance at mass responding to the prayers that normally were reserved for the altar servers. A related movement emphasized the importance of individuals seeing relationships between what happened in worship and what happened in the world around them, especially in terms of promoting social justice.

Such developments, however, were not sufficient to satisfy those calling for change in a church that, in the middle of the twentieth century, was still centrist and highly bureaucratized. As Cornwell has put it, "whatever the strengths and virtues of the Church during that period, whatever its disciplines, its unassailable unity, its loyalty to the Pope in Rome, the post–Second World War era found it ripe for sweeping change."[14] This was the situation faced by Cardinal Angelo Roncalli when he was elected Pope John XXIII, on October 28, 1958. Very soon he was calling for an aggiornamento "to open up the windows of the Church, allowing her to experience this world and for the world to experience the Church anew."[15] Developments set in train led to the opening of the first session of the Second Vatican Council on October 11, 1962. The primary goals of the council were to revitalize Catholics in their spirituality, to adapt church observances to the requirements of the age, to unite all Christians, and to strengthen the church's mission to all peoples. Pope John died on June 3, 1963, just under six months after the end of the first session. The council, however, continued under Cardinal Giovanni Montini, who was elected Pope Paul VI.

In historical sequence, there are five periods related to the council.[16] The first period, which covered the initial exploratory work and the establishment of the preparatory commissions to form the significant basis of the formal council debates, commenced in October 1959 and concluded in September 1962. The second period covered the first session of the formal council proceedings; it commenced on October 11, 1962, with the papal opening address and concluded on December 8, 1962. Bishops from all around the world, as well as abbots and theologians, were invited to be council members. "Observers," including representatives from other faith denominations, also attended. The third period covered the second session of the council proceedings. This session commenced on September 29, 1963, and ended on December 4 of the same year. Pope Paul VI, having been elected following the death of Pope John XXIII in June 1963, increased the council membership by inviting 63 non-Catholic observers, as well as 11 laymen. The fourth period, marking the third formal session of the council, commenced on September 14, 1963, and concluded on November 21, 1964. Eight female religious, as well as seven lay single women, were invited to this session as auditors. The final period covered the fourth session of the council proceedings. Commencing on September 14, 1965, it lasted for three months. Pope Paul then formally closed the council on December 8, 1965, by which stage it had approved 16 documents by a significant majority.

Educationally Relevant Principles Emerging from the Council

The bulk of the proceedings of the council dealt with matters other than education. Nevertheless, much of what was agreed upon had educational implications. Thus, Donohoe[17] was able to deduce a set of educationally relevant principles from the documents produced. The first of these principles is that the council gave a strong endorsement to the positive value of what the church traditionally termed "secular culture," that is, the arts, sciences, technology, and politics of the human community. In doing so, the work of Catholic educators, who for centuries had attempted to combine an education in faith with an education for life in society, was given positive recognition. In a similar vein, Donohoe has concluded, the thrust of the council's declarations also gave legitimacy to those advocating for the continuing education of Catholic adults on the grounds of being a contemporary necessity, and also to those emphasizing the importance in schools and other educational institutions of relating Catholic teaching to contemporary issues and problems.

A second principle identified by Donohoe that had implications for education was the affirmation of the role and the responsibility of the laity, both in human society and in the life and structures of the church. This was clearly a principle that contested those claiming that since membership of religious teaching orders was in decline and priests, brothers, and nuns would no longer be able to take the lead in these spheres, the laity were now to be welcomed as principals and managers of Catholic schools, and parents should have much more of a say in policy decisions regarding the nature and structure of Catholic education. Rather, the church affirmed that the laity, as members of the church, had rights and responsibilities in education equal to those of the religious. Furthermore, it followed from this principle that Catholic communities and institutions needed to offer an education that would provide lay people with the knowledge, skills, and dispositions for assuming such a role.

McLaughlin has elaborated at length on how this second principle has been reiterated in various documents of the Vatican-based Congregation of Catholic Education. The essential focus of these documents, he states, is one of:

> Catholic education being the nurturing of the humanity of its students, and that the Christ experience for many students will be conveyed primarily through the humanity of dedicated and pastoral Catholic educators—emphasizing that the Catholic school be focused on serving the common good; nurturing a community dynamic and committing itself to the service of the poor—having its educational mission based on love and generating an inclusive community. [18]

McLaughlin then reminds us that, in pursuing such an educational vision, religious and lay personnel are equal partners. Indeed, he states that Vatican 2 makes it clear that within this sphere, the distinction between the religious and the lay is an artificial one. Among the powerful statements he has marshaled in support of this position are those of Pope Paul VI, who stated that "it is the whole Church that receives the mission to evangelize, and the work of each individual member is important to the whole,"[19] and Lakeland[20], who has interpreted Vatican 2 as proclaiming that for Christians, "our common humanity, not lay-religious distinction, is the primary vehicle for us to transform the world and nurture Christ's kingdom." In other words, McLaughlin concludes, both the religious and the lay embrace a common calling to be God's people and share a common mission.

A third principle identified by Donohoe on examining the record of the proceedings of Vatican 2, and that has implications for education, "underscored human freedom as the basis for personal worth and dignity."[21] This principle of freedom, as Elias points out, "governs many aspects of education: rights of teachers and students, proper modes of instruction, elimination of indoctrination and manipulation, and the rights of parents." He quotes as follows from the council's *Declaration on Religious Liberty* to make clear that the principle was extended to religious education:

> In spreading religious belief and in introducing religious practices everybody must at all times avoid any action which seems to suggest coercion or dishonest or unworthy persuasion especially when dealing with the uneducated or the poor. Such a manner of acting must be considered an abuse of one's own right and an infringement of the rights of others.[22]

This was a radical departure from the position of previous times that members of the Catholic Church claimed not only a right but also an obligation to seek conversions through all lawful means.

Donohoe's fourth principle for education, which again he deduced from the record of the proceedings of Vatican 2, emphasizes "the value of community in bringing about the unity of the human family and the common bond of humankind."[23] It follows from this, Elias argues, that education should be seen not as an individualistic enterprise, but as an activity that takes place within a group that shares common values and aspirations. He also states that it was a position which was given prominence in various official church documents written after the council.

To Donohoe's four principles, one could add a fifth. It emanates from *The Pastoral Constitution on the Church in the Modern World*. This, as Dosen points out, was the one document of Vatican 2 that developed on the floor of the council, rather than from the planning commissions. He went on:

> The spirit of this document is revolutionary for the Church. For the first time, the Church admits that She not only has something to give to the world, but that the world has something to give to the Church. There is a reciprocity, a dialogue that can take place between church and secular society...the Church lives in the world and shares its common history. Together with the "Declaration on Religious Freedom," the Church opens itself to the development of social and scientific research initiatives. The Church also admits to the legitimate possibility of pluralism around political and social issues, recommending that people not be classified as more or less Christian because of their personal preferences on these particular issues.[24]

The implications of this particular position for curriculum and pedagogy at all levels of education were not spelt out. However, it did constitute a framework for anyone interested in adopting a revolutionary approach for Catholic education relative to the church's traditional dogmatic position in both areas. Furthermore, various correspondences with the position can be found in those specific education declarations from the proceedings of Vatican 2. A broad overview on these declarations will now be provided.

Specific Education Declarations

While the bulk of the proceedings of Vatican 2 dealt with matters other than education, albeit with many educational implications, there were some specific educational declarations. The central document in this regard was *Gravissimum Educationis*. Elias[25] has summarized the enunciations of this document, stating that it showed an interest in all forms of education, not only Catholic education. He went on:

> It affirmed the rights of all individuals to an education to prepare them for life in the world and for their ultimate end. This education should utilize the advances of psychology and pedagogy in order to promote a proper sense of responsibility and freedom. In addressing the social goal of education the statement broadened the goals of Catholic education to include not only that students worship God properly as mature persons in the faith, but also that they help in the Christian formation of the world and work for the good of the whole society. The inclusion of a broader social goal for Christian education is in keeping with the Council's thrust in showing interest in and concern for not just the life of the Church but also for all of society.

He goes on to state that the declaration spelt out the goals of education as both individual and social. The primary role of Catholic schools should be to educate its members "for the fullness of life in the hereafter and the goodness of the earthly community." This requires the provision of catechetical instruction, preparation for an active and intelligent participation in the liturgy and engagement in "good works." It was recognized, however, that there is also a duty to provide a high-quality secular education and to encourage participation in extracurricular activities through youth associations in order to help the individual achieve his, or her, full potential. In a similar vein, the document encouraged efforts to establish professional and technical schools, adult education centers, schools for those with disabilities, and also colleges for the preparation of religious education teachers. While the church had long been involved to some extent in such activity, this was the first clear articulation that Catholic education should not be seen as prioritizing primary and secondary school education. Rather, the view was that Catholic education should be multifaceted.

Particular emphasis was placed in the document on what has since come to be termed "the Church's option for the poor." Teachers were encouraged to see schools as a vehicle for providing for the needs of those who are materially, or emotionally, deprived. Also, for the first time, secular schools were praised for their work in this regard, as well as in the education of children more generally. This move away from disparaging state-run institutions was further evidence of the church recognizing that, while it wished to teach the world, it also had much to learn from it.

Religious education also underwent change as a result of the deliberations of Vatican 2. Specifically in relation to theological faculties where priests are trained, teachers are prepared, and research is conducted, *Gravissimum Educationis* stated that the research task is as follows:

> To make more penetrating inquiry into the various aspects of the sacred sciences so that even deepening understanding of sacred Revelation is obtained, the legacy of Christian wisdom handed down by our forefathers is more fully developed, the dialogue with our separated brethren and with non-Christians is fostered, and answers are given to questions arising from the development of doctrine.[26]

This emphasis on an ecumenical approach in theological work again reflects the new, more open approach being advocated throughout all of the work of the council.

Various new guidelines for the teaching of religion in schools were also forthcoming as ideas originating from earlier decades were beginning to break through.[27] Some suggest that these ideas went back to the work of the German Jesuit theologian Josef Jungmann, in the 1930s. He was concerned that the church's emphasis on doctrine and formulae had made these things "ends in themselves."[28] Jungmann's central notion was that the focus should be on the essential message of Christian teaching, the *kerygma*; hence the name "kerygmatic catechesis." As he saw it, the conveyance of knowledge was not as important as an examination of the central basis of "the faith." He emphasized that Christianity should be seen not just as a system of truths, or a code of rules, but as a message, the "good news." Thus, it was argued, catechetics should be personalized, following the behavior of human intercourse, and be "christocentric," that is, molding all its elements around the central figure of Christ.

The emphasis on the kerygmatic approach resulted in the appearance, with general episcopal approval, of several new texts throughout the Catholic world. A noticeable feature of these works was their dependence on the Bible, and the pedagogical methods used by Jesus were recommended.[29] Also, they found expression in *Gravissimum Educationis*, where it is stated:

> For her part Holy Mother Church, in order to fulfill the mandate she received from her divine founder to announce the mystery of salvation to all men and to renew all things in Christ, is under an obligation to promote the welfare of the whole life of man, including his life in this

> world insofar as it is related to his heavenly vocation, she has therefore a part to play in the development and extension of education.[30]

While the place of the church and the home in education was considered in this declaration, most of the focus was on the schools. The accompanying argument was that due weight should be given "to advances in psychological, pedagogical and intellectual sciences" so that children and young people could "be helped to develop harmoniously their physical, moral and intellectual qualities."[31] This position reflected both the reevaluation of religious education occurring within the church internationally and comparable movements in the government and other non-Catholic sectors in relation to the teaching of the "secular" subjects on the curriculum.

Redefining the Religious, with Implications for Their Involvement in Education

From the early Middle Ages until Vatican 2, Catholics, as Sammon puts it, "accepted unchallenged a three tiered hierarchical ranking of the clerical, religious and lay states within the Church,"[32] with the priesthood being the highest state, religious life coming in second, and the lay state being at the bottom. Furthermore, he states, "Catholics were taught that only vowed members of religious orders could achieve spiritual perfection."[33] These positions were seriously contested by the council, which was faced with the task of trying to reconstitute the church so that it could engage fully with the modern world, while at the same time preserving its essential dogma. In particular, there was a very strong movement aimed at moving the spotlight away from the clergy as being at the center of the church's work and onto the laity as being their partners in the enterprise.[34] The most significant document produced to guide developments in this regard was the "Decree on the Apostolate of the Laity." In it, lay people were provided with an official pronouncement on their status in the statement that their aim should be "to penetrate and perfect the temporal sphere with the spirit of the gospel."[35]

Members of many religious orders welcomed the opportunities presented by this new declaration on the laity. The general position was to declare that it was both a restatement and reinstatement of the position held by lay people in the early Christian Church. Those religious embracing the change found that they now had a much wider set of peers with whom they could work in helping them realize their vocation. For others, however, it presented a huge challenge. While priests were still considered to be elevated within the church by virtue of the fact that they were ordained, and thus were the only ones who could celebrate the sacraments, the nonordained religious, namely, nuns and religious brothers, were now, essentially, lay people. This, as Schneider, puts it, "resulted in a virtual crisis for many."[36] He depicts the religious in the pre–Vatican 2 Church sociologically quasiclergy, stating:

> Like the clergy, they lived apart from other Catholics, wore distinguishing garb, were addressed by special titles, carried on full-time ministries to which they were assigned by ecclesiastical authorities and which guaranteed their livelihood. They were essentially unaccountable to the laity they served, enjoyed sacralised (though not canonical) authority in relation to the laity, and most importantly, did not marry...they were for all practical purposes second-class-clergy rather than (even first-class) laity.[37]

The declarations of Vatican 2, however, and the subsequent revision of canon law, suggested that even this "second class" status was not warranted, thus leaving many religious "'displaced,' or even 'placeless,' in the official self-description of the Church."[38] The new situation was that the church divided its members into two groups, the ordained and the nonordained, with no room for overlap. Thus, Schneider concludes, those religious who were not ordained were, "by the process of elimination, defined as laity at least in relation to the hierarchical structure of the Church."[39]

The problem now for the religious was one of how to redefine themselves. Many felt, on witnessing the nature and extent to which lay people were becoming more and more involved in the work of the church at the parish level, that they themselves had been demoted. If, as Schneider puts it, there was nothing that they could do that separated them from the laity, their very reason for existence could be called into question. Indeed, in terms of their appearance, many now did not even look any different from the laity. This was due to those changes encouraged by the Vatican Council that resulted in a move toward wearing ordinary clothes. Concurrently, there was a dropping of religious titles and a growth in such practices as visiting one's family regularly, having friends outside of the religious life, and taking part in various social and cultural activities in society.[40]

In the 1970s and 1980s, large numbers left religious life and the numbers joining were greatly reduced. The departures cannot be attributed just to the change in the official position of the church on the nonordained religious since there had been the beginnings of an increase in departures even before the council met for the first time, while large numbers also left the priesthood. Nevertheless, it is difficult to ignore the likelihood that it was a major factor contributing to the overall decline in the numbers of those in religious life, including those who were religious teaching brothers.[41]

Those who remained in religious life were left with the task of trying to work out where they fitted into the life of the church. In this, they were assisted by the emphasis that the council had placed on each religious order working out its "charism," which was defined as "a grace given for the sake not only of recipient but also and primarily for the upbuilding of the Church."[42] In the first instance, they were expected to make the Gospel their supreme rule. Then, they had to become involved in establishing and reflecting on the ideas and works of their founders and early members in order to establish what was, and should be, distinctive about themselves. To this end also, they were expected to study the sources of their own spirituality. This helped many to establish for themselves a new place within the church, one consistent with the ideals of their order's founder, but adapted to the realities of contemporary life.[43]

The first changes made in most communities had to do with the prayer structure and the daily schedule. Members usually still gathered at least once a day for Mass, and again in the evening to pray together with the assistance of the psalms and other readings from Scripture.[44] Often, however, some of the other previously scheduled periods for meditation and spiritual reading were set aside, leaving it to the individual to read and meditate privately according to one's own need. Other changes soon followed. Dooley, for example, has noted how the members of the St. Patrick's Province of the Irish Christian Brothers in Australia, in trying to move back to the original charism and intuitions of their founder, Edmund Rice, [45] changed to embrace a form of dress more on the lines of laymen, wearing a black tie and cross with black suit, or white open-necked shirt and cross with black trousers in hot weather. The only time they continued to wear the distinctive religious habit was at the community spiritual exercises and in school.

Other freedoms followed, "freedom to use the telephone, to correspond with friends, to drive out alone in a car, to use the media, to visit home."[46] Johann goes on:

> Most of the old formalities have given way to less formal and more natural type of interpersonal relationships—members sit wherever

> they like and with whomever they wish at meals and on other occasions. They may go out alone if they so desire…since they use the telephone freely, they make their own appointments and arrange for their own transportation. Recreation and relaxation are seen as a personal responsibility, as are private prayer, reading and professional updating.[47]

All of these changes meant that, in sharp contrast to the pre–Vatican 2 days, there was now an emphasis on engaging in personal decision making. These, indeed, were new times for religious orders, including those of teaching brothers.

This chapter opened by providing a broad overview on the radical changes brought about by the Second Vatican Council. It went on to outline those educationally relevant principles that emerged from the council, along with its specific education declarations. Attention was also given to how the religious, including teaching brothers, were redefined by the council and the implications that this had for education. Brothers, like priests and nuns, now also mixed more freely with lay people as more and more of them began to enroll in university degrees. In some cases, this meant enrollment in courses of teacher preparation in secular institutions. The religious also opened up many of their own colleges to allow attendance by nonreligious, and not just in programs of teacher preparation, but also in theology and philosophy, as well as in new courses on social justice, often accredited by old established secular universities. While all of these developments were welcomed by some, they were not welcomed by others, often causing "dissension, some bitterness, and for varying lengths of time, distrustful polarization among the members."[48] These problems of dissension within the ranks of the religious faded into insignificance for the authorities of the orders, however, when they were hit by a host of scandals across the world, many of them concerned with child sexual abuse. Soon, it was becoming apparent that an era that initially seemed to be heralding in a bright new future for religious orders, might just be about to become one during which their collapse would be witnessed.

CHAPTER 8

Child Abuse

> *There is a tendency to hide from the public knowledge of any incident of unnatural practice in institutions to which children are committed by the courts... When they do occur the citizens ought to be told. Only by knowing can they take a helpful interest in the welfare of those children for whom they, too, have a moral responsibility.*[1]

Thus wrote Peadar Cowan in the 1960s, particularly in relation to Catholic institutions run by the teaching religious. His, however, was very much a lone voice at the time, and not just in relation to Ireland, about which he was specifically speaking. Up until about 25 years ago, the vast majority of expositions on the teaching religious in Catholic schools and other educational institutions, as pointed out in Chapter One, were both historical and hagiographic. In the main, they were produced by the religious orders themselves to commemorate what they viewed as the heroic sacrifices of their predecessors. In more recent years, however, there has been an awakening of interest in this group of teachers across society more generally. The interest has been generated largely by accounts demonstrating that it was not all a tale of heroism and achievement, that there was a darker side to what went on in schools and other institutions run by the church, involving both physical and sexual abuse of minors. The popular press was particularly active in the associated project, revealing the shameful side of the life and deeds of some of those who were members of religious orders. It was not long until scholarly accounts of what took place also started to appear.[2]

Much of the early exposure of child abuse in church-run institutions was in the United States. In 1997, Isely reported that over the previous ten years, the American public had been "saturated with media reports regarding criminal and civil cases against religious ministers accused of sexually assaulting children," with the majority of them involving "the criminal and sexual misuse of male adolescents and children while under the supervision of male ordained Christian ministers."[3] He also pointed out that while clergy from various denominations had been accused, or convicted, of child sexual abuse, the Roman Catholic Church dominated the cases in which individual offenders were "accused of molesting from several to over 100 children apiece during their tenure as religious professionals."[4]

It was not long until allegations of such abuse were made in relation to events in other countries. The nature and extent of the evidence is irrefutable. Also, the horrific nature of what took place has not been made more palatable on considering the very legitimate observations that the state resources provided to church-run institutions were low, thus leading to physical and psychological frustration among those involved in child welfare. It has been diluted neither by the argument that such welfare was provided to protect society, not the child, nor by accounts that demonstrate that abuse was not peculiar to Catholic-managed institutions.

For quite some time, much of the reporting of abuse outside of the United States centered on the work of Catholic religious brothers, with abuse by priests and nuns, including that carried out by regular diocesan clergy and some members of the hierarchy, only surfacing in more recent times.[5] Consequently, it would be remiss to overlook here this shameful episode that has rocked the Catholic Church time and again, but particularly over the last ten years. The remainder of the chapter addresses the matter in a general way, with the emphasis being largely on trying to provide some perspective on a situation that is very much deserving of a comprehensive work in its own right. If one is after the gory details, one will need to follow up many of the references in the footnotes. They provide very graphic descriptions of incidents and events, and make for very depressing reading.

The chapter commences with a brief section indicating that there is nothing new within the greater course of church history in reports on the sexual abuse of minors by those in religious life. This is followed by a consideration of accounts from more recent times that excessive use of corporal punishment was a characteristic of education in brothers' schools, particularly those of the Irish Christian Brothers who, arguably, have come under the spotlight more than other orders in this regard. The third part of the chapter then provides an overview on the accounts of terrible atrocities carried out by members of this order in three parts of the world—Newfoundland, Western Australia, and Ireland—where the indications are that the lines between physical and sexual abuse of minors were very much blurred. The chapter concludes with a brief overview on some tentative historical insights that go some way toward providing an understanding of the situation, while in no way seeking to condone it.

Sexual Abuse of Minors within the Church

Isely[6] draws on a substantial body of evidence in the historical and anthropological record to demonstrate that the sexual use of children has a long history.[7] Some of the states in Ancient Greece permitted such use of pubescent boys, while others prohibited it.[8] At the other end of Europe, as Coogan has pointed out, Celtic warriors in pre-Christian Ireland were not averse to homosexual relationships with young boys.[9] Historical accounts from the eighteenth century also show that such practices were prevalent in China, Japan, Africa, Turkey, Arabia, Egypt, and Islamic areas of India.[10]

Payer[11] also deals with this matter. He points out that while, with the advent of Christianity, pederasty was condemned in ancient Rome, deterioration in the moral life of the Catholic Church was evident in the tenth and eleventh centuries, particularly in the case of clerical sexual immorality. This explains the issuing of a series of regulative documents by the early medieval church, in which pederasty, incest, bestiality, and homosexual practices were condemned. Indeed, early church history evidences a persistent fear by church authorities of sexual contact between men and boys. For example, St. Basil, a Benedictine monk, issued strict penalties on adult treatment of children in monasteries, and his writings show great concern about the sexual attraction of an adult monk toward his young male pupils.[12] Quinn has concluded that such decreeing of penalties was justified, considering the number of documents in which tenth- and eleventh-century monks wrote love poems celebrating "paederastia."[13]

The Benedictine practice of "child oblation" in the Early Middle Ages was also of concern.[14] This involved parents sending a male child, usually between the ages of five and seven, to a monastery, where he stayed until he had reached the age of profession, normally about ten years afterward.[15] Because the order was clearly aware of the possibility that monks would misbehave sexually with such children, it was prompted to draw up the "Penitential." This consisted of a series of rules to regulate behavior to try to ensure that sexual relations did not take place between a monk and a boy, a situation considered "particularly undesirable and offensive."[16] Fr. Damien, an influential Benedictine monk of the eleventh century, also condemned sexual activities between boys and monks in *Liber Gomorrhianus* (Book of

Gomorrah)[17] and advocated the expulsion from holy orders of any monk who engaged in pederasty, calling such acts "molestation" and "spiritual infanticide." He was also explicit in laying responsibility for any transgressions on the monks, whether the child was a "willing" or an "unwilling" participant.[18]

Isely also draws attention to ecclesiastical records indicating sexual abuse by Catholic clergy in later centuries. He points to the example of a Jesuit priest who, in 1570, was "defrocked, sentenced to death, and decapitated for engaging in sodomy and other sexual acts with an adolescent choirboy."[19] Others have detailed incidents since then. Burkett and Bruni, for example, relate the case of a German priest who was imprisoned in the mid-eighteenth century for exposing himself to small girls and masturbating boys.[20] Then, at the beginning of the twentieth century, there was the situation of a young 17-year-old woman who was raped by a Catholic priest on the church grounds, and this was heard in a civil case by the Supreme Court of Massachusetts in 1914.[21] It is not clear if these were extremely isolated incidents, but what seems beyond doubt is that sexual contact between the religious and the youths is not just a twentieth-century phenomenon, and that it has at all times been officially considered by the church to be a very serious offense indeed.

Corporal Punishment

Schools of various religious orders of brothers throughout the English-speaking world have developed a reputation for being fearsome places, especially up until the 1970s, with corporal punishment being a part of the "normal" daily rhythm of schooling. The production of a rich popular literature on American Catholicism has contributed to this reputation, although, as Perko has pointed out, "what is true of American education generally is also true of Catholic schooling: it is difficult to generalize about the experience as a whole because it took such different forms."[22] Nevertheless, for those who did write, albeit fictional literature, it is reasonable to assume that they wrote about what they knew. Powers depicted teaching brothers as follows:

> "You got Brother Gruppi? Oh, man, he's the worst. He's got this huge leather strap and when it gets going, you can hear the thing all over the school." "Whatever you do, don't talk in Brother Courtdown's class. If he gets pissed off at you, he'll punch you right in the face. He damn nearly broke some kid's nose last year."[23]

In summarizing the depiction of the male teaching religious in the work of Farrell,[24] Benard,[25] and Powers,[26] Perko concludes that what is revealed is a philosophy of education governing Catholic education in the United States up to the 1970s, which does not "view the child as one to be gently guided toward discovery and personal setting of limits." Rather, it is one in which "children tend to be seen as unruly animals which need to be kept in their place."[27] The Irish Christian Brothers have become particularly infamous in the latter regard. Much of the associated evidence has been assembled by Coldrey.[28] As he puts it, "every novel, memoir, autobiography or oral reflection" that makes reference to the brothers refers to their incessant use of corporal punishment in the classroom.[29]

Coldrey has made a sterling effort to place the negative reputation of the Irish Christian Brothers on corporal punishment within a historical context, noting that they were no more uncontrolled than members of other orders, teachers of many other religious denominations, and those working within various state school systems. He has drawn attention to the "ferocious discipline of the Great Public Schools educating upper-class youth, both before and after the reforms initiated by Thomas Arnold of Rugby in the 1840s."[30] He points out that Edmund Rice, the founder of the Irish Christian Brothers, "emphasized a mild compassionate approach to teaching and the children."[31] He has also drawn attention to the large number of pupils from the poorest class in society who inhabited the classrooms of the brothers for much of their history, arguing that there could hardly have been any way of engaging in what, for many teachers, must have been akin to "crowd control" as we would refer to it today, other than through corporal punishment. A further factor that needs to be considered, he has argued, is that in the late eighteenth and early nineteenth centuries, children were seen as "defective adults, the fruits of original sin, whose evil propensities were to be beaten out of them."[32] A consequence was that "discipline of children was similar throughout the British Isles among the major religious affiliations. Severity towards children was non-sectarian; nor did attitudes differ between social classes."[33]

The leather strap was synonymous with the pedagogical approach of the Irish Christian Brothers for much of their history. A prominent university academic in Melbourne recalled this implement of discipline from his days in a brothers' school in the state of Victoria:

> It was a vicious looking thing about 12 inches long and consisting of six or eight black and brown thin strips of dried leather stitched

> amateurishly together. It was the stitching that was alleged to make it so painful.[34]

The brothers imported the strap to Ireland from the De La Salle Brothers in France in the 1820s. This "leather slapper," as it was popularly named, was 13 inches long and 0.25 inches thick. It was meant to be used only on the hand and to be carefully regulated; normally, it was to be one slap only, and even then it was not to be given on a boy's writing hand. Over the next century-and-a-half, however, a great range of literary, biographical, and autobiographical works emerged indicating that there was widespread deviation from this regulation.

Much of the latter work has come out of Ireland. It includes a number of novels, most notably O'Brien's *The Hard Life*,[35] which provides an austere portrait of life in a prominent Irish Christian Brothers' school in Dublin, Farrell's[36] *Thy Tears Might Cease* where the hero, Martin Reilly, lives in terror of the same brothers' brutality, and Plunkett's *Farewell Companions*, where their approach is described as follows: "[they] coax it into them or beat it into them, but they do a bloody good job—that's the motto of the Brothers." [37] Among the most prominent autobiographical works relating to the situation from the beginning to the middle of the twentieth century are those of Browne,[38] Byrne, [39] and Ó Fáoláin, [40] the first two commenting on life in Irish Christian Brothers' schools, and the latter on life at Presentation Brothers College, Cork, also in Ireland. They all relate a regular regime of physical punishment, not just for misbehavior but, as Ó Fáoláin has put it, as "the sole spur [to achievement] within the school."[41] Fr. Flanagan, made famous by the Spencer Tracy movie *Boys Town*, visited Ireland in the 1940s and also condemned the level of punishment that he witnessed, in this case in the industrial schools. The severity of the regime contrasted greatly for him with the level of care at the farm for poor and wayward boys that he had established in Omaha, Nebraska, and that had its genesis in an earlier initiative of his in 1917.[42]

A similar set of writings and related academic works has come out of Australia. One of the most well-known academic works within this collection is that of Angus.[43] In his ethnography of an Irish Christian Brothers' school in the 1980s, he has commented stridently on the "firm, sometimes repressive or even brutal discipline which has historically been associated with the Brothers' schools in Australia."[44] The Australian dramatist Barry Oakley has related his experience of this regime at a school in Melbourne in the 1940s, recalling a brother who delivered regular "leather fusillades" with his strap "carried gun-manhandy in the hip pocket of his shabby black habit."[45] Others have depicted the scene in fictional works, with Koch relating the use of the leather slapper "by a bare-knuckle, old working-class, Irish-Australian Brother" at St Virgil's College, Hobart, Tasmania,[46] and O'Grady in *Deschooling Kevin Carew* saying that "he felt fear and loathing when the brothers adopted roughhouse methods."[47]

It is true that the use of physical punishment throughout much of the English-speaking world, particularly in the first half of the twentieth century, was not confined to schools of the Irish Christian Brothers. What has increased their reputation for abuse, however, has been the extraordinary number of revelations, especially since the 1980s, of the brutal treatment of boys committed to their care in residential institutions—boys' homes, borstals, and orphanages—until the reorganization of child care throughout the Western world. These institutions had their origins in the 1860s, when the British government subsidized the establishment in Ireland and Britain of industrial schools and reformatories for illegitimate, abandoned, poverty-stricken, and delinquent youth.[48] The principal religious groups were quick to respond in availing of this initiative, which, over time, was replicated overseas. Among the Catholic religious orders involved was the Irish Christian Brothers.

In recent years, terrifying autobiographical accounts of life in these institutions, such as those of Flynn[49] and Touher,[50] have appeared, especially in relation to Ireland up to the 1960s. It is clear, however, that the combination of physical and sexual abuse involved was also a feature of the work of the brothers in various other parts of the world. The next part of this chapter now provides an overview on the background to the revelations that have appeared in relation to Newfoundland, Western Australia, and Ireland.

Abuse in Newfoundland, Western Australia, and Ireland

Newfoundland

In 1898, Michael Francis Howley, Catholic Archbishop of St. John's, the principal town in Newfoundland, donated land for an orphanage. It was named the Mount Cashel Boys' Home after the ancient Christian monastery at the Rock of Cashel in County Tipperary, Ireland.[51] After Newfoundland joined the Canadian Confederation in 1949, the provincial government began to place wards of the state at the orphanage, which, for the last 40 years of its operation, was run by the Canadian Province of the Irish Christian Brothers.

The first signs of concern regarding the operation of Mount Cashel were raised in 1975, when the Royal Newfoundland Constabulary (RNC) investigated allegations that physical and sexual abuse had been carried out there. While five members of staff were reported by 20 residents, the investigation was brought to a halt by the chief of the RNC, on instruction from the Department of Justice, even though two of the brothers admitted sexual wrongdoing and were placed in treatment centers outside the province. A second investigation commenced in 1982, resulting in a brother being convicted of sexual offenses and receiving a sentence of four months in jail and three years probation.[52] It was in 1989, however, that the extent of the abuse at Mount Cashel began to be aired publically for the first time. It started with a caller to a radio call-in program stating suspicion of a cover-up by the Government of Newfoundland and Labrador about sexual and physical abuse within the institution. A justice of the Supreme Court of Newfoundland and Labrador followed up on the issue, and the RNC was instructed to complete its 1975 investigation. Very soon, a local weekly newspaper, *The Sunday Express*, began to publish allegations of sexual abuse, cruelty, and severe physical punishment perpetrated by staff at the orphanage over the previous quarter of a decade.

The public outcry that ensued following the revelation of the gruesome details of what took place resulted in the appointment on March 31, 1989, of a royal commission led by a retired justice of the Supreme Court of Ontario, Samuel Hughes, to investigate the obstruction of justice. The Hughes Commission commenced its investigation on June 1, 1989, and took evidence from dozens of witnesses over the next two years. Its report, which became public in April 1992, found that the Irish Christian Brothers who had been investigated by the RNC investigation in 1975, should have been charged, and that the Department of Justice had interfered with the police investigation. It went on to recommend that the Government of Newfoundland and Labrador establish a compensation fund for the abuse victims. By now, the orphanage was permanently shut. Shortly afterward, the brothers formally apologized to the victims. Mount Cashel was then demolished, the land was sold to property developers, and financial compensation was paid to victims.

In 1997, the Government of Newfoundland and Labrador acknowledged its responsibility as a result of having sent wards of the state to the orphanage and paid a settlement of $11.25 million to approximately 40 former residents who were victims of sexual and physical abuse. The provincial government then began a process of seeking to reclaim this money from the Canadian-based assets of the Irish Christian Brothers. Overall, by 2004, approximately $27 million had been paid in compensation to around 100 victims of physical and sexual abuse at the Mount Cashel Orphanage by the Government of Newfoundland and Labrador and by the brothers.[53] As of May 2009, however, there were still approximately 50 civil lawsuits being processed through the courts in relation to victims of the sexual and physical abuse perpetrated there.

In his analysis of the whole affair, Overton has highlighted the extent to which church officials, the police, politicians, and even a newspaper editor "had participated in covering up details of what had been happening at Mount Cashel, at least since the 1970s, when a police investigation resulting from a complaint had been stopped."[54] The kind of questioning of institutions, attitudes, and practices that this stimulated, he held, was positive. At the same time, he pointed out that the situation in which powerful interests in Newfoundland "played a key role in not just ignoring, but suppressing, efforts to make public the abuse," deeply shocked and disturbed many people in the province. Equally, he concluded that there was great fear that the discovery of abuse would undermine young people's respect for authority, and that this would, in turn, "weaken discipline and lead to an increase in delinquency, vandalism, crime and violence amongst the young."[55]

Western Australia

Australia, as has already been pointed out, is one country regarding which a significant body of biographical and autobiographical literature has appeared detailing abuse in brothers' schools and other educational institutions, including sexual abuse. Also, it is clear that engagement in this abuse was not the sole preserve of the Irish Christian Brothers. In his account of the Marist Brothers in Australia, Braniff has stated that "in the light of the contemporary concern about child abuse by Catholic clergy and members of religious orders, in Australia and elsewhere," it is "necessary to point out that this problem is not simply a modern phenomenon."[56] He noted that various Marist Brothers were dismissed from the order in the latter half of the nineteenth century after '"acts of immodesty," others were disciplined for "undue familiarity with some students" and "for hugging certain students," while a former novice complained of being "deprived of his innocence" in the novitiate. Donovan,[57] in his history of the De La Salle order in Australia, Papua New Guinea, and New Zealand, is also open in recognizing that there were brothers within that order who abused the trust of their students and violated their vows. He also makes it clear that it is difficult to gauge the extent and the degree of molestation since perpetrators were clever in hiding their activities from their peers.

Within the reporting of the abuse committed by a variety of orders, including orders of brothers, the events at the orphanages in Western Australia run by the Irish Christian Brothers received the most publicity nationally. These orphanages at Castledare, Clontarf, Bindoon, and Tardun received some 4,000 boys between 1901 and 1983, most of whom were from deprived backgrounds. While 259 of the total were Maltese child migrants who arrived between 1950 and 1965, the majority, about 1,400, "were British child migrants received initially in 1938–1939, and in larger numbers after 1947."[58] This migration was facilitated by a scheme initiated by the Australian government to help it populate the nation, and it had the cooperation of several voluntary organizations, including the Australian Catholic Church. The scheme picked up pace when the impoverished post–World War II British government saw it as a way of relieving its financial outlay on the large population within children's homes.

Those children who came into the care of the Irish Christian Brothers in Western Australia were divided according to age and perceived ability. Infants were sent to Castledare. Older boys deemed to have academic ability were sent to Clontarf, while those deemed suited to learning a trade were sent either to St. Joseph's Farm and Trade School at Bindoon, or St. Mary's Agricultural School at Tardun. In 1987, a Western Australian newspaper, *The Western Mail*, reported on abuse by brothers at these institutions under such headings as "The Lost Children of Britain Sent Away to Australia" and "The Nightmare at Bindoon." Two years later the topic was reopened and beamed to a national audience on a TV program entitled "Christian Brothers," in which four former Bindoon residents related the violence they experienced at the hands of brothers. By now, the broader historical context within which such activity took place was being exposed through the best-selling book, *Lost Children of the Empire*,[59] and an associated television documentary. These developments, in turn, stimulated the writing and publication within Australia of a number of biographical accounts by former child residents.[60]

The Irish Christian Brothers investigated the situation and went on, in July 1993, to publish a public apology in the national press in regard to physical and sexual abuse committed by members of their order in their Western Australian orphanages. By now, however, concern was mounting that such abuse also took place beyond the confines of the four Western Australian institutions, and also not just at the hands of the Irish Christian Brothers. Increasing public disquiet and agitation by pressure groups representing victims meant that cries for full exposure of the nature and extent of what took place could not be ignored by the Australian government, which had been responsible for receiving child migrants, and by the British government, which had been responsible for sending them.

The outcome was two major government inquiries into child migration, namely, a 1998 report of the UK Health Committee and a 2001 report of the Australian Senate Community Affairs Reference Committee. Both inquiries identified the Irish Christian Brothers as having been particularly culpable in the manner in which they ran their orphanages in Western Australia.[61] They related horrendous accounts of sexual abuse and assault.[62] Following this, and responding to a lawsuit, the Irish Christian Brothers, in 1997, once again officially apologized to the child migrants and agreed to pay out $5.1 million, of which $3.7 million was for compensation to victims."[63]

The British government also faced up to its responsibilities. By now, the general public had been made well aware of the fact that under the *Empire Settlement Act* of 1922 and 1937, private organizations had been in receipt of British state financial assistance to help people settle in His Majesty's Overseas Dominions. This legislation was availed of by certain organizations, including those associated with the Christian churches, to send child migrants to various parts of the British Empire. This child migration increased following World War II under conditions made available by the *Children's Act 1948*. The situation has been portrayed thus:

> About 150,000 children with an average age of eight years and nine months emigrated from the United Kingdom, the majority to Canada, until the scheme ended in 1967. A key motivation for child migration was to maintain the racial unity of the Empire and populate the Dominions of Canada, Rhodesia, New Zealand and Australia with "good white stock"...in Australia, a feature of the scheme was the care of children in residential institutions rather than by foster care adoption.[64]

The financial backing for this project was provided both by the British government and the governments of the receiving countries, while the nongovernment organizations receiving the assistance usually had direct charge of most of the children at the recruitment stage, during their passage, and after their arrival in the receiving countries.

In 1998, the British House of Commons Health Committee tabled its report, *The Welfare of Former British Child Migrants*,[65] in which it was concluded that the policies of previous governments in promoting child migration were misguided. In December of that year government assistance to former child migrants was promised. This resulted in the setting up of a central database in the United Kingdom to help such migrants trace their records and in the establishment of a support fund to help pay for family reunions. Three years later, a similar report, *Lost Innocents: Righting the Record—Report on Child Migration*,[66] which was the culmination of an investigation carried out by a committee of the Australian Senate, also accepted responsibility for the misguided role played by previous Australian governments in facilitating child migration to Australia. This was soon followed by the announcement that financial assistance was going to be made available for travel funding to assist former child migrants to return to Britain, and to establish state memorials to commemorate their lives and those of their predecessors. Finally, in Western Australia, the state that has been most associated with child abuse, particularly in the orphanages run by the Irish Christian Brothers, the state government issued an apology in April 2005, to people who were harmed in institutional care. This was followed up two years later by the establishment of a government fund to provide counseling services and compensation payments for those abused and harmed while in such care.[67]

Ireland

As has been pointed out in Chapter Two, the gains made by the church in education, in the latter decades of British rule, were solidified in newly independent Ireland, much to the satisfaction of the hierarchy. This is not surprising since church personnel had been centrally involved in the development of new curricula for primary and secondary schools, which had a strong religious ethos. This foundation meant that throughout the first four decades following Irish independence, the church maintained its dominant role in Irish education irrespective of the political party in power. While this dominance continued over the next 20 years, it began to weaken somewhat as many religious left their orders in the post–Vatican 2 era, and the

Irish state began to take a more active role in making educational provision.

A further dent was made in the church's hegemonic position in Irish society, including education, with the revelation that various high-profile Catholic clerics had been engaged in heterosexual relations. The Irish public, who took it as the norm that its priesthood was celibate and chaste, and that engaging in sexual activity outside of marriage was sinful, was shocked. It was accustomed to the church regularly reminding its members not to use artificial contraception, campaigning strongly against abortion, and publicly disapproving of unmarried cohabitating couples and illegitimacy. Therefore, it came as a considerable surprise when the Irish media started to report allegations of lapses in these areas in the priesthood itself. More was to follow. Starting in the 1990s, a series of criminal cases and Irish government enquiries established that hundreds of priests had abused thousands of children in previous decades and that church authorities, instead of reporting such matters to the police, moved the offenders to other parishes to avoid scandal.

Some of the worst cases of abuse that came to light related to those who were among the approximately 35,000 orphans, petty thieves, truants, unmarried mothers, or members of dysfunctional families who had been sent to a network of 250 church-run industrial schools, reformatories, orphanages, and hostels from the 1930s to the early 1990s.[68] While this abuse was initially highlighted in the press and through a numbers of biographical and autobiographical works, it really came to the attention of the general public through a series of television programs during the 1990s that publicized allegations of systemic abuse in Ireland's Roman Catholic–run childcare system, primarily in the reformatory and industrial schools. While England had closed such institutions in the 1930s, Ireland persisted with them and with their religious-run management structures up until the early 1990s.

The Irish government eventually responded by establishing what has come to be known as the Ryan Commission. The resulting 2,600-page Ryan Report, which drew on testimony from thousands of former inmates and officials from more than 250 church-run institutions, and which took nine years to complete, was published in May 2009. It documents a shocking scenario of priests, brothers, and nuns terrorizing thousands of boys and girls for decades and of government officials turning a blind eye to what many knew were taking place.[69] Among the very few orders to come out of this unscathed were the Dominican Sisters and the Daughters of Liege. Various levels of physical abuse were reported as having taken place at the hands of members of other orders of female religious-run institutions. Male orders, however, were exposed for the very high levels of both physical and sexual abuse that took place under their tutelage. These included the Rosminian Order of priests and the Oblates of Mary Immaculate, which is an order composed of both religious brothers and priests.

Religious orders composed of only brothers, however, dominated the scene. The Presentation Brothers ran an industrial school up until 1959, when there were reports of physical and sexual abuse. Particularly disturbing accounts of sexual abuse of boys with special needs were also related regarding a school run by the Brothers of Charity. However, the abuse perpetrated at the institutions of the Irish Christian Brothers, the largest provider of residential care for boys in the country, received most attention. The stories ranged from embracing and fondling boys, to beatings and rape, as well as to sexual abuse and peer sexual activity at a school for the deaf. Following the publication of the Ryan Report, Ireland's prime minister apologized to the victims for the government's failure to intervene in the terrible atrocities perpetrated against them in the twentieth century. Also, while the religious orders put aside various sums of money to compensate the victims, the archbishop of Dublin, Diarmuid Martin, severely criticized them on the grounds that the amounts they were offering were insufficient.

Some Historical Insights

Trying to explain the horrors of the child abuse scandals that have rocked the Catholic Church brings one into professional and academic fields extending well beyond those of the historian. Nevertheless, one can still offer some insights that arise from adopting a historical perspective.[70] Hopefully, in the fullness of time they can inform in-depth interdisciplinary fora on, and analyses of, this shameful period in the history of Catholic education and child care. In view of the focus of this book, the few insights offered here relate largely to the world of religious brothers. It is recognized that some of them may also apply to the abuse perpetrated by the female religious and by both diocesan and religious-order priests.

A useful way of commencing this exposition is to highlight the view taken by some that the all-male nature of the life of religious brothers attracted those with a sexual orientation toward members of their own sex, both young and old. Given, however, that the great majority were recruited in their early adolescent years, the argument hardly holds; at this stage of life they were most unlikely to have even considered their sexual orientation, much less to have acted in accordance with it. What is more plausible is the contention that the nature of religious "formation," or training, and the nature of the religious life itself, contributed to enormous sexual repression for many.[71] Furthermore, when it became apparent to the authorities of the various religious orders that this repression was redirected into areas where its expression was least likely to be discovered, namely, toward young boys, the overwhelming response was to cover this up, lest discovery by the general public give rise to scandal and threaten the church's hegemonic position.

The tendency to cover up physical and sexual abuse also has to be viewed in the light of the church's embattled position historically. Especially since the loss of the Papal States in 1870, it was particularly sensitive to criticism of those within its ranks. Concurrently, in its all-out war on Liberalism, its condemnation of all things modern and its assertion of its exclusive claims to truth and authority, it promoted a fortress mentality throughout the Catholic world right up to the early 1970s.[72] The associated belief that developed was that it was only through loyalty and obedience that the church could remain strong.

The all-pervasive view was that nothing should ever be mentioned in public that might harm the church and that the church must be protected at all costs. This is not to say that problems were not being aired and discussed behind the scenes. Individual acts of abuse certainly came to the attention of the superiors of individual schools and institutions. The common practice was to move the perpetrators on to somewhere else, rather than expose their conduct to the civil authorities. So far, however, it has not been possible to calibrate the extent to which the superiors in question did this simply to remove the immediate problem and make life easier for themselves, or whether they reported it higher up the ranks, requesting that the perpetrator be confronted and be treated medically, or be charged with a crime. This is one of the areas seriously in need of in-depth research. Such work should also probe the extent to which there was an understanding, if any, of recidivism among child abusers, or whether the belief was that a change of environment would lead to a change in behavior. Furthermore, it is necessary to ask if the superiors of religious orders were under pressure to hold on to members they knew to be abusive toward pupils because of the intense pressure they were under at the time to increase the numbers within the ranks as more and more schools and other institutions were built. Could it be that the pressures to maintain such a huge unpaid labor force for work "in the service of God" were so great that the notion prevailed that it was more important to maintain an abusing member of a religious order within the educational system than seek to raise the finances to replace him, or her, with a lay member of staff?

Some observers not familiar with the internal politics of the Catholic Church are also wont to point out the extent to which Catholic bishops have spoken and acted with a powerful authority and ask why they did not put pressure on the superiors of religious orders to deal with abusers. However, as Grace has so aptly put it, despite its "array of awesome authority, episcopal jurisdiction within Catholic schooling has never achieved total hegemonic domination, and examples of power and control struggles"[73] existed. As pointed out in Chapter Three, two broad divisions existed within religious orders, namely, pontifical orders and diocesan orders. Because the pontifical orders operated almost exclusively under the governing authority of their own superiors, they were not subjected to any official surveillance systems by the bishops of the various diocese in which they were located.

To point out such matters is not to exonerate the members of the hierarchy from all blame. It is most unlikely that no cases of child abuse committed by members of religious orders were reported to them. Also, while their power in terms of church law and protocol was as already described, it is difficult to imagine why they did not find ways to handle reported cases of abuse. This question becomes particularly pertinent when one realizes that ways were certainly found by local bishops to exercise control over members of religious orders who were critical of them on various matters.

It should also not be assumed that there was no anticipation that abuse would be unlikely to take place within institutions run by religious orders. Not only did various sections of the rules and constitutions of different orders make it quite clear that problems were foreshadowed, they also indicated a confidence that methods had been developed to deal with them successfully. At the most basic level, the idea was that everybody was meant to be so busy there would be no time for anything untoward to happen. The training of priests, religious brothers, and nuns was specifically aimed at ensuring such a scenario through developing in them a capacity for hard work. This was seen as providing essential preparation to ensure that on becoming a fully-fledged member of the order, every member would make sure he, or she, was sufficiently occupied that, as it is tended to be put, "the Devil did not find work for idle hands." Also, strict rules operated to ensure that the emergence of interpersonal relationships between members of an order would not be tolerated. These rules, as has been pointed out in previous chapters, went so far as to insist that when it came to recreation, the brothers were expected to walk in threes rather than in twos, as anything bordering on "particular friendships" was frowned upon.

All religious orders also had a rule making it clear that members who were teachers should never allow themselves to be alone with pupils in a classroom, or anywhere else. Unfortunately for the many victims of abuse, these rules were not implemented appropriately or, where they were, steps were rarely taken to ensure that there would be no repeat offenses. There is also the likelihood that, for many members of orders, the nature of the formation geared toward regulating their lives, which, as pointed out in Chapter Four, was "perfection" 'by "dying to themselves and the world,"[74] had the unintended effect of suppressing their physical and sexual energy. This was particularly so in the case of members of religious orders of brothers, many of whom were recruited in their early teens. The regime they experienced is likely to have generated a bitterness that was eventually to gain an outlet through the adoption of an aggressive disposition toward those in their care. As I have put it elsewhere, the "normal" turmoil of early-to-middle adolescent years is unsettling enough psychologically, without having to subdue desires and passions to come to be able to live within the extraordinary authoritarian framework of the consecrated celibate life.[75]

What also seems clear is that there was no cognizance among those responsible for the "religious formation" of members of the orders that the bitterness being alluded to could be generated by some of their practices. While the emphasis was on the notion that what made the religious life an elevated one was the great stress placed on renouncing one's sexual role and function to attain a neutral personhood, there seems to have been little account taken of the devastating effect upon the individual personality of what was required. The emphasis on "quitting the world" meant, in the case of certain religious orders, as has been pointed out already, that a member could not even visit a dying relative, or attend a parent's funeral without special permission, which was rarely given. It is not going too far to suggest that what would now be considered very cruel behavior caused some to take out their bitterness on those they taught and looked after in the schools and educational institutions. Also, to simply ask why members who felt aggrieved did not leave is to fail to understand a particular element of the Catholic culture of the period; leaving was not considered a good thing to do, and if one did, it often brought shame not only on oneself, but also on one's family. Indeed, the immediate point of departure was constructed as a painful and shameful one. Stanton, in his introduction to a work on individuals who were once Salesian brothers in the United States and left before taking final vows has depicted how "the superiors of the community moved quickly and quietly" to bustle the departing brother out without the rest of the community knowing. There was, as he recalled, "no chance to say goodbye to your brothers. Just out and gone."[76]

Finally, before leaving this matter of the possible bitterness generated among members of religious orders because of their experiences within the ranks, it is important to recall that some had more status than others, a situation that is also likely to have contributed to frustration and aggression, which was then channeled in the direction of those under their care. For example, there were clear hierarchies in terms of how those with different teaching abilities were treated; the best teachers went into the prestigious colleges and elite boarding schools. The situation was compounded by the fact that the schools for the lower social orders usually had the highest pupil-teacher ratios, resulting in many turning to corporal punishment as a behavioral management strategy. Also, when it came to the orphanages, it was often the case that the children were under the care of those who could not perform to expectations in the more prestigious institutions. It is not difficult to imagine how the sense of self-worth of these individuals was, as a consequence, devalued. To add to the pressure they were under in such settings, they were often, for seven days a week, placed in charge of huge numbers of children from troubled backgrounds, at a time when there was no professional child-care training.

To offer the historical insights outlined so far is not to excuse any of the vile practices that took place as a result of the conditions under which those teachers in the religious life lived. Rather, it is to put as much emphasis on the depersonalizing structures maintained by the institution as on the individual perpetrators. Also, it needs to be recognized that there is a very large research agenda that needs to be pursued. The main aim of this final section of the present chapter has been to try to offer some food for thought and hopefully try to stimulate readers to a realization that this is a complex subject and one on which the historian can throw some light. Coupled with insights from a range of other disciplines, especially psychology and sociology, it should be possible to generate a more comprehensive and nuanced understanding of the situation than is currently available and, hopefully, make a contribution to try and ensure that such a shocking episode in the history of the Catholic Church, including that of religious teaching brothers, never takes place again.

CHAPTER 9

Looking Backward, Looking Forward

Religious life, as we know it, is over, or dying across the world. I'm more than ever convinced of it. In some parts of the world it is just over. There is absolutely no one joining.[1]

This view was offered in January 2011, by the Indian brother Philip Pinto, who heads the Congregation of the Edmund Rice Christian Brothers.[2] While it provides sobering food for thought, he was speaking specifically in relation to Catholic teaching religious brothers only. In the context of the overall history of religious orders within the Catholic Church, this particular group is of recent origin.[3] Thus, while their future may not be assured, it is important to view recent developments in context and to point out that it certainly does not mean we are witnessing the disappearance of a great number of other religious orders.

The religious way of life commenced way back with the ascetics of the desert, who are primarily associated with the period 250 A. D.–500 A. D. This was followed by the monastic movement, between 500 A. D. and 1200 A. D., with the Benedictines and the Cistercians being especially prominent. Over the next three centuries, from 1200 A. D. to 1500 A. D., the mendicant orders, most notably the Franciscans, the Dominicans, the Augustinians, the Carmelites, and the Servites, emerged and grew. The next group to flourish, from 1500 A. D. to 1800 A. D., consisted of the apostolic orders, which included the Jesuits.

The final group to emerge, primarily from the middle of the 1700s, comprised those orders deemed to be especially involved in "institutional ministries." The orders of religious teaching brothers that have been the focus of attention throughout the book belong to this last era in the age of religious life within the Catholic Church.

It has been indicated that, like religious orders of nuns, these orders of religious brothers can be distinguished from priests in that their members are not ordained clergy. Attention has also been given to another distinguishing feature, namely, that, like nuns and religious orders of priests, but unlike diocesan priests, they live in community. Furthermore, up until the Second Vatican Council, religious orders of brothers, like most religious orders of priests, had "domestic brothers," who usually assisted with domestic work, maintenance, and farm work, as did "lay sisters" in convents.

Historically, religious orders of brothers have been involved in work of different types, including nursing and social work of various kinds, but they have been primarily involved in teaching. The most central characteristic of their way of life for most of the period under consideration is that, while they worked in the world, they also had to divorce themselves from the world as much as possible. It is this characteristic of teaching brothers that has been foregrounded as the principal theme running throughout this book, the argument being that they were religious first and foremost, and that teaching, while deemed to be a very important role, was always in accord with and, where necessary, took second place to, that life. Indeed, the expectation in this regard was made crystal clear to all aspiring to be brothers ever before they took one step over the threshold of the cloister. Once inside, the message continued to be reinforced among recruits of the orders, with great regularity, and with increasing intensity from year to year, as they proceeded through the various stages of the brotherhood. In this way, they became more and more socialized into what Goffman has termed a "total institution."[4]

Goffman defined a "total institution" as "a place of residence and work where a large number of like-situated individuals cut off from the wider society for an appreciable period of time together lead an enclosed formally administered round of life."[5] Religious brothers certainly lived a life that conformed to this definition. It was distinguished from the basic social arrangements in modern Western society whereby the individual "tends to sleep, play and work in different places with different co-participants, under different authorities and without an overall rational plan."[6] For brothers, the barriers separating these various spheres of activity were broken down, so that, as with members of other total institutions, their life conformed to the following characteristics identified by Goffman:

> First, all aspects of life are conducted in the same place and under the same single authority. Second, each phase of the member's daily

> activity is carried out in the immediate company of a large batch of others, all of whom are treated alike and required to do the same things together. Third, all phases of the day's activities are tightly scheduled with one activity leading at a pre-arranged time into the next, the whole sequence of events being imposed from above by a series of explicit, formal rulings and a body of officials. Finally, the various enforced activities are brought together into a single rational plan purportedly designed to fulfill the official aims of the institutions.[7]

It is true that certain deviations from these characteristics could be pointed out in the case of the life of teaching brothers. These, however, were minor rather than major. Regarding the first characteristic, for example, namely, that all aspects of life are conducted in the same place, it is certainly the case that brothers had to venture away from the monastery if the school, or church, were not also located on the one site, but their rules were designed to ensure they remained as oblivious as possible to "the outside" world as they moved through it daily.

At this juncture, it is apposite to recall the point made in Chapter One that this is a pioneering book, being the first general work to appear on the life of Catholic religious teaching brothers across the English-speaking world for the period 1891–1965. It was made clear that it relates to teaching brothers as a whole, rather than focusing specifically on any particular order, even though examples from the experiences of a variety of orders had to be drawn upon to illustrate the arguments put forward. It was also made clear that the emphasis is more on delineating the broad parameters within which the life of teaching brothers was constructed and regulated, rather than with capturing lived experience, notwithstanding the fact that some of the available material on the lived experience has been used throughout.

It is hoped that other scholars will now respond by engaging in more detailed, nuanced, and fine-grained works on particular orders, in particular geographical locations, and during various subperiods. For example, there is no significant body of work based upon the reminiscences of religious teaching brothers themselves,[8] those of former pupils (apart from those who attended orphanages and "special schools"),[9] and those who left the brotherhood. Equally, there is a dearth of scholarship on those who went to work on the mission fields and on the adaptations, if any, that they made in their lives when they were far removed from their orders' centers of power at a time when policies and directives were much slower in reaching their destinations than is the situation today. A related area in which there has been no research is that of brothers recruited from the mission fields and how these personnel lived their lives in relation to the expectations both of the societies into which they had been born and of the brothers of American, European, Australian, and New Zealand origins with whom they lived in community.

Studies along the lines outlined above should facilitate engagement in comparative projects aimed at elaborating upon, refining, and perhaps even contesting various aspects of the account offered in this book. The changes that took place in the lives of teaching brothers over the last few decades is also in need of investigation. The remainder of this chapter now sketches out, in a very general way, some of the avenues one might traverse in the latter regard.

By the middle of the 1960s, influenced especially by the proceedings of the Second Vatican Council, the "totality" of the life of members of religious orders was beginning to break down. Among the many challenges posed by the council were those aimed at promoting change in the nature of the life of the religious, including moving members of religious communities away from a religious formation based on blind obedience within a hierarchical institution, to one based on rational choices within more democratic structures. Various orders welcomed these and associated changes to varying degrees. While no major calibration of the responses has been conducted, anecdotal evidence indicates that, initially, they were embraced much more enthusiastically by female orders than by male orders. Nevertheless, brothers, including teaching brothers, did respond over time and began to act on the initiatives more and more. These meant not only more flexible prayer structures and daily schedules, but also dressing more along the lines of lay people, engaging much more than heretofore in personal decision making, and having more freedom to relax, develop friendships, and partake in recreational activities.

New developments in the educational life of brothers also took place. Teaching in coeducational institutions became much more the norm than previously. Brothers also began to interact more regularly with females as, more and more, they enrolled in university degrees and other courses in secular educational institutions. In some orders a regulation that had lasted for over a century requiring that one could not become a secondary schoolteacher without first gaining a qualification as a primary schoolteacher, was dropped. Also, as has been pointed out in Chapter Eight, many orders opened up their own post–high school courses at college and university level to lay people, and not just in programs of teacher preparation, but also in theology, philosophy, and related studies on social and economic development, spirituality, and social justice.

Following extensive engagement in trying to work out where they fitted into the life of the church following the challenge offered by the Second Vatican Council that the members of each order reflect on the ideas and works of their founders, some of the more well-known orders of teaching brothers also took new directions. In some cases, this still meant involvement in education, but with a somewhat different focus relative to what had been traditional practices. The Australian branch of the Irish Christian Brothers, for example, who took the radical step of pulling out of their schools totally and reestablishing them as "trust" institutions run by a board of lay people, have established some new projects in developing countries. One of these involves working in the Philippines in two small cities, Kabankalan on the island of Negros, and Hilongos on the island of Leyte. Here they are involved in building the capacity of principals and teachers in Catholic schools to provide special programs for young people at risk and assisting out-of-school children to gain access to education.[10]

Such action by the Irish Christian Brothers in various parts of the world is in accord with the new vision of their work for the poor and the marginalized, a position that was codified as follows at their 1996 general chapter:

The following strategies are directed to making the call to the margins of society a reality in our congregation:

- We will situate all our new ventures at the margins having reviewed our present ministries in the light of our call to new beginnings;
- We will review and evaluate our mission statements on a regular basis to ensure a faithfulness to our shared faith-vision of life;
- We will work in partnership with others in order to challenge structural injustices in society wherever we meet them;
- We will maintain a global perspective in redistributing our human and material resources, committing a percentage of our substance as well as our surplus to the marginalized.[11]

Some of the other major orders of teaching brothers have taken a similar position and have become engaged in related projects. For example, in the late 1990s, the Marist Brothers began providing assistance in refugee camps in the Indonesian border area of West Sepik

Province in Papua New Guinea. The refugees found themselves there as a result of separatist military activity by their indigenous peers. At the time, there was a fear that the Indonesian military would carry out reprisals against the refugees in the camps, forcing them to return to the areas from which they had fled. The Papua New Guinea government did not have the resources to assist the refugees, but the Catholic Church provided some limited relief. Later, when border crossers set up more camps in Papua New Guinea's Western Province, a humanitarian crisis loomed. The urgent needs were for food, medical attention, and schools. Again, the brothers went to help, especially as nurses and teachers.[12]

Some of the lesser known orders have also been active in pursuing an agenda informed by a commitment to social justice, particularly in developing countries. As early as the 1930s, American Brothers of the Sacred Heart began founding schools in Africa. Since then they have opened educational and other institutions in Kenya, Lesotho, Uganda, Zambia, and Zimbabwe. Today, most of the brothers of the order in these countries are indigenous. They direct and staff high schools, minister to street children and AIDS orphans, and run agricultural projects and retreat centers.[13] The Gabrielite Brothers, on the other hand, took the initiative of trying to promote social justice through university-level programs aimed at social and economic development.[14] To this end, they established the Assumption School of Business in Thailand in 1969 (having opened schools in the country as early as 1901), which became the Assumption Business Administration College in 1972, and the Assumption University in 1990. This is a comprehensive university in terms of its discipline offerings and, along with local students, attracts large numbers of students from India, China, Myanmar, Russia, Bangladesh, and Pakistan.[15] In a similar vein, the De La Salle Brothers opened the Bethlehem University in Palestine, in 1973, making it the first university in the West Bank.[16]

Notwithstanding such developments, the number of teaching brothers around the world continues to decline at a very steep rate.[17] Recognizing that their days might be numbered, some have set up networks so that they can continue to have an influence through affiliated groups of lay people, including men who have left the order, but continue to be practicing Catholics. What the future holds is not at all certain. Some of the main orders may, in fact, be disestablished as a result not just of falling numbers, but also due to the possibility of going bankrupt from payments arising out of lawsuits connected with child abuse.[18] What does seem clear, however, is that even if orders of Catholic religious teaching brothers do continue to exist, it will only be at the margins, in contrast to the centerstage they held for so long in Catholic education throughout much of the English-speaking world.

Notes

1 Introduction

1. E. Smyth, "Much Exertion of the Voice and Great Application of the Mind: Teacher Education within Congregations of the Sisters of St. Joseph of Toronto, Canada, 1851–1920," *History of Education Review/ Historical Studies in Education* (Joint Issue) 6, no. 3 (1994): 27.
2. P. Wittberg, *The Rise and Fall of Catholic Religious Orders: A Social Movement Perspective* (Albany: SUNY Press, 1994), 53.
3. Ibid.
4. See M. Peckham-Magray, *The Transforming Power of the Nuns: Women, Religion and Cultural Change in Ireland, 1750–1900* (New York: Oxford University Press, 1998).
5. In this book the terms "the Catholic Hierarchy" and "the Hierarchy" refer to Catholic bishops, archbishops, and cardinals. Furthermore, the term "Catholic" refers to the Roman Catholic Church, thus following common usage.
6. See T. A. O'Donoghue, *Come Follow Me and Forsake Temptation: Catholic Schooling and the Recruitment and Retention of Teachers for Religious Teaching Orders, 1922–1965* (Bern: Peter Lang, 2004), 11.
7. J. Whyte, *Church and State in Modern Ireland* (Dublin: Gill and Macmillan, 1980), 21.
8. T. Inglis, *Moral Monopoly: The Rise and Fall of the Catholic Church in Modern Ireland* (Dublin: University College Dublin Press, 1998), 211.
9. S. Dunn, "Education, Religion and Cultural Change in the Republic of Ireland" in *Christianity and Educational Provision in International Perspective*, eds. W. Tulasiewicz and C. Brock (London: Routledge, 1988), 101.
10. T. Inglis, *Moral Monopoly: The Rise and Fall of the Catholic Church in Modern Ireland*, 58.
11. See T. A. O'Donoghue, *The Catholic Church and the Secondary School Curriculum in Ireland, 1922–1962* (New York: Peter Lang, 1999), 87–110.
12. See T. A. O'Donoghue, *Bilingual Education in Pre-Independent Irish-speaking Ireland, 1800–1922. A History* (New York: Edwin Mellen Press, 2006), 31–42.

13. Throughout the remainder of this chapter where I refer to "the brothers" and the "Christian brothers," I am referring to the Irish Christian brothers, the terms by which I knew them in my younger years. In the remaining chapters, I use the official title of each order of brothers.
14. The Legion of Mary was founded by Frank Duff in Dublin on September 7, 1921, and is operational even today. His idea was to help Catholic lay people to live their dedication to the church in an organized structure, supported by the fraternity and prayer. Its members first started out by visiting hospitals and then moved on to engaging in other "good works."
15. I have dealt with this in detail in T. A. O'Donoghue, "Rescuing Lay Teachers in Catholic Schools from Anonymity for the Period 1870–1970," *Education Research and Perspectives* 26, no. 2 (2004): 78–93.
16. For a comprehensive review of this work see B. Hellinckx, F. Simon, and M. Depaepe, *The Forgotten Contribution of the Teaching Sisters: An Historiographical Essay on the Educational Work of Catholic Women Religious in the Nineteenth and Twentieth Centuries* (Leuven: Leuven University Press, 2009).
17. Smyth, "Much Exertion," 28–29.
18. Ibid.
19. J. A. K. McNamara, *Sisters in Arms: Catholic Nuns through Two* Millennia (Cambridge: Harvard University Press, 1996).
20. Wittberg, *The Rise and Fall of Catholic Religious Orders.*
21. E. Smyth, "Sisters in Culture: Ethnicity and Toronto's Teaching Communities of Women Religious" (Proceedings of the ISCHE XXI Conference, University of Sydney, Australia. July 12–16, 1999).
22. S. Burley, "The Silent Sisterhood(s): Catholic Nuns, Their Public Work and Influence for Social Change in Australia, in Particular South Australia, 1880–1930" (Unpublished Research Paper, Graduate School of Education, The University of Adelaide, 2000).
23. J. Collins, "Hidden Lives: The Teaching and Religious Lives of Eight Dominican Sisters, 1931–1961." (MEd. thesis, Massey University, New Zealand, 2001).
24. F. M. Perko, "Religious Schooling in America: An Historiographic Reflection," *History of Education Quarterly* 40, no. 3 (2000): 320–338.
25. C. Clear, *Nuns in Nineteenth Century Ireland* (Dublin: Gill and Macmillan, 1988).
26. Peckham-Magray, *The Transforming Power of the Nuns.*
27. B. Walsh, *Roman Catholic Nuns in England and Wales, 1800–1937* (Dublin: Irish Academic Press, 2002).
28. C. M. Mangion, *Catholic Women Religious in Nineteenth Century England and Wales* (Manchester: Manchester University Press, 2008). The broad range of work that has been produced internationally has also been expertly reviewed in B. Hellinckx, F. Simon, and M. Depaepe, *The Forgotten Contribution*

29. A notable exception is D. Plowman. *Enduring Struggle: St. Mary's Tardun Farm School* (Perth: Scholastic Press, 2003). Here we get some insights into the fact that the cloister was not always a place where divisions of power and authority were accepted without resistance.
30. Perko, "Religious Schooling in America," 337.
31. This point is made regularly throughout J. Braniff, "The Marist Brothers' Teaching Tradition in Australia: 1872–2000" (PhD thesis, University of Sydney, 2005).
32. Clear, *Nuns in Nineteenth Century Ireland*, xviii.

2 The Church and Its Teaching Orders

1. E. O. Hanson, *The Catholic Church in World Politics* (Princeton, NJ: Princeton University Press, 1987), 85.
2. A more sophisticated picture could be provided by also considering the situation in a number of other countries, particularly Canada and South Africa. Such a picture could lead not only to cross national comparisons, but also to an analysis of differences within countries; contrasts between French Canada and English Canada immediately come to mind in the latter regard. See, for example, T. J. Fay, *A History of Canadian Catholics: Gallicanism, Romanism, and Catholicism* (Montreal and Kingston: McGill-Queen's University Press, 2002). In this chapter, however, the purpose is to promote a general appreciation of the role of teaching brothers within Catholic education historically by highlighting a number of very important examples of individual country "cases."
3. W. Tulasciewitcz and C. Brock (eds.), *Christianity and Educational Provision in International Perspective* (London: Routledge, 1989), 3.
4. Ibid.
5. Ibid.
6. Ibid.
7. S. J. Curtis and M. E. A. Boultwood, *A Short History of Educational Ideas* (London: University Tutorial Press Ltd., 1970), 100.
8. A. S. Bryk, V. E. Lee, and P. B. Holland, *Catholic Schools and the Common Good* (Cambridge, MA: Harvard University Press, 1993), 19.
9. Ibid.
10. For an account of this see J. Cornwell, *Hitler's Pope: The Secret History of Pius XII* (London: Penguin Books, 1999).
11. Hanson, *The Catholic Church in World Politics*, 33.
12. Ibid., 34.
13. Ibid.
14. S. Connolly, *Religion and Society in Nineteenth Century Ireland* (Dundalk: Dundalgan Press, 1985), 27.
15. Ibid., 13.
16. Hanson, *The Catholic Church in World Politics*, 31.
17. Ibid., 173.

18. Ibid., 50.
19. See M. J. Hickman, "Catholicism and the Nation State in Nineteenth Century Britain" in *Commitment to Diversity: Catholics and Education in a Changing World*, eds. M. Eaton, J. Longmore, and A. Naylor (London and New York: Cassell, 2000), 47–66.
20. See M. Peckham-Magray, *The Transforming Power of the Nuns: Women, Religion and Cultural Change in Ireland, 1750–1900* (New York: Oxford University Press, 1998), 5–11.
21. E. Smyth, "Teacher Education within the Congregation of the Sisters of St. Joseph of Toronto, Canada, 1851–1920," *History of Education Review* 23, no. 3 (1994): 97–113.
22. See E. M. Hogan, *The Irish Missionary Movement: A Historical Survey, 1830–1980* (Dublin: Gill and Macmillan, 1992), 55–61.
23. Ibid., 2.
24. T. A. O'Donoghue, *Upholding the Faith: The Process of Education in Catholic Schools in Australia, 1922–1965* (New York: Peter Lang, 2001), 22–23.
25. This section of the chapter is largely a summary of my account in T. A. O'Donoghue, *Come Follow Me and Forsake Temptation: Catholic Schooling and the Recruitment and Retention of Teachers for Religious Teaching Orders, 1922–1965* (Bern: Peter Lang, 2004), 37–61.
26. R. Stark and R. Finke, "Catholic Religious Vocations: Decline and Revival," *Review of Religious Research* 42, no. 2 (2000): 125.
27. Ibid.
28. Ibid.
29. M. A. Grant and T. C. Hunt, *Catholic School Education in the United States: Development and Current Concerns* (New York: Garland Publishing, Inc., 1992), 19. For an outline of the growth of Catholicism in the United States within the context of the growth of the Christian religions as a whole, along with a brief overview on the history of Christianity in Canada and Mexico, see M. A. Noll, *The Old Religion in the New World: The History of North American Christianity* (Grand Rapids, MI: Wm. B. Edermans Publishing, 2002).
30. Grant and Hunt, *Catholic School Education in the United States: Development and Current Concerns*, 231.
31. There is an extensive list of works that outlines the arrival of different religious orders in different diocese and the expansion of their work. Typical in this regard is L. W. Tentler, *Seasons of Grace: A History of the Catholic Church in the Archdiocese of Detroit* (Detroit: Wayne State University Press, 1990).
32. See H. Judge, *Faith-Based Schools and the State: Catholics in America, France and England* (Wallingford, Oxford, United Kingdom: Symposium Books, 2002), 189–206.
33. Grant and Hunt, *Catholic School Education in the United States: Development and Current Concerns*, 43.
34. Ibid.

35. Murphy, *A History of Irish Emigrant and Missionary Education* (Dublin: Four Courts Press, 2000), 247.
36. T. Walch, "United States Catholic History: American Catholic Education—Historical Contours and Future Directions," *Catechist* 34, no. 6 (2001), 46–51.
37. See J. M. Lee (ed.), *Catholic Education in the Western World* (Notre Dame, IN: University of Notre Dame Press, 1966), 300.
38. See A. S. Bryk., V. E. Lee, and P. B. Holland, *Catholic Schools and the Common Good* (Cambridge, MA: Harvard University Press, 1994), 33.
39. Judge, *Faith-Based Schools and the State: Catholics in America, France and England*, 201.
40. J. P. White, "A Short History of English Catholic Education" in *Catholic Education in the Western World*, ed. J. M. Lee (Notre Dame, IN: University of Notre Dame Press, 1966), 211.
41. Ibid., 213.
42. For separate treatment of the history of the Catholic Church in Wales see D. Atwater. *The Catholic Church in Modern Wales* (London: Burns Oates and Washbourne, 1935) and T. O. Hughes, *Winds of Change. The Roman Catholic Church and Society in Wales, 1916–1962* (Cardiff: University of Wales Press, 1999).
43. Ibid.
44. B. O'Keefe, "Reordering Perspectives in Catholic Schools" in *Catholics in England 1950–2000: Historical and Sociological Perspectives*, ed. M. P. Hornsby-Smith (London: Cassell, 1999), 244.
45. See T. Buchanan, "Great Britain" in *Political Catholicism in Europe, 1918–1965*, eds. T. Buchanan and M. Conway (Oxford: Clarendon Press, 1996), 250.
46. Ibid.
47. M. P. Hornsby-Smith, "Catholic Schooling in England and Wales" in *Commitment to Diversity: Catholics and Education in a Changing World* (London and New York: Cassell, 2000), 187–188.
48. Ibid., 188.
49. M. P. Hornsby-Smith, *Catholic Education: The Unobtrusive Partner* (London: Sheed and Ward, 1978), 3.
50. Murphy, *A History of Irish Emigrant and Missionary Education*, 165.
51. For an overview of the expansion of male religious in England from the 1850s to the 1960s see D. A. Bellenger, "Religious Life for Men" in *From without the Flamian Gate: 150 Years of Catholicism in England and Wales,1850–2000*, ed. V. A. McClelland (London: Darton, Longman and Todd, 1999), 142–166.
52. Buchanan, "Great Britain," 250.
53. See Judge, *Faith-Based Schools and the State*, 229.
54. Ibid., 240.
55. See B. Titley, *Church, State and the Control of Schooling in Ireland 1900–1944* (Kingston, ON: McGill-Queen's University Press. Titley, 1983), 5–6.

56. T. A. O'Donoghue, "The Catholic Church and the Promotion of a Gaelic Identity in Irish Secondary Schools," *The Australian Journal of Irish Studies* 2 (2002): 149–165.
57. See P. Duffy, *The Lay Teacher* (Dublin: Fallons, 1967), 79.
58. Ibid., 72.
59. Ibid., 49.
60. J. Weafer and A. Breslin, *A Survey of Irish Catholic Clergy and Religious, 1970–1981.* (Maynooth: Council for Research and Development, Report No. 17, 1983).
61. T. Inglis, *Moral Monopol* (Dublin: University College Dublin Press, 1998), 225. See also T. O'Donoghue and J. Harford, "A Comparative History of Church-State Relations in Irish Education," *Comparative Education Review*, 55 no. 3 (2011): 315–341.
62. See D. White, *Education and the State: Federal Involvement in Educational Policy Development* (Victoria, Australia: Deakin University Press, 1987).
63. Ibid., 7.
64. See Australian Schools Commission (Report of the Interim Committee for the Australian Schools Commission) (P. Karmel, Chairman), *Schools in Australia* (Canberra, Australia: Australian Government Printing Service, 1973).
65. R. Fogarty, *Catholic Education in Australia: 1806–1950* (Melbourne: Melbourne University Press, 1959), 257–303.
66. I have dealt with the expansion of the religious teaching orders in Australia in O'Donoghue, *Upholding the Faith*, 22–27.
67. See K. Canavan, "The Quiet Revolution in Catholic Schooling in Australia," *Catholic Education: Journal of Inquiry and Practice* 2, no. 1 (1998): 47.
68. For a comprehensive overview of Irish settlement in New Zealand see D. H. Akenson, *The Irish Diaspora: A Primer* (Belfast: Queen's University Belfast, Institute of Irish Studies, 1996), 59–90.
69. See Murphy, *A History of Irish Emigrant and Missionary Education*, 404–415.
70. Ibid., 19–20.
71. Ibid., 157. See also R. Sweetman, *A Fair and Just Solution? A History of the Integration of Private Schools in New Zealand* (Palmerston North, New Zealand: Dunmore Press, 2002).
72. See F. J. O'Hagan, *The Contribution of the Religious Orders to Education in Glasgow during the Period 1847–1918* (Lampeter, Wales: The Edwin Mellen Press), 101–102.
73. See B. C. Manion, *A Centenary of Service: The Christian Brothers in Queensland, 1875–1975* (Sydney: Christian Brothers of Australasia, 1975), 22.
74. The work of Catholic religious orders, including orders of brothers, is not dealt with in such standard works on the history of disability as P. L. Safford and E. J. Safford, *A History of Childhood and Disability*

(New York: Teachers College Press, Columbia University, 1996) and M. Winzer, *The History of Special Education: From Isolation to Integration* (Washington, DC: Gallaudet University Press, 1993).

75. For a comprehensive overview on the history of different approaches to the teaching of the deaf see L. Monaghan, C. Schmaling, K. Nakamura, and G. H. Turner (eds.), *Many Ways to Be Deaf: International Variation in Deaf Communities* (Washington, DC: Gallaudet University Press, 2003). Brothers, however, are rarely mentioned in such general works on the history of the teaching of the deaf. Nuns fare a little better. See C. Mitchell, "Exclusion and Integration: The Case of the Sisters of Providence of Quebec" in *Deaf History Unveiled: Interpretations from New Scholarship*, ed. J. V. Van Cleve (Washington, DC: Gallaudet University Press, 2003), 146–171.
76. See J. Towey, *Irish De La Salle Brothers in Christian Education* (Dublin: De La Salle, 1980).
77. See K. J. Griffin, "A History of Teacher Education in the Seven Colleges Conducted by the American Christian Brothers" (PhD thesis, Saint Louis University, 1976).
78. See International Association of Lasallian Universities http://www.aiul.net/portal/index.php?page=universities (Accessed November 3, 2009).
79. See details on the International Federation of Catholic Universities at http://www.fiuc.org/cms/index.php?page=homeENG (Accessed November 3, 2009).See also:http://collegeapps.about.com/od/collegerankings/tp/top-catholic-colleges.htm(Accessed November 3, 2009).
80. Nevertheless, colleges and universities run by brothers get hardly a mention in two of the most significant works on Catholic higher education which have emerged in the United States since the Second Vatican Council, namely, A. Galin, *Negotiating Identity: Catholic Higher Education since 1960* (Notre Dame, IN: University of Notre Dame Press, 2000) and R. Hassenger (ed.), *The Shape of Catholic Higher Education* (Chicago, IL: The University of Chicago Press, 1967). This contrasts with the extensive attention given to institutions run by orders of priests, diocesan priests, and orders of nuns.
81. http://www.cbu.edu/cbu/AboutCBU/OverviewHistory/index.htm(Accessed November 3, 2009).
82. http://www.manhattan.edu/ (Accessed November 3, 2009).
83. http://www.lasalle.edu/univcomm/glance.php (Accessed November 3, 2009).
84. http://www.stmarys-ca.edu/ (Accessed November 3, 2009).
85. http://www.smumn.edu/ (Accessed November 3, 2009).
86. http://www.lewisu.edu/welcome/lewis.htm (Accessed November 3, 2009).
87. http://www.catholic.org/encyclopedia/view.php?id=2922 (Accessed November 3, 2009).

88. Ibid.
89. Ibid.
90. Towey gives a very good account of the spread of the De La Salle order to America, with brothers establishing themselves first in French-Canada, and expanding from there into English-Canada and the USA. He also provides a very detailed account of their spread in the 1850s to Malaya and Singapore, in the 1860s to India, Burma and Ceylon, to Hong Kong in the 1870s, to the Philippines in the early 1900s, and to South Africa, Mauritius, Nigeria, and Australia from the 1900s onward. See J. Towey, *Irish De La Salle Brothers in Christian Education* (Dublin: De La Salle Brothers, 1980). See also H. K. Wong, "An Investigation into the Work of the De La Salle Brothers in the Far East," *Paedagogica Historica* 6, no. 2 (1966): 440–504.
91. W. J. Battersby, *The De La Salle Brothers in Great Britain* (London: Burns and Oates, 1954), 77.
92. http://www.maristoz.edu.au/main.php?name+%22history%22 (Accessed March 10, 2009).
93. By far the best accounts of Rice are provided in D. Keogh, *Edmund Rice and the First Christian Brothers* (Dublin: Four Courts Press, 2008) and D. McLaughlin, *The Price of Freedom: Edmund Rice, Educational Leader* (Melbourne: David Lovell Publishing, 2007).
94. Similarities of titles can be very confusing. There is another order of brothers yet again known as the Brothers of Christian Instruction, more correctly named the De La Mennais Brothers. They were established in 1819 by two Catholic priests in France, Fr. Gabriel Deshayes and Fr. Jean-Marie de Lamennais, for the education of poor boys. Over time they spread into Bulgaria, Turkey, Egypt, Spain, England, Canada, and the United States, along with other countries.
95. These should not be confused with a thriving order of brothers also entitled the Brothers of the Sacred Heart, founded by Pere Andre Coindre in Lyons, France, in 1821. See http://www.coindre.org/FR/statistiques/pays.htm (Accessed August 12, 2011).
96. The fortunes of the order are considered throughout M. D. Curran, *A History of the Christian Brothers in India* (Dublin: The Irish Christian Brothers, nd.).
97. See, for example, D. S. Blake, *Jerome Colm Keating (1928–1999): Christian Brother Extraordinary* (Rome: Christian Brothers, 2004), 346.
98. Buetow details a number of such failed attempts. See H. A. Buetow, *Of Singular Benefit: The Story of Catholic Education in the United States* (London: The Macmillan Company, 1970), 78–88.

3 Brothers, Not Priests

1. Blessed Sacrament Brothers, *The Vocation of the Blessed Sacrament Brother* (Sydney: O'Loughlin Bros., 1963), 3.

2. The Christian Brothers, *Directory and Rules of the Congregation of the Brothers of the Christian Schools of Ireland* (Dublin: The Christian Brothers, 1927), 258.
3. M. S. Thompson, "Sisterhood and Power: Class, Culture and Ethnicity in the American Convent," *Colby Library Quarterly* 25 (1989): 149–175.
4. See, for example, Sisters of Saint Joseph of the Most Sacred Heart of Jesus, *Customs and Practices of the Sisters of St. Joseph of the Most Sacred Heart of Jesus* (Sydney: Sisters of Saint Joseph of the Most Sacred Heart of Jesus, 1950), 14–15. See also J. Graham, *Breaking the Habit: Life in a New Zealand Convent 1955–1967* (Dunedin, New Zealand: John McIndoe Ltd., 1992), 82.
5. Thompson, "Sisterhood and Power, 149–175.
6. P. Wittberg, *The Rise and Fall of Catholic Religious Orders: A Social Movement Perspective* (Albany, NY: SUNY Press, 1994), 13.
7. Ibid.
8. Ibid.
9. M. R. A. MacGinley, *A Dynamic of Hope: Institutes of Women Religious in Australia* (Sydney: Crossing Press, 1996), 2.
10. Ibid.
11. The Religious Hospitallers of Saint Joseph, *Constitutions of The Religious Hospitallers of Saint Joseph* (Montreal: The Religious Hospitallers of Saint Joseph, 1953), 21.
12. The Sisters of Mercy, *Constitutions of the Congregation of the Australian Union of the Sisters of Our Lady of Mercy* (London: Robson and Son, 1866), 2. See also, The Brigidine Congregation, *The Constitutions of the Sisters of the Brigidine Congregation* (New South Wales, Australia: The Brigidine Congregation, 1956), 1. Here the following is stated: "The primary aim of this Congregation is that common to every Religious Institute with simple vows—viz., to perfect the member by observance of the three vows of religion and by the Constitutions."
13. Brigidine Congregation, *The Constitutions of the Sisters of the Brigidine Congregation*, 154.
14. The Institute of the Blessed Virgin Mary, *Rules IBVM* (Dublin: IBVM, 1914), 8.
15. Congregation of the New Zealand Dominican Sisters, *Constitutions* (Auckland: Dominican Sisters, 1933), 1–2.
16. Wittberg, *The Rise and Fall of Catholic Religious Orders*, 111.
17. Ibid.
18. Ibid.
19. Pope Pius XII, *Sacra Virginitas: Encyclical of Pope Pius XII on Consecrated Virginity March 25, 1954.* http://www.papalencyclicals.net/Pius12/P12SACRA.HTM (Accessed July 1, 2009).
20. R. Sullivan, *Visual Habits: Nuns, Feminism, and American Postwar Popular Culture* (Toronto: University of Toronto Press, 2005), 83.

Jansenism is a theological position emphasizing original sin and human depravity. It originated in Holland in the early 1600s and thrived in France, even though it was condemned by the Catholic Church.

21. D. Bollen, *Up On the Hill: A History of St. Patrick's College, Goulburn* (Sydney: University of New South Wales Press, 2008), 260.
22. Ibid.
23. Ibid., 259.
24. Ibid.
25. Ibid.
26. Ibid, 260.
27. See D. Strong, *Jesuits in Australia* (Richmond, Victoria, Australia: Aurora Books, 1995), 60.
28. Ibid.
29. Brigidine Congregation, *The Constitutions of the Sisters of the Brigidine Congregation*, 122.
30. Ibid., 62.
31. Sisters of Saint Joseph of The Most Sacred Heart of Jesus, *Constitutions of The Sisters of the Most Sacred Heart of Jesus* (Sydney: Sisters of Saint Joseph of The Most Sacred Heart of Jesus, 1949), 3.
32. The Brigidine Sisters, *Directory of the Brigidine Sisters* (New South Wales, Australia: The Brigidine Sisters, 1955), 1.
33. The Sisters of Mercy, *Constitutions of the Congregation of the Australian Union of the Sisters of Our Lady of Mercy* (Canberra, Australia: The Sisters of Mercy, General Motherhouse, 1960), 3.
34. See Sisters of Mercy, *A Guide for the Religious Called Sisters of Mercy* (London: Robson and Son, 1866), 5.
35. Christian Brothers, *Christian Brothers General Chapter 1968* (Dublin: The Christian Brothers, 1968), 13–14.
36. Ibid.
37. Wittberg, *The Rise and Fall of Catholic Religious Orders*, 15.
38. The Oxford Movement originated among High Church Anglicans associated with the University of Oxford, and it developed into what came to be known as Anglo-Catholicism. The principal aim of the movement, also known as Tractarianism, was the reinstatement of many Roman Catholic traditions of faith and their inclusion in Anglican liturgy and theology. See C. B. Faught, *The Oxford Movement: A Thematic History of the Tractarians and Their Times* (University Park: Pennsylvania State University Press, 2003).
39. Ibid.
40. The Taize Community, in Taize, Burgundy, France, was founded by a Catholic religious brother, Br. Roger Schutz in 1940. It is an ecumenical monastic order devoted to promoting peace and justice through prayer and meditation. See http://www.taize.fr/ (Accessed on May 9, 2011).
41. This exposition is based on that in http://www.mb-soft.com/believe/txh/chrisbro.htm (Accessed on August 11, 2006).

42. The Divine Office is also known as the Liturgy of the Hours. It is the official set of daily prayers prescribed by the Catholic Church to be recited at appointed times by priests, brothers, and nuns.
43. K. Armstrong, *Through the Narrow Gate* (London: Pan Books Ltd., 1982), 68–69.
44. M. Sturrock, *Women of Strength, Women of Gentleness: The Brigidine Sisters, Victoria Province* (Melbourne: David Lovell Publishing, 1995), xi.
45. See J. Collins, "Hidden Lives: 'The Teaching and Religious Lives of Eight Dominican Sisters, 1931–1961." (MEd thesis, Massey University, 2001), 113.
46. See E. Smyth, "Much Exertion of the Voice and Great Application of the Mind: Teacher Education within Congregations of the Sisters of St. Joseph of Toronto, Canada, 1851–1920," *History of Education Review/Historical Studies in Education* (Joint Issue) 6, no. 3 (1994): 97–113. See also Collins, "Hidden Lives, 114.
47. M. Peckham-Magray, *The Transforming Power of the Nuns: Women, Religion and Cultural Change in Ireland, 1750–1900* (New York: Oxford University Press, 1998), 42.
48. This account is based on that in C. Trimingham Jack, "The lay sister in educational history and memory" (Proceedings of the Australian and New Zealand History of Education Society Annual Conference, Auckland, New Zealand, 1998).
49. C. Trimingham Jack, *Growing Good Catholic Girls. Education and Convent Life in Australia* (Melbourne: Melbourne University Press, 2003), 8.
50. Ibid.
51. www.ewtn.com (Accessed on August 11, 2006).
52. I have dealt with this in relation to the work of lay brothers of the Missionaries of the Sacred Heart in Papua New Guinea in T. A. O'Donoghue, "The Sacred Heart Mission and Education in Papua 1885–1942," *Journal of Educational Administration and History* 25, no. 1 (1993): 58–71.
53. http://www.ewtn.com/library/papaldoc/jp2f2295.htm (Accessed on August 18, 2011).
54. The Christian Brothers, *Directory and Rules of the Congregation of the Brothers of the Christian Schools of Ireland* (Dublin: The Christian Brothers, 1927), 278.
55. The Christian Brothers, *Directory and Rules of the Congregation of the Brothers of the Christian Schools of Ireland*, 278.
56. J. Arthur, *The Ebbing Tide: Policy and Principles of Catholic Education* (Leominster, Herefordshire, UK: Gracewing, 1988), 22.
57. Ibid.
58. Arthur also points out that in Canon Law (the law of the Catholic Church) it is the bishop of each diocese who is charged with the responsibility for all schools that bear the title "Catholic."

59. G. Grace, *Catholic Schools: Mission, Markets and Morality* (London: Routledge, 2002), 30.
60. See, for example, W. A. Greening, "The Adaptation of the Irish Christian Brothers' Education System to Australian Conditions in the Nineteenth Century" (PhD thesis, University of Melbourne, 1988).
61. The Irish Christian Brothers, to select an example, is a pontifical order. To take one point in time—the late 1950s—the order was governed by a "general council" in Rome, consisting of a superior-general and four assistants. Each of these assistants represented four groups of provinces. The first group consisted of two Irish provinces and one English province; the second group consisted of two provinces in the United States and one province in Canada; the third group consisted of one South African province and one Indian province; and the fourth group consisted of one New Zealand province and four Australian provinces. The situation in the case of the De La Salle brothers in the United States (another pontifical order) also illustrates how an order divided up a country into a number of provinces. In the mid-1970s there were eight De La Salle provinces in the United States. These administrative units were the Long Island-New England District, the New York District, the Baltimore District, the St. Louis District, the Central States District, the Winona District, the New Orleans-Santa Fe District, and the California District. See K. J. Griffin, "A History of Teacher Education in the Seven Colleges Conducted by the American Christian Brothers" (PhD thesis, Saint Louis University, 1976), 3.
62. This account is based on that in S. F. Dooley, "The Changing Nature of the Congregation of the Christian Brothers within the Province of St. Patrick and Its Response to the Second Vatican Council" (PhD thesis, La Trobe University, 1998), 30–31.
63. For an outline of this situation see D. McLaughlin, *The Price of Freedom: Edmund Rice—Educational –Leader* (Melbourne: David Lovell Publishing, 2007), 357.

4 Recruitment

1. The Sisters of Saint Joseph of the Sacred Heart, *My Yoke Is Sweet* (Sydney: Sisters of Saint Joseph of the Sacred Heart, 1948), 3.
2. Pope Pius XII, *Sacra Virginitas: Encyclical of Pope Pius XII on Consecrated Virginity March 25, 1954.* http://www.papalencyclicals.net/Pius12/P12SACRA.HTM (Accessed July 1, 2009).
3. Ibid.
4. K. Lowden, 'Women Religious and Teacher Education: A Case Study of the Sisters of Notre Dame in the Nineteenth Century" in *Commitment to Diversity: Catholics and Education in a Changing World*, eds. M. Eaton, J. Longmore, and A. Naylor (London: Cassell, 2000), 67–93. This point is also taken up for the New Zealand context in J. Graham,

Breaking the Habit: Life in a New Zealand Dominican Convent 1955–1967 (Dunedin, New Zealand: John McIndoe Ltd., 1992), 37. See also, J. Bennett and R. Forgan (eds.), *There's Something about a Convent Girl* (London: Virago Press, 1991), 161. Here they quote as follows from John Walsh, literary editor of the *Sunday Times* in London, who spoke regarding his education in England: "When I was thirteen I decided I was going to be a Jesuit and I remember telling my mother as she was closing the curtains in the living room and she stopped half way. There are some people, you can tell when they are moved, just from the back of their heads, you could tell she had huge tears in her eyes. She said how pleased, and how happy I had made her by what I'd said."

5. Quoted in S. Kennedy, *Faith and Feminism: Catholic Women's Struggle for Self-Expression* (Sydney: Studies in the Christian Movement, 1985), xv.
6. O. Thorpe, *Ecclesiastical Vocations* (Sydney: Pelegrini, 1944), 40.
7. This theme for the New Zealand context runs through J. Sullivan, *Catholic Boys* (Auckland, New Zealand: Penguin Books, 1996).
8. Thorpe, *Ecclesiastical Vocations*, 36.
9. Ibid., 45.
10. See A Brother of the Christian Schools, *Instructions on Vocation* (New York: La Salle Bureau, 1938), 14.
11. Ibid., 36.
12. Ibid., 19.
13. Ibid., 36.
14. Quoted in A. Henderson, *Mary MacKillop's Sisters: A Life Unveiled* (Sydney: Harper-Collins, 1997), 10.
15. D. S. Blake, *Jerome Colm Keating* (Rome: Christian Brothers, 2004), 16.
16. P. C. Power, *Once a Brother: An Irish Christian Brother's Story* (Dublin: Appletree Press, 2008), 6.
17. Blake, *Jerome Colm Keating*, 20. The matter of siblings joining orders of religious brothers is one that has not been studied to date, but merits serious attention. Reading through the many individual histories of the fortunes of the orders across the world, and of individual communities, one cannot fail but to be struck by the fact that sibling recruitment was not uncommon. However, there has been no work undertaken on the extent to which this happened, what the forces were that brought it about, and what processes operated.
18. The Society of Jesus, *Jesuit Brother* (Melbourne: The Society of Jesus, nd.), 2.
19. The Hospitaller Brothers of St. John of God, *Modern Samaritans* (Christchurch, New Zealand: The Hospitaller Brothers of St. John of God, 1958), 8.
20. Congregation of the Mission, *Meet the Vincentians* (Eastwood, New South Wales: Congregation of the Mission, 1959), 2.

21. Blessed Sacrament Brothers, *The Vocation of the Blessed Sacrament Brother* (Sydney: O'Loughlin Bros., 1963), 5.
22. The Hospitaller Brothers of St. John of God, *Modern Samaritans* (Christchurch, New Zealand: The Hospitaller Brothers of St. John of God, 1958), 2.
23. Passionist Brothers, *Help Wanted: Good Sincere Catholic Young Men to Labour for Jesus Christ as Passionist Brothers* (Marrickville, New South Wales: Passionist Brothers, nd.), 9.
24. Brother of the Christian Schools, *Instructions on Vocation*, 56.
25. D. Donnelly, *Have I A Vocation*? (Dublin: Irish Messenger Office, 1935), 3.
26. Ibid., 4.
27. Passionist Brothers, *Help Wanted*, 6.
28. Ibid., 4.
29. Blessed Sacrament Brothers, *The Vocation of the Blessed Sacrament Brother*, 3.
30. Thorpe, *Ecclesiastical Vocations*, 5.
31. Ibid., 13.
32. D. Donnelly, *Have I A Vocation*? 8.
33. The Hospitaller Brothers of St. John of God, *Modern Samaritans*, 2
34. Congregation of the Mission, *Meet the Vincentians*, 2.
35. Ibid.
36. T. A. O'Donoghue, *Come Follow Me and Forsake Temptation: Catholic Schools and the Recruitment and Retention of Teachers for Religious Teaching Orders, 1922–1965* (Bern: Peter Lang, 2004), 80.
37. Ibid.
38. Congregation of the Mission, *Meet the Vincentians*, 3.
39. The Hospitaller Brothers of St. John of God, *Modern Samaritans*, 16.
40. The Society of Jesus, *Jesuit Brother*, 4–5.
41. Thorpe, *Ecclesiastical Vocations*, 13.
42. Ibid.
43. Passionist Brothers, *Help Wanted*, 12.
44. Pope Pius XII, *Sacra Virginitas: Encyclical of Pope Pius XII on Consecrated Virginity March 25, 1954*. http://www.papalencyclicals.net/Pius12/P12SACRA.HTM (Accessed July 1, 2009).
45. Congregation of the New Zealand Dominican Sisters, *Constitutions* (Auckland: Dominican Sisters, 1933), 34.
46. R. Orsi, "Material History of American Religion Project: The Material World of Catholic Childhood." http://www/materialreligion.org/journal/children.html#Vocations (Accessed May 10, 2006). The results of a small project involving conversations with six De La Salle Brothers at De La Salle Hall, Lincroft, New Jersey, indicates that all of the participants had themselves been students at a De La Salle high school. See Gilder Lehrman Center, A Conversation with Six De La Salle Brothers. http://www.yale.edu/glc/archive/1024.htm (Accessed August 16, 2011).

47. J. Morris, *Moon in My Pocket* (Sydney: Australasian Publishing Co. Ltd., 1945), 20.
48. M. Hastings, *Jesuit Child* (London: Michael Joseph, 1971), 54.
49. Quoted in J. Sullivan, *Catholic Boys* (Auckland, New Zealand: Penguin Books, 1996), 180.
50. Ibid.
51. http://www.comms.dcu.ie/sheehanh/portrait.htm (Accessed February 4, 2005). Reflecting specifically on her own experience in a Catholic school in Australia during the 1950s, Nelson comments as follows: "To the nuns my destiny was obviously the convent, and in the later years of school the pressure began to be applied, subtly at first, then openly." See V. Nelson, "My Father's House" in *Sweet Mothers, Sweet Maids: Journeys from Catholic Childhoods*, eds. K. Nelson and D. Nelson (Ringwood, Victoria, Australia: Penguin Books, 1986), 204. Hobbs also takes up this issue of pressure, relating the emphasis that the nuns who taught her in New Zealand placed on the notion that if you wanted to do your very best "you had to be a nun, to give up your life for God." The latter quotation is from J. Tolerton, *Convent Girls* (Auckland, New Zealand: Penguin Books, 1994), 94.
52. Marist Brothers of the Schools, *Common Rules of the Institute of the Marist Brothers of the Schools* (np: np, 1947), 68.
53. Ibid.
54. Quoted in Sullivan, *Catholic Boys*, 158.
55. The Christian Brothers, *Directory and Rules of the Congregation of the Brothers of the Christian Schools of Ireland* (Dublin: The Christian Brothers, 1927), 328.
56. Ibid., 328.
57. Ibid., 330.
58. An exception in this regard was the De La Salle order, whose members were not allowed to teach Latin throughout much of the nineteenth century and in the early years of the twentieth century. This matter is dealt with in detail in Chapter Six.
59. See K. O'Reilly, "Roman Catholic Reactions to the Thomas Committee Report," *New Zealand Journal of Educational Studies* 12, no. 2 (1997): 124.
60. The Christian Brothers, *Directory and Rules*, 333.
61. These individuals were sometimes able to draw upon specially written handbooks to guide them on how to go about recruiting potential members for their respective orders. Various Protestant churches were also engaged in formal recruiting practices in order to try to recruit young men to become ministers and lay preachers. They also had specially prepared manuals to guide them in their recruitment practices. A good example of such a text produced at the beginning of the twentieth century is J. T. Stone, *Recruiting for Christ* (New York: Fleming H. Revell Company, 1910).

62. P. Connole, "Strathfield Revisited: A Look at Recruiting," *Educational Record* 36, no. 2 (1963): 69.
63. Ibid.
64. Morris, *Moon in My Pocket*, 18.
65. J. Redrup, *Banished Camelots: Recollections of a Catholic Childhood. A Celebration and a Requiem* (Sydney: Bookpress, 1997), 227.
66. C. Geraghty, *Cassocks in the Wilderness: Remembering the Seminary at Springwood* (Melbourne: Spectrum Publications, 2001), 5. By the early 1960s, a number of texts appeared that were meant to provide guidance on the approach to be taken before someone was to be considered a suitable candidate for consideration for training for the priesthood. It is reasonable to assume that the same procedures were used in the recruitment of members for religious orders of brothers and also that they simply codified sets of practices that had been used for some time. These included determining that the potential recruit had the necessary intelligence, interest, aptitudes, and personality for the role, inquiring into his personal and medical condition, and investigating his family background. Among the texts produced see B. Frison, *Selection and Incorporation of Candidates for the Religious Life* (Milwaukee: Bruce Publishing, 1961); R. Hostie (translated by M. Barry), *The Discernment of Vocations* (London: Geoffrey Chapman, 1963); G. Poage, *Recruiting for Christ* (Milwaukee: Bruce Publishing, 1950); G. Poage, *For More Vocations* (Milwaukee: Bruce Publishing, 1955).
67. Quoted in Sullivan, *Catholic Boys*, 123.
68. Redrup, *Banished Camelots*, 227.
69. Ibid., 228.
70. Ibid.
71. Boudreau, S. and Stanton, G. (eds.), *We Were Brothers: The Stories of Salesian Seminarians Who Followed A Dream* (London: Routledge, 1988), 50.
72. K. O'Malley, *Inside* (Victoria, Canada: Trafford Publishing, 2004), 61.
73. Ibid., 64.
74. The remainder of this chapter is based on a longer analysis published in A. Chapman and T. A. O'Donoghue, "The Recruitment of Religious as Teachers: A Case Study from 1960s Australia," *Cambridge Journal of Education* 37, no. 4 (2007): 561–577.
75. J. L. Lemke, *Classroom Communication of Science* (Final report to the US National Science Foundation) (Arlington, VA: ERIC Documents Reproduction Service No. ED 222 346, 1982), 12.
76. K. Armstrong, "Introduction," in *I Leap Over the Wall*, ed. M. Baldwin (London: Hamish Hamilton, 1987), 7.

5 Learning the Rule

1. B. Bradley, *James Joyce's Schooldays* (New York: St. Martin's Press, 1982), 16.

2. D. S. Blake, *Jerome Colm Keating* (Rome: Christian Brothers, 2004), 25.
3. T. Dunne, *Rebellions: Memoir, Memory and 1798* (Dublin: The Lilliput Press, 2004), 34.
4. P. C. Power, *Once a Brother: An Irish Christian Brother's Story* (Dublin: Appletree Press, 2008); K. O'Malley, *Inside* (Victoria, Canada: Trafford Publishing, 2004).
5. This is true even of Catholic education in "regular" Catholic schools. Among the small body of work on the latter is J. J. Irvine and M. Foster, *Growing Up African American in Catholic Schools* (New York: Teachers College Press, Columbia University, 1996).
6. J. L. Heenan, *Not the Whole Truth* (London: Hodder and Stoughton, 1971), 37.
7. J. Redrup, *Banished Camelots: Recollections of a Catholic Childhood. A Celebration and a Requiem* (Sydney: Bookpress, 1997), 251.
8. Ibid.
9. Ibid.
10. Very few studies have been conducted on those who left. Dillon's work is one of the very few to address this matter. See J. T. Dillon, "The Religious Life of Ex-Religious: A Study of Former Christian Brothers in Old Age," *Review of Religious Research* 46, no. 2 (2004): 201–205.
11. See P. Stanosz, "Reproducing Celibacy: A Case Study in Diocesan Seminary Formation" (PhD thesis, Fordham University, 2004).
12. The Christian Brothers, *Directory and Rules of the Congregation of the Brothers of the Christian Schools of Ireland* (Dublin: The Christian Brothers, 1927), 40.
13. Ibid.
14. Marist Brothers of the Schools, *Common Rules of the Institute of the Marist Brothers of the Schools* (np: np, 1947), 45–46.
15. Christian Brothers, *Directory and Rules,* 43.
16. Ibid., 287.
17. Ibid.
18. Marist Brothers, *Common Rules of the Institute of the Marist Brothers of the Schools* (Belgium: Marist Brothers, 1947), 46.
19. Brothers of the Christian Schools, *Common Rules and Constitutions of the Brothers of the Christian Schools* (Rome: Brothers of the Christian Schools, 1947).
20. Ibid., 101.
21. Marist Brothers, *Common Rules of the Institute of the Marist Brothers of the Schools,* 51.
22. Ibid, 50.
23. Ibid., 50.
24. Ibid., 49.
25. Ibid., 63–64.
26. Ibid., 50.
27. Christian Brothers, *Directory and Rules,* 169.

28. Pope Pius XII, *Sacra Virginitas, Encyclical of Pope Pius XII on Consecrated Virginity March 25, 1954.* http://www.papalencyclicals.net/Pius12/P12SACRA.HTM (Accessed July1, 2009).
29. Pope Pius XII, *Counsel to Teaching Sisters. An Address by His Holiness, Pope Pius XII, given September 15, 1951 to the First International Congress of Teaching Sisters.* http://www.papalencyclicals.net/Pius12/P12T.CHRS.HTM (Accessed July 1, 2009).
30. Pope Pius XII, *Sacra Virginitas.*
31. Ibid.
32. Ibid., 169–170.
33. C. Geraghty, *Cassocks in the Wilderness: Remembering the Seminary at Springwood* (Melbourne: Spectrum Publications, 2001), 133.
34. Ibid., 152.
35. Ibid., 107.
36. Marist Brothers, *Common Rules of the Institute of the Marist Brothers of the Schools*, 52–53.
37. Ibid.
38. S. Boudreau and G. Stanton (eds). *We Were Brothers: The Stories of Salesian Seminarians Who Followed A Dream* (London: Routledge, 1988), 70.
39. Marist Brothers, *Common Rules of the Institute of the Marist Brothers of the Schools*, 52–53.
40. P. C. Power, *Once a Brother*, 38.
41. See M. B. Bernstein, *Nuns* (Glasgow: Collins, 1978), 87.
42. Brothers of the Christian Schools, *Common Rules and Constitutions*, 91.
43. O'Malley, *Inside*, 5–6.
44. W. J. Keenan, "Clothed in Authority: The Rationalization of Marist Dress-culture" in *Undressing Religion: Commitment and Conversion from a Cross-cultural Perspective*, ed. L. B. Arthur (Oxford: Berg, 2000), 86–87.
45. Ibid., 87.
46. For changes over time in the "school dress," "house dress," and "street dress" of the Irish Christian Brothers, see D. McLaughlin, *The Price of Freedom: Edmund Rice—Educational Leader* (Melbourne: David Lovell Publishing, 2007), 407.
47. P. McLaren, "Making Catholics: The Ritual Production of Conformity in a Catholic Junior High School," *Journal of Education* 168, no. 2 (1986): 55–77.
48. Power, *Once a Brother*, 38–40.
49. Marist Brothers, *Common Rules of the Institute of the Marist Brothers of the Schools*, 52–53.
50. Ibid., 15.
51. Ibid., 71.
52. See G. Danaher, T. Schirato, and J. Webb, *Understanding Foucault* (Sydney: Allen and Unwin, 2000), 75.

53. Ibid., 20.
54. Ibid., 21.
55. Ibid.
56. Ibid.
57. Ibid.
58. Christian Brothers, *Directory and Rules,* 84. For what the De La Salle rule outlined as "model regulation for retreat time," see Brothers of the Christian Schools, *Common Rules and Constitutions,* 201–203.
59. W. J. Keenan, "Death Culture in Religious Life: Components of Marist Death Culture 1817–1997," *Mortality* 3, no. 1 (1998): 8.
60. Ibid.
61. Ibid., 19.
62. Ibid., 8.

6 An Education Rigid and Unbending

1. V. Thomas, "The Role of the Laity in Catholic Education in South Australia from 1836 to 1986" (PhD. thesis, The Flinders University of South Australia, 1989), 183.
2. H. Praetz, *Building a School System: A Sociological Study of Catholic Education* (Melbourne: Melbourne University Press, 1980), 19.
3. Institute of the Blessed Virgin Mary, *Constitutions of the Institute of the Blessed Virgin Mary for the House Dependent on the General Mother-House, Rathfarnham, Dublin* (Dublin: Institute of the Blessed Virgin Mary, 1938), 44.
4. E. O. Hanson, *The Catholic Church in World Politics* (Princeton, NJ: Princeton University Press, 1987), 34.
5. Evidence furnished by Cullen before the Powis Commission and printed in P. F. Moran (ed.), *The Pastoral Letters and Other Writings of Cardinal Cullen, Archbishop of Dublin, Vol. 3.* Dublin: Browne and Nolan, 1882), 677.
6. Episcopal Committee for Catholic Action, Social Justice Statement, *Christian Education in a Democratic* Community (Carnegie, Victoria, Australia: Renown, 1949), 4.
7. Ibid.
8. T. T. McAvoy, *Father O'Hara of Notre Dame* (Notre Dame: University of Notre Dame Press, 1967), 411.
9. R. Rodriguez, *Hunger of Memory: The Education of Richard Rodriguez* (Boston: David R. Godine, 1981), 83.
10. K. Lawlor, "Bishop Bernard D. Stewart and Resistance to the Reform of Religious Education in the Diocese of Sandhurst, 1950–1979" (PhD thesis, La Trobe University, 1999), 258.
11. E. Campion, "Irish Religion in Australia," *The Australasian Catholic Record* 55, no. 1 (1978): 11.
12. See S. MacSweeney, "Poetic Perspectives on Education" (MEd thesis, Trinity College Dublin, 1982), 93.

13. Rodriguez, *Hunger of Memory*, 88.
14. Campion, "Irish Religion in Australia," 11.
15. Ibid.
16. Praetz, *Building a School System*, 33.
17. Ibid.
18. Christian Brothers, *Directory and Rules of the Congregation of the Brothers of the Christian Schools of Ireland* (Dublin: The Christian Brothers, 1927), 294.
19. Ibid., 295.
20. Rodriguez, *Hunger of Memory*, 93.
21. Ibid.
22. R. Fogarty, *Catholic Education in Australia: 1806–1950* (Melbourne: Melbourne University Press, 1959), 413.
23. Ibid.
24. J. Arnold, *Mother Superior Woman Inferior* (Blackburn, VIC: Dove Communications, 1985), 141.
25. See S. MacSweeney, "Poetic Perspectives," 59.
26. See L. Finnegan, "Dramatic Perspectives on Education" (MEd thesis, Trinity College Dublin, 1986), 94.
27. See J. Ryan, "Artistic Perspectives on Education" (MEd thesis, Trinity College Dublin, 1984), 122–123.
28. Ibid., 36.
29. L. Angus, "Class, Culture and the Curriculum: A Study of Continuity and Change in a Catholic School" in *Continuity and Change in Catholic Education: An Ethnography of Christian Brothers College*, ed. R. Bates, L. Smith, L. Angus, and P. Watkins (Melbourne, VIC: Deakin University, 1982), 60.
30. D. Bollen, *Up On The Hill: A History of St. Patrick's College, Goulburn* (Sydney: University of New South Wales Press, 2008), 135.
31. Rodriguez, *Hunger of Memory*, 89.
32. J. Braniff, "The Marist Brothers' Teaching Tradition in Australia: 1872–2000" (PhD thesis, University of Sydney, 2005), 130.
33. See P. Donovan, *For Youth and the Poor: The De La Salle Brothers in Australia, Papua New Guinea and New Zealand 1906–2000* (Kensington, NSW: De La Salle Provincialite, 2001), 45.
34. See J. Collins, "From Apprentice to Professional," *History of Education Review* 34, no. 2 (2005): 27–40.
35. See Thomas, "The Role of the Laity," 182.
36. Ibid.
37. Ibid.
38. Christian Brothers, *Directory and Rules of the Congregation*, 169.
39. Ibid.
40. Brother A. Jacq, "Brothers and Lay Teachers Associating for the Same Mission. The Policy of the Brothers of the Christian Schools, 1950–2000 (in Britain)."http://www.dlsnet.demon.co.uk/DOCS/ajacq.htm (Accessed March 1, 2005).

41. W. A. Greening, "The Adaptation of the Irish Christian Brothers' Education System to Australian Conditions in the Nineteenth Century" (PhD thesis, The University of Melbourne, 1988), 58.
42. Ibid., 78.
43. Ibid.
44. Christian Brothers, *Directory and Rules of the Congregation*, 169.
45. Ibid.
46. Ibid., 294.
47. M. T. Kehoe, "Lay Teachers in Melbourne Catholic Parish Primary Schools, 1872–1972" (MEd thesis, University of Melbourne, 1982), 81.
48. See Brothers of the Christian Schools, *Common Rules and Constitutions of the Brothers of the Christian Schools* (Rome: Brothers of the Christian Schools, 1947), 53.
49. H. J. O'Donnell, "The Lay Teacher in Catholic Education" in *Enlightening the Next Generation: Catholics and Their Schools 1830–1980*, ed. F. M. Perko (New York: Garland Publishing Inc., 1988), 256.
50. E. A. Fitzpatrick, "Lay Teachers and Religious Perfection," *Catholic School Journal* (December 1941): 341.
51. See T. E. Shields, "Co-education" in *The Catholic Encyclopedia* published in 1908 and available at http://www.newadvent.org/cathen/04088b.htm. See also J. C. Albiseti, "Catholics and Coeducation: Rhetoric and Reality in Europe before *Divini Illius Magistri*", *Paedagogica Historica* 35, no. 3 (1999): 668.
52. Ibid.
53. Ibid.
54. Ibid.
55. Ibid., 673.
56. Pope Pius XI, *Divini Illius Magistri*, December 31, 1929. http://www.vatican.va/holy_father/pius_xi/encyclicals/documents/hf_p-xI_enc_31121929_divini-illius-magistrI_en.html (Accessed June 21, 2006).
57. See Donovan, *For Youth and the Poor*, 66.
58. D. Bollen, *Up on The Hill*, 30.
59. P. Connole, "Educating the Christian Brothers in Australia" *The Educational Record* 42, no. 1 (1969): 56–63.
60. Ibid.
61. D. Bollen, *Up on The Hill*, 56.
62. See Collins, "From Apprentice to Professional," 7–40.
63. Braniff, J. "The Marist Brothers' Teaching Tradition in Australia:1872–2000," 36.
64. J. F. Murphy, "Professional Preparation of Catholic Teachers in the Nineteen Hundreds" in *Enlightening the Next Generation: Catholics and Their Schools 1830–1980*, ed. F. M. Perko (New York: Garland Publishing, Inc., 1988), 243–253.

65. Ibid., 245.
66. Ibid., 249.
67. See M. J. Oates, "The Professional Preparation of Parochial School Teachers 1870–1940," *Historical Journal of Massachusetts* 12 (1984): 60–72.
68.. A. S. Bryk, V. E. Lee, and P. B. Holland. *Catholic Schools and the Common Good* (Cambridge, MA: Harvard University Press, 1993).
69. Ibid.
70. Ibid.
71. Ibid., 31.
72. This is illustrated for New Zealand by Collins in J. Collins, "Schooling for Faith, Citizenship and Social Mobility: Catholic Secondary Education in New Zealand, 1924–1944," *Journal of Educational Administration and History* 37, no. 2 (2005): 157–172.
73. Pope Pius XI, *Divini Illius Magistri*, December 31, 1929..
74. This matter and the ensuing controversy was dealt with back in 1948, in A. Gabriel, *The Christian Brothers in the United States. 1848–1948: A Century of Catholic Education* (New York: Declan X. McMullan Co., 1948), 478–484.
75. Ibid.
76. See R. E. Isetti, "The Latin Question: A Conflict in Catholic Higher Education between Jesuits and Christian Brothers in Late Nineteenth-century America," *The Catholic Historical Review* 76, no. 3 (1990): 526–548.
77. Ibid.
78. This point is also made in relation to schools of all Christian denominations across the world in A. R. King and J. A. Brownell. *The Curriculum and the Disciplines of Knowledge* (New York: John Wiley and Sons, 1966).
79. F. M. Perko, 'With All Those Nuns Watching You: Popular Literature and the Culture of Catholic Schooling, 1900–1970," *U.S. Catholic Historian* 6, nos. 2–3 (1987): 211.
80. J. H. Fichter, *Parochial School* (Garden City: Anchor Books, 1964), 86.
81. Perko, "With all those Nuns Watching You," 211.
82. H. Praetz, *Building a School System: A Sociological Study of Catholic Education* (Melbourne: Melbourne University Press, 1980), 16.
83. The Brigidine Sisters, *Directory of the Brigidine Sisters* (NSW: The Brigidine Sisters, 1955), 55.
84. Quoted in Fogarty, *Catholic Education in Australia: 1806–1950*, 410.
85. Ibid.
86. Ibid.
87. K. Massam, *Sacred Threads: Catholic Spirituality in Australia 1922–1962* (Sydney: University of New South Wales Press, 1996), 42.
88. See G. Wills, *Bare Ruined Choirs: Doubt, Prophecy and Radical Religion* (New York: Doubleday and Co., Inc., 1972), 33.

89. Ibid.
90. Ibid.
91. Ibid.
92. Pope Pius XI, *Vigilanta Cura: On Motion Pictures*, Encyclical of Pope Pius XI promulgated on June 29, 1936. http://www.papalencyclicals.net/Pius11/P11VIGIL.HTM (Accessed September 2005).
93. I have dealt with this at length in T. A. O'Donoghue, *The Catholic Church and the Secondary School Curriculum in Ireland, 1922–1962* (New York: Peter Lang, 1999), 48–51.
94. Christian Brothers, *Directory and Rules of the Congregation*, 258.
95. Ibid.
96. T. A. O'Donoghue. *Upholding the Faith: The Process of Education in Catholic Schools in Australia, 1922–1965* (New York: Peter Lang, 2001), 88.
97. Ibid.
98. J. Joyce, *Portrait of the Artist as a Young Man* (London: Collector's Library, 2005). 80. See also P. J. Ledden, "Education and Social Class in Joyce's Dublin," *Journal of Modern Literature* 22, no. 2 (1998–1999): 329–336.
99. C. Koch, J. Calligan, and J. Gros (eds), *John Baptist De La Salle: The Spirituality of a Christian Educator* (Mahwah, NJ: Paulist Press, 2004), 27.
100. W. Swan, *Christian Politeness and Counsels for Youth* (Dublin: The Christian Brothers, 1912).
101. C. M. Devlin and J. V. Horan, *Courtesy for Boys and Girls* (Dublin: The Christian Brothers, 1962).
102. Christian Brothers, *Fortifying Youth or Religion in Intellect and Will* (Dublin: The Christian Brothers, 1926), vi.
103. Ibid.
104. "Notes on New Books," *The Irish Monthly* 55, no. 651 (1927): 501–503.
105. See P. Connole, "The Christian Brothers in Secondary Education in Queensland, 1875 1965," (MEd thesis, The University of Queensland, 1964), 261.
106. Ibid.
107. I have dealt with this in similar terms in O'Donoghue. *Upholding the Faith*, 108.
108. R. W. Connell, *Masculinities* (London: Polity Press, 1995).
109. See I. Brice. "Ethnic Masculinities in Australian Boys' Schools—Scots and Irish Secondary Schools in Late Nineteenth Century Australia" (Proceedings of the ISCHE Annual Conference, Sydney, Australia, 1998).
110. Ibid.
111. I have dealt with this in similar terms in O'Donoghue. *Upholding the Faith*, 109.

112. M. Scott, "Masculinities and National Identity in Adelaide Boys' Secondary Schools, 1800–1911" (Proceedings of the ANZHES Annual Conference, Auckland, New Zealand, 1998).
113. J. Hamilton, "Faith and Football: Masculinities at Christian Brothers' College, Wakefield Street, 1879–1912" (MEd thesis, The University of Adelaide, 2000), 164.
114. I. Brice, "Ethnic Masculinities in Australian Boys' Schools—Scots and Irish Secondary Schools in Late Nineteenth Century Australia."
115. T. J. L. Chandler, "Manly Catholicism: Making Men in Catholic Public Schools, 1945–80" in *With God on Their Side: Sport in the Service of Religion*, ed. T. Magdalinski and T. J. L. Chandler (London: Routledge, 2002), 116.
116. See F. J. O'Hagan, *The Contribution of the Religious Orders to Education in Glasgow during the Period 1847–1918* (Lampeter, Wales: The Edwin Mellen Press), 176–177.
117. See M. De Búrca, *The GAA (Gaelic Athletic Association): A History* (Dublin: Gill and Macmillan Ltd., 1999).
118. See G. R. Gems, "Selling Sport and Religion in American Society: Bishop Sheil and the Catholic Youth Organization," *The International Journal of the History of Sport* 10, no. 2 (1993): 233–241.
119. B. Kelty, "Catholic Education: The Historical Context" in *The Catholic School: Paradoxes and Challenges*, ed. D. McLaughlin (Strathfield, NSW: St. Paul's Publications, 2000), 13.

7 Responding to the Second Vatican Council

1. M. P. Hornsby-Smith, "Social and Religious Transformations in Ireland: A Case of Secularization?" in *The Development of Industrial Society in Ireland*, eds. J. H. Goldthorpe and C. T. Whelan (Oxford: Oxford University Press, 1994), 271.
2. A. S. Bryk, V. E. Lee, and P. B. Holland, *Catholic Schools and the Common Good* (Cambridge, MA: Harvard University Press, 1993), 46.
3. A. J. Dosen, *Catholic Education in the 1960s: Issues of Identity and Governance* (Charlotte, NC: Information Age Publishing, 2009), 11.
4. See T. P. McLaughlin (ed.), *The Church and the Reconstruction of the Modern World: The Social Encyclicals of Pius XI* (New York: Image, 1957).
5. For a detailed exposition on, and analysis of, Catholic social teaching for the period see C. Curran, *Catholic Social Teaching: A Historical, Theological and Ethical Analysis* (Washington, DC.: Georgetown University Press, 2002).
6. J. Whyte, *Church and State in Modern Ireland* (Dublin: Gill and Macmillan, 1971), 62.
7. Ibid.
8. This is not to overlook the following point made by Cornwell: "From the first decade of the twentieth century Catholic theology and social

teaching had been in deep freeze following the suppression of the 'modernist' movement under Pius X. Catholic social teaching leaned without embarrassment towards corporatism (selection rather than election), thus favouring the early rule of Mussolini of Italy and the entire era of Generalissimo Franco of Spain. Pius XI had influenced the withdrawal of Catholic democratic parties in the form of the Italian Partito Popolare (the People's party), and Cardinal Secretary of State Eugenio Pacelli (the future Pope Pius XII) had encouraged the demise of the German Zentrum, the Centre Party, despite the viable challenge posed by the Popular and centre parties to Fascism and Nazism." See J. Cornwell, *Breaking Faith: The Pope, the People and the Fate of Catholicism* (London: Penguin Books, 2001), 39.

9. Ibid.
10. 'Quadragesimo Anno', paragraph 79, translation in McLaughlin (ed.), *The Church and the Reconstruction of the Modern World*,np.
11. Whyte, *Church and State in Modern Ireland*, 63.
12. See J. Cornwell, *Breaking Faith: The Pope, the People and the Fate of Catholicism* (London: Penguin Books, 2001), 42–43.
13. See Dosen, *Catholic Education in the 1960s*, 12.
14. Cornwell, *Breaking Faith*, 43.
15. Ibid.
16. See S. F. Dooley, "The Changing Nature of the Congregation of the Christian Brothers within the Province of St Patrick and Its Response to the Second Vatican Council (1959–1977)" (PhD thesis, La Trobe University, 1998), 42–44.
17. See. J. L. Elias, *A History of Christian Education: Protestant, Catholic and Orthodox Perspectives* (Malabar, FL: Krieger Publishing Company), 206.
18. D. McLaughlin, "Educating Together in Catholic Schools: A Shared Mission between Consecrated Persons and the Lay Faithful," *Journal of Catholic School Studies* 80, no. 2 (Nov/Dec 2008): 37–53.
19. Pope Paul VI, "Evangelisation in the Modern World" in *Vatican Council II.*, ed. A. Flannery (Collegeville: Liturgical Press, 1982), 15.
20. P. Lakeland, *Catholicism at the Crossroads: How the Laity Can Save the Church* (New York: Continuum, 2007).
21. Elias, *A History of Christian Education*, 206.
22. Ibid., 207.
23. Ibid.
24. Dosen, *Catholic Education in the 1960s*, 16.
25. Elias, *A History of Christian Education*, 207.
26. W. M. Abbott (ed.) *Documents of Vatican II* (London: Geoffrey Chapman, 1966), 11.
27. For an overview in changes in religious education in Catholic schools see M. T. Buchanan, "Pedagogical Drift: The Evolution of New Approaches and Paradigms in Religious Education," *Religious Education* 51, no. 4 (2003): 22–30.

28. K. Lawlor, "Bishop Bernard D. Stewart and Resistance to the Reform of Religious Education in the Diocese of Sandhurst, 1950–1979" (PhD thesis, La Trobe University, 1999), 263.
29. Ibid.
30. See A. Flannery (ed.), *Vatican Council 11. The Conciliar and Post Conciliar Documents* (Dublin: Dominican Publications, 1975), 725.
31. Ibid., 726.
32. S. D. Sammon, "By Their Fruits you Shall Know Them: The Challenge of Renewal Among Men Religious in the USA Today," *Social Compass* 48, no. 2 (2001): 213.
33. Ibid.
34. Dosen, *Catholic Education in the 1960s*, 14.
35. 'Declaration on Christian Education—*Gravissimum Educationis.* Proclaimed by His Holiness Pope Paul VI on October 28, 1965. http://www.vatican.va/archive/hist_councils/ii_vatican_council /documents/vat-ii_decree_19651118_apostolicam-actuositatem _en.html (Accessed May 19, 2009).
36. S. M. Schneider, *Religious Life in a New Millenium* (New York: Paulist Press, 2000), 210. Change, however, was already underway before Vatican 2. In the late 1950s, the then existing Sacred Congregation for Religious convened in Rome its first general assembly of religious. At this assembly, Pope Pius XI encouraged the religious to modify dated and nonessential customs and to relax their excessively strict cloister restrictions.
37. Ibid.
38. Ibid., 211.
39. Ibid.
40. Ibid., 213.
41. See Sammon, "By Their Fruits you Shall Know Them, 209–228.
42. Schneider, *Religious Life in a New Millenium*, 283.
43. Dosen, *Catholic Education in the 1960s*, 15.
44. Dooley, "The Changing Nature of the Congregation," 340.
45. Ibid.
46. E. Johann, "We Are Asking for More Voice" in *Climb Along the Cutting Edge: An Analysis of Change in Religious Life*, ed. J. Chittister, S. Campbell, M. Collins, E. Johann, and J. Putnam (New York: Paulist Press), 20.
47. Ibid., 21.
48. Ibid., 19.

8 Child Abuse

1. P. Cowen, *Dungeons Deep: A Monograph on Prisons, Borstals, Reformatories and Industrial Schools in the Republic of Ireland, and Some Reflections on Crime and Punishment and Matters Relating Thereto* (Dublin: Marion Printing, 1960), 31.

2. For just two such accounts see B. M. Coldrey, *Child Migration and the Western Australian Boys Homes* (Moonee Ponds, VIC: Tamanaraik Publishing, 1991), and M. Raftery and E. O'Sullivan, *Suffer Little Children: The Inside Story of Ireland's Industrial Schools* (Dublin: New Island Books, 1999). For an overview of the situation in the United States and of explanations put forward by some psychologists, see T. C. Fox, *Sexuality and Catholicism* (New York: George Braziller, 1995), 184–197.
3. P. J. Isely, "Child Sexual Abuse and the Catholic Church: An Historical and Contemporary Review," *Pastoral Psychology* 45, no. 4 (1997): 277.
4. Ibid.
5. When abuse by priests did eventually become well known, it was dealt with at length in J. Berry, *Lead Us into Temptation: Catholic Priests and the Sexual Abuse of Children* (Chicago, IL: University of Chicago Press, 2000). For a recent powerful, albeit short, account, see R. Donadio, "A Culture of Denial and Foot-Dragging Endures," *International Herald Tribune*, July 2, 2010.
6. Isely, "Child Sexual Abuse and the Catholic Church," 277–299.
7. M. A. Ames and D. A. Houston, "Legal, Social and Biological Definitions of Paedophilia," *Archives of Sexual Behavior* 19, no. 4 (1990): 333–342.
8. B. Sergent, "Paederasty and Political Life in Archaic Greek Cities," *Journal of Homosexuality* 25, nos. 1–2 (1993): 147–164.
9. T. P. Coogan, *Wherever Green Is Worn: The Story of the Irish Diaspora* (London: Arrow Books, 2000), 15.
10. Ames and Houston, "Legal, Social and Biological Definitions of Paedophilia."
11. P. J. Payer, *Book of Gommorah: An Eleventh-century Treatise against Clerical Homosexual Practices* (Waterloo, ON: Wilfrid Laurier University Press, 1982), 11.
12. St. Basil: Regula Fructuosi, 1107 A.D., quoted in P. J. Payer, *Book of Gommorah*, 61.
13. P. A. Quinn, *Better Than the Sons of Kings* (New York: Peter Lang Publishing, 1989).
14. Ibid.
15. Isely, "Child Sexual Abuse and the Catholic Church," 280.
16. Payer, *Book of Gommorah*, 10.
17. J. Boswell, *Christianity, Social Tolerance, and Homosexuality: Gay People in Western Europe from the Beginning of the Christian Era to the Fourteenth Century* (Chicago, IL: University of Chicago Press, 1980), 365–366.
18. Quinn, *Better Than the Sons of Kings*, 184.
19. Isely, "Child Sexual Abuse and the Catholic Church," 282.
20. E. Burkett and F. Bruni, *A Gospel of Shame* (New York: Viking, 1993).

21. Isely, "Child Sexual Abuse and the Catholic Church," 283.
22. F. M. Perko, 'With All Those Nuns Watching You: Popular Literature and the Culture of Catholic Schooling, 1900–1970," *U.S. Catholic Historian* 6, nos. 2–3 (1987): 204.
23. J. R. Powers, *Do Black Patent Leather Shoes Really Reflect Up?* (New York: Popular Library, 1976), 30.
24. J. T. Farrell, *Father and Son* (New York: The Vanguard Press, 1940); J. T. Farrell, *Studs Lonigan* (New York: Avon Books, 1977).
25. R. Benard, *A Catholic Education* (New York: Holt, Rinehart and Winston, 1982).
26. J. R. Powers, *The Last Catholic in America* (New York: Warner Books, 1973); Powers, *Do Black Patent Leather Shoes Really Reflect Up?*
27. Perko, "With All Those Nuns Watching You," 209.
28. B. Coldrey, "A Most Unenviable Reputation: The Christian Brothers and School Discipline over Two Centuries," *History of Education* 21, no. 3 (1992): 277–289.
29. Ibid., 277.
30. Ibid., 280.
31. Ibid.
32. Ibid.
33. Ibid.
34. L. Clancy, *A Collapsible Man* (Melbourne: St. Martin's Press, 1975), 55.
35. F. O'Brien, *The Hard Life: An Exegesis of Squalor* (Dublin: Dalkey Archive Press, 1961), 25.
36. M. Farrell, *Thy Tears Might Cease* (London: Arena Arrow,1963), 93–98.
37. J. Plunkett, *Farewell Companions* (London: Random House, 1977), 25.
38. N. Browne, *Against the Tide* (Dublin: Gill and Macmillan, 1987), 31.
39. G. Byrne, *The Time of My Life* (London: Sidgwick and Jackson, 1989), 10.
40. S. Ó. Fáoláin, *Vive Moi: An Autobiography* (London: Atlantic Monthly Press, 1965).
41. Ibid., 96.
42. See J. Fay, "Boys Town Founder, Fr. Flanagan, Warned Irish Church about Abuse in the 1940s," http://www.irishcentral.com/news/Boys-Town-founder-Fr Flanagan (Accessed September 28, 2011).
43. L. B. Angus, *Continuity and Change in Catholic Schooling* (London: Falmer Press, 1988).
44. Ibid., 21.
45. B. Oakley, "Years of Sawdust, the Crack of the Whip," *The Secondary Teacher* (Feb. 1967): 13.
46. C. J. Koch, *The Doubleman* (London: Avon, 1955), 38.
47. D. O'Grady, *Deschooling Kevin Carew* (Melbourne: Wren, 1974), 15.

48. B. Coldrey, "A Strange Mixture of Caring and Corruption: Residential Care in Christian Brothers Orphanages and Industrial Schools during the Last Phase, 1940s to 1960s," *History of Education* 29, no. 4 (2000): 343–356.
49. M. Flynn, *Nothing to Say* (Dublin: Lilliput Press, 1983), 67.
50. P. Touher, *Fear of the Collar: My Terrifying Childhood in Artane* (Dublin: O'Brien Press, 2001).
51. For a graphic depiction of life and events at Mount Cashel, see M. Harris, *Unholy Orders: Tragedy at Mount Cashel* (Markham, ON: Viking, 1990).
52. See http://www.nwac-hq.org/en/documents/InstitutionalAbuse PublicResponse.pdf. (Accessed March 2, 2009).
53. See http://eassyrvet,wirdoress,cin/2009/05/ (Accessed March 2, 2009).
54. J. Overton, "Child Abuse, Corporal Punishment, and the Question of Discipline: The Case of Mount Cashel," *Critical Social Policy* 12 (1993): 83.
55. Ibid., 84.
56. J. Braniff, "The Marist Brothers' Teaching Tradition in Australia: 1872–2000" (PhD thesis, The University of Sydney, 2005), 123.
57. P. Donovan, *For Youth and the Poor: The De La Salle Brothers in Australia, Papua New Guinea and New Zealand 1906–2000* (Kensington, NSW: De La Salle Provincialite, 2001), 317.
58. See http://religionandmorality.net/church-state/B-brothers.html (Accessed March 2, 2009).
59. J. Melville and P. Bean, *Lost Children of the Empire* (Sydney: Harper Collins, 1990).
60. For a more recent work see B. Blyth, *Counting the Cost: Christian Brothers and Child Abuse in Australian Orphanages* (Perth: P and B Press, 1999).
61. See http://religionandmorality.net/church-state/B-brothers.html (Accessed March 2, 2009).
62. See "Senate Committee, Part of 'Lost Innocents: Righting the Record', August 2001" http://www.aph.gov.au/senate/committee/clac_cttee /child-migrat/c04.doc (Accessed March 2, 2009).
63. http://www.abc.net.au/lateline/stories/s17579.htm (Accessed March 2, 2009).
64. http://www/aph.gov.au/library/pubs/bn/sp/childmigrants.htm (Accessed March 2, 2009).
65. Great Britain Parliament, House of Commons. Health Committee, *Welfare of Former British Child Migrants* (London: Stationery Office, 1998).
66. See "Senate Committee, Part of "Lost Innocents: Righting the Record," August 2001. http://www.aph.gov.au/senate/committee /clac_cttee/child-migrat/c04.doc (Accessed March 2, 2009).

67. Ibid.
68. Ibid.
69. Ibid.
70. The following account is a variation on that which I have provided in T. A. O'Donoghue "Child-Abuse Scandals and the Catholic Church: Are We Asking the Right Historical Questions?" *History of Education Review* 32, no. 1 (2003): 1–15.
71. P. McGarry, "Roots of a Warped View of Sexuality," *The Irish Times*, June 20, 2009.
72. G. Grace, *Catholic Schools: Mission, Markets and* Morality (London: Routledge, 2002), 26.
73. Ibid., 30.
74. Ibid.
75. See T. A. O'Donoghue, *Come Follow Me and Forsake Temptation: Catholic Schooling and the Recruitment and Retention of Teachers for Religious Teaching Orders, 1922–1965* (Bern: Peter Lang, 2004), 185–186.
76. G. Stanton, "Introduction" in *We Were Brothers: The Stories of Salesian Seminarians Who Followed A Dream*, ed. S. Boudreau and G. Stanton (London: Routledge, 1988), 101.

9 Looking Backward, Looking Forward

1. See http://www.ucanews.com/2011/01/05/keep-the-dangerous-memory-of-jesus-alive-christian-brother/ (Accessed February 22, 2012).
2. This is the title by which the Irish Christian Brothers have become more commonly known over the last ten years.
3. See J. Fitz, "Historical Development of Brother-Priest Relationships" in *Who Are My Brothers?* ed. P. Armstrong (New York: Alba House, 1988), 3–34.
4. E. Goffman, *Asylums* (Harmondsworth: Penguin, 1968).
5. Ibid., 11.
6. Ibid., 17.
7. Ibid., 22.
8. A recent addition to the small corpus of work that does exist, and that has been outlined at various points throughout this book, is C. Barry, *Brother Charles Barry's Papua New Guinean Reminiscences and Recollections 1968–1994* (Sydney: Patrician Brothers, 2011).
9. Again, a notable exception in this regard is the extensive account on the teaching of the Marist Brothers in Glasgow in the early 1870s in F. J. O'Hagan, *The Contribution of the Religious Orders to Education in Glasgow during the Period 1847–1918* (Lampeter, Wales: The Edwin Mellen Press): 172–173. It details the approach used in teaching the catechism. The layout of the schoolroom is also described, relating how 200 boys were controlled and taught in one room.

10. See http://www.edmundrice.org/The-Philippines-Ministry-Updates (Accessed August 26, 2011).
11. Congregation of Christian Brothers, *New Beginnings with Edmund* (Esselen Park, Johannesburg: Congregation of Christian Brothers, 1996), 7.
12. See L. McCane, *Melanesian Stories: Marist Brothers in Solomon Islands and Papua New Guinea 1845–2003* (Madang: Divine Word University, 2004), 330–331.
13. See http://www.africanmissionappeals.org/missions.htm (Accessed August 24, 2011).
14. See http://www.enotes.com/topic/Montfort_Secondary_School (Accessed August 24, 2011).
15. The order also established the Montfort Agricultural Secondary School in Rujewa, Tanzania, in 1988 on 538 acres of land provided by the government. The farm has orchards, paddy fields, fish ponds, and livestock, and funds itself by selling its products.
16. See http://www.bethlehem.edu (Accessed August 27, 2011).
17. See R. McLory, "Despite Steep Decline, Brothers See Hope for their Vocation's Future," *National Catholic Reporter*, September 20, 2010. For example, the 4,700 religious brothers in the United States in 2010, as reported by the Center for Applied Research in the Apostolate (CARA), represent a 62 percent drop from the 1965 figures.
18. For example, on May 11, 2011, it was announced that Br. Philip Pinto, superior-general of the Edmund Rice Christian Brothers (formerly the Irish Christian Brothers), stated that the order's future is uncertain because of costly settlements in child abuse cases. The order sought to seek bankruptcy protection in New York on April 28, 2011. The North American Province of the order, Pinto stated, was especially vulnerable to disappearing because of claims related to its schools in Oregon and Newfoundland.

Bibliography

A Brother of the Christian Schools. *Instructions on Vocation.* New York: La Salle Bureau, 1938.

Abbott, W. M. (ed.). *Documents of Vatican II.* London: Geoffrey Chapman, 1966.

Akenson, D. H. *The Irish Diaspora: A Primer.* Belfast: Queen's University Belfast, Institute of Irish Studies, 1996.

Albiseti, J. C. "Catholics and Coeducation: Rhetoric and Reality in Europe before *Divini Illius Magistri.*" *Paedagogica Historica* 35, no. 3 (1999): 666–696.

Ames, M. A. and Houston, D. A. "Legal, Social and Biological Definitions of Paedophilia." *Archives of Sexual Behavior* 19, no. 4 (1990): 333–342.

Angus, L. "Class, Culture and the Curriculum: A Study of Continuity and Change in a Catholic School." In *Continuity and Change in Catholic Education: An Ethnography of Christian Brothers College*, edited by R. Bates, L. Smith, L. Angus, and P. Watkins, 1–66. Geelong, VIC: Deakin University, 1982.

Angus, L. B. *Continuity and Change in Catholic Schooling.* London: Falmer Press, 1988.

Armstrong, K. *Through the Narrow Gate.* London: Pan Books Ltd., 1982.

Arnold, J. *Mother Superior Woman Inferior.* Blackburn, VIC: Dove Communications, 1985.

Arthur, J. *The Ebbing Tide: Policy and Principles of Catholic Education.* Leominster, Herefordshire, UK: Gracewing, 1988.

Atwater, D. *The Catholic Church in Modern Wales.* London: Burns Oates and Washbourne, 1935.

Australian Schools Commission (Report of the Interim Committee for the Australian Schools Commission (P. Karmel, Chairman). *Schools in Australia.* Canberra, Australia: Australian Government Printing Service, 1973.

Baldwin, M. *I Leap over the Wall.* London: Hamish Hamilton, 1987.

Barry, C. *Brother Charles Barry's Papua New Guinean Reminiscences and Recollections 1968–1994.* Sydney: Patrician Brothers, 2011.

Battersby, W. J. *The De La Salle Brothers in Great Britain.* London: Burns and Oates, 1954.

Bellenger, D. A. "Religious Life for Men." In *From without the Flamian Gate: 150 Years of Catholicism in England and Wales, 1850–2000*, edited by V. A. McClelland, 142–166. London: Darton, Longman and Todd.

Benard, R. *A Catholic Education*. New York: Holt, Rinehart and Winston, 1982.

Bennett, J. and Forgan, R. (eds.). *There's Something about a Convent Girl*. London: Virago Press, 1991.

Bernstein, M. B. *Nuns*. Glasgow: Collins, 1978.

Berry, J. *Lead Us into Temptation: Catholic Priests and the Sexual Abuse of Children*. Chicago, IL: University of Chicago Press, 2000.

Blake, D. S., *Jerome Colm Keating (1928–1999): Christian Brother Extraordinary*. Rome: Christian Brothers, 2004.

Blessed Sacrament Brothers. *The Vocation of the Blessed Sacrament Brother*. Sydney: O'Loughlin Bros., 1963.

Blyth, B. *Counting the Cost: Christian Brothers and Child Abuse in Australian Orphanages*. Perth: P and B Press, 1999.

Bollen, D. *Up on the Hill: A History of St. Patrick's College, Goulburn*. Sydney: University of New South Wales Press, 2008.

Boswell, J. *Christianity, Social Tolerance, and Homosexuality: Gay People in Western Europe from the Beginning of the Christian Era to the Fourteenth Century*. Chicago, IL: University of Chicago Press, 1980.

Boudreau, S. and Stanton, G. (eds.). *We Were Brothers: The Stories of Salesian Seminarians Who Followed A Dream*. London: Routledge, 1988.

Bradley, B. *James Joyce's Schooldays*. New York: St. Martin's Press, 1982.

Braniff, J. "The Marist Brothers' Teaching Tradition in Australia: 1872–2000." PhD thesis, University of Sydney, 2005.

Brice, I. "Ethnic Masculinities in Australian Boys' Schools—Scots and Irish Secondary Schools—in Late Nineteenth Century Australia." Proceedings of the ISCHE Annual Conference, Sydney, Australia, 1998.

Brothers of the Christian Schools. *Common Rules and Constitutions of the Brothers of the Christian Schools*. Rome: Brothers of the Christian Schools, 1947.

Browne, N. *Against the Tide*. Dublin: Gill and Macmillan, 1987.

Bryk, A. S., Lee, V. E., and Holland, P. B. *Catholic Schools and the Common Good*. Cambridge, MA: Harvard University Press, 1993.

Buchanan, M. T. "Pedagogical Drift: The Evolution of New Approaches and Paradigms in Religious Education." *Religious Education* 51, no. 4 (2003): 22–30.

Buchanan, T. "Great Britain." In *Political Catholicism in Europe, 1918*–1965, edited by T. Buchanan and M. Conway, 240–260. Oxford: Clarendon Press, 1996.

Buetow, H. A. *Of Singular Benefit: The Story of Catholic Education in the United States*. London: The Macmillan Company, 1970.

Burkett, E. and Bruni, F. *A Gospel of Shame*. New York: Viking, 1993.

Burley, S. "The Silent Sisterhood(s): Catholic Nuns, Their Public Work and Influence for Social Change in Australia, in Particular South Australia, 1880–1930." Unpublished Research Paper, Graduate School of Education, The University of Adelaide, Australia, 2000.

Byrne, G. *The Time of My Life*. London: Sidgwick and Jackson, 1989.

Campion, E. "Irish Religion in Australia." *The Australasian Catholic Record* 55, no. 1 (1978): 10–14.

Canavan, K. "The Quiet Revolution in Catholic Schooling in Australia." *Catholic Education: Journal of Inquiry and Practice* 2, no. 1 (1998): 46–54.

Chandler, T. J. L. "Manly Catholicism: Making Men in Catholic Public Schools, 1945–1980." In *With God on Their Side: Sport in the Service of Religion*, edited by T. Magdalinski and T. J. L. Chandler, 100–119. London: Routledge, 2002.

Chapman, A. and O'Donoghue, T. A. "The Recruitment of Religious as Teachers: A Case Study from 1960s Australia." *Cambridge Journal of Education* 37, no. 4 (2007): 561–577.

Christian Brothers. *Christian Brothers General Chapter 1968*. Dublin: The Christian Brothers, 1968.

———. *Fortifying Youth or Religion in Intellect and Will*. Dublin: The Christian Brothers, 1926.

Clancy, L. *A Collapsible Man*. Melbourne: St. Martin's Press, 1975.

Coldrey, B. M. *Child Migration and the Western Australian Boys Homes*. Moonee Ponds, VIC: Tamanaraik Publishing, 1991.

———. "A Most Unenviable Reputation: The Christian Brothers and School Discipline over Two Centuries." *History of Education* 21, no. 3 (1992): 277–289.

———. "A Strange Mixture of Caring and Corruption: Residential Care in Christian Brothers Orphanages and Industrial Schools during the Last phase, 1940s to 1960s." *History of Education* 29, no. 4 (2000): 343–356.

Collins, J. "Hidden Lives: The Teaching and Religious Lives of Eight Dominican Sisters, 1931–1961." MEd thesis, Massey University, New Zealand, 2001.

———. "From Apprentice to Professional." *History of Education Review* 34, no. 2 (2005): 27–40.

Collins, J. "Schooling for Faith, Citizenship and Social Mobility: Catholic Secondary Education in New Zealand, 1924–1944." *Journal of Educational Administration and History* 37, no. 2 (2005): 157–172.

Commonwealth of Australia, Senate Committee. "Lost Innocents: Righting the Record, August 2001." http://www.aph.gov.au/senate/committee/clac_cttee/child-migrat/c04.doc (Accessed March 2, 2009).

Concilium Legionis Mariae. *The Official Handbook of the Legion of Mary*. Dublin: The Legion of Mary, 1969.

Congregation of the Mission. *Meet the Vincentians*. Eastwood, NSW: Congregation of the Mission, 1959.

Congregation of the New Zealand Dominican Sisters. *Constitutions*. Auckland: Dominican Sisters, 1933.

Connell, R. W. *Masculinities*. London: Polity Press, 1995.

Connole, P. "The Christian Brothers in Secondary Education in Queensland, 1875–1965." MEd thesis, The University of Queensland, 1964.

———. "Educating the Christian Brothers in Australia." *The Educational Record*, 42, no. 1, 1969: 56–63.

———. "Strathfield Revisited: A Look at Recruiting." *Educational Record*, 36, no. 2 (1963): 65–72.

Connolly, S. *Religion and Society in Nineteenth Century Ireland*. Dundalk: Dundalgan Press, 1985.

Coogan, T. P. *Wherever Green Is Worn: The Story of the Irish Diaspora*. London: Arrow Books, 2000.

Cornwell, J. *Breaking Faith: The Pope, the People and the Fate of Catholicism*. London: Penguin Books, 2001.

———. *Hitler's Pope: The Secret History of Pius XII*. London: Penguin Books, 1999.

Cowen, P. *Dungeons Deep: A Monograph on Prisons, Borstals, Reformatories and Industrial Schools in the Republic of Ireland, and Some Reflections on Crime and Punishment and Matters Relating Thereto*. Dublin: Marion Printing, 1960.

Curran, C. *Catholic Social Teaching: A Historical, Theological and Ethical Analysis*. Washington, DC.: Georgetown University Press, 2002.

Curran, M. D. *A History of the Christian Brothers in India*. Dublin: The Irish Christian Brothers, nd.

Curtis, S. J. and Boultwood, M. E. A. *A Short History of Educational Ideas*. London: University Tutorial Press Ltd., 1970.

Danaher, G., Schirato, T., and Webb, J. *Understanding Foucault*. Sydney: Allen and Unwin, 2000.

De Búrca, M. *The GAA (Gaelic Athletic Association): A History*. Dublin: Gill and Macmillan Ltd., 1999.

Devlin, C. M. and Horan, J. V. *Courtesy for Boys and Girls*. Dublin: The Christian Brothers, 1962.

Dillon, J. T. "The Religious Life of Ex-Religious: A Study of Former Christian Brothers in Old Age." *Review of Religious Research*, 46, no. 2 (2004): 201–205.

Donadio, R. "A Culture of Denial and Foot-Dragging Endures." *International Herald Tribune*, July 2, 2010.

Donnelly, D. *Have I A Vocation?* Dublin: Irish Messenger Office, 1935.

Donovan, P. *For Youth and the Poor: The De La Salle Brothers in Australia, Papua New Guinea and New Zealand 1906–2000*. Kensington, NSW: De La Salle Provincialite, 2001.

Dooley, S. F. "The Changing Nature of the Congregation of the Christian Brothers within the Province of St. Patrick and Its Response to the Second Vatican Council." PhD thesis, La Trobe University, 1998.

Dosen, A. J. *Catholic Education in the 1960s: Issues of Identity and Governance*. Charlotte, NC: Information Age Publishing, 2009.

Dunn, S. "Education, Religion and Cultural Change in the Republic of Ireland." In *Christianity and Educational Provision in International*

Perspective, edited by W. Tulasiewicz and C. Brock, 90–104. London: Routledge, 1988.

Dunne, T. *Rebellions: Memoir, Memory and 1798*. Dublin: The Lilliput Press, 2004.

Elias, J. L. *A History of Christian Education: Protestant, Catholic and Orthodox Perspectives*. Malabar. FL: Krieger Publishing Company, 2002.

Episcopal Committee for Catholic Action, Social Justice Statement. *Christian Education in a Democratic Community*. Carnegie, VIC: Renown, 1949.

Farrell, J. T. *Father and Son*. New York: The Vanguard Press, 1940.

———. *Studs Lonigan*. New York: Avon Books, 1977.

Farrell, M. *Thy Tears Might Cease*. London: Arena Arrow, 1963.

Faught, C. B. *The Oxford Movement: A Thematic History of the Tractarians and Their Times*, University Park: Pennsylvania State University Press, 2003.

Fay, T. J. *A History of Canadian Catholics: Gallicanism, Romanism, and Catholicism*. Montreal and Kingston: McGill-Queen's University Press, 2002.

Fichter, J. H. *Parochial School*. Garden City: Anchor Books, 1964.

Finnegan, L. "Dramatic Perspectives on Education." MEd thesis. Trinity College Dublin, 1986.

Fitz, J. "Historical Development of Brother-Priest Relationships.' In *Who Are My Brothers?* edited by P. Armstrong, 3–34. New York: Alba House, 1988.

Fitzpatrick, E. A. "Lay Teachers and Religious Perfection." *Catholic School Journal* (December 1941): 338–345.

Flannery, A. (ed.). *Vatican Council 11. The Conciliar and Post Conciliar Documents*. Dublin: Dominican Publications, 1975.

Flynn, M. *Nothing to Say*. Dublin: Lilliput Press, 1983.

Fogarty, R. *Catholic Education in Australia: 1806–1950*. Melbourne: Melbourne University Press, 1959.

Fox, T. C. *Sexuality and Catholicism*. New York: George Braziller, 1995.

Frison, B. *Selection and Incorporation of Candidates for the Religious Life*. Milwaukee, WI: Bruce Publishing, 1961.

Gabriel, A. *The Christian Brothers in the United States. 1848–1948: A Century of Catholic Education*. New York: Declan X. McMullan Co., 1948.

Galin, A. *Negotiating Identity: Catholic Higher Education since 1960*. Notre Dame, IN: University of Notre Dame Press, 2000.

Gems, G. R. "Selling Sport and Religion in American Society: Bishop Sheil and the Catholic Youth Organization." *The International Journal of the History of Sport* 10, no. 2 (1993): 233–241.

Geraghty, C. *Cassocks in the Wilderness: Remembering the Seminary at Springwood*. Melbourne: Spectrum Publications, 2001.

Gilder Lehrman Center. "A Conversation with Six De La Salle Brothers." http://www.yale.edu/glc/archive/1024.htm (Accessed August 16, 2011).

Goffman, E. *Asylums*. Harmondsworth: Penguin, 1968.

Government of Newfoundland and Labrador—Canada. "Government Forgoes Claim in Favour of Mount Cashel Victims." http://www.releases.gov.nl.ca/releases/2002/just/1213n07.htm (Accessed March 2, 2009).

Grace, G. *Catholic Schools: Mission, Markets and Morality.* London: Routledge, 2002.

Graham, J. *Breaking the Habit: Life in a New Zealand Dominican Convent 1955–1967.* Dunedin, New Zealand: John McIndoe Ltd., 1992.

Grant, M. A. and Hunt, T. C. *Catholic School Education in the United States: Development and Current Concerns.* New York: Garland Publishing Inc., 1992.

Great Britain Parliament. House of Commons. Health Committee. *Welfare of Former British Child Migrants.* London: Stationery Office, 1998.

Greening, W. A. "The Adaptation of the Irish Christian Brothers' Education System to Australian Conditions in the Nineteenth Century." PhD thesis, University of Melbourne, 1988.

Griffin, K. J. "A History of Teacher Education in the Seven Colleges Conducted by the American Christian Brothers." PhD thesis, Saint Louis University, 1976.

Hamilton, J. "Faith and Football: Masculinities at Christian Brothers' College, Wakefield Street, 1879–1912." MEd thesis, The University of Adelaide, 2000.

Hanson, E. O. *The Catholic Church in World Politics.* Princeton, NJ: Princeton University Press, 1987.

Harris, M. *Unholy Orders: Tragedy at Mount Cashel.* Markham, ON: Viking, 1990.

Hassenger, R. (ed.). *The Shape of Catholic Higher Education*, Chicago, IL: The University of Chicago Press, 1967.

Hastings, M. *Jesuit Child.* London: Michael Joseph, 1971.

Heenan, J. L. *Not the Whole Truth.* London: Hodder and Stoughton, 1971.

Hellinckx, B., Simon, F., and Depaepe, M. *The Forgotten Contribution of the Teaching Sisters: An Historiographical Essay on the Educational Work of Catholic Women Religious in the 19th and 20th Centuries.* Leuven: Leuven University Press, 2009.

Henderson, A. *Mary MacKillop's Sisters: A Life Unveiled.* Sydney: Harper-Collins, 1997.

Hickman, M. J. "Catholicism and the Nation State in Nineteenth Century Britain." In *Commitment to Diversity: Catholics and Education in a Changing World*, edited by M. Eaton, J. Longmore, and A. Naylor, 47–66. London and New York: Cassell, 2000.

Hogan, E. M. *The Irish Missionary Movement: A Historical Survey, 1830–1980.* Dublin: Gill and Macmillan, 1992.

Hornsby-Smith, M. P. *Catholic Education: The Unobtrusive Partner.* London: Sheed and Ward, 1978.

Hornsby-Smith, M. P. "Social and Religious Transformations in Ireland: A Case of Secularization?" In *The Development of Industrial Society in*

Ireland, edited by J. H. Goldthorpe and C. T. Whelan, 265–290. Oxford: Oxford University Press, 1994.

Hornsby-Smith, M. P. "Catholic Schooling in England and Wales." In *Commitment to Diversity: Catholics and Education in a Changing World*, edited by M. Eaton, J. Longmore, and A. Naylor, 184–209. London and New York, Cassell, 2000.

Hostie, R. *The Discernment of Vocations*, translated by M. Barry. London: Geoffrey Chapman, 1963.

Hughes, T. O. *Winds of Change. The Roman Catholic Church and Society in Wales, 1916–1962*. Cardiff: University of Wales Press, 1999.

Inglis, T. *Moral Monopoly: The Rise and Fall of the Catholic Church in Modern Ireland*. Dublin: University College Dublin Press, 1998.

Institute of the Blessed Virgin Mary. *Constitutions of the Institute of the Blessed Virgin Mary for the House Dependent on the General Mother-House, Rathfarnham, Dublin*. Dublin: Institute of the Blessed Virgin Mary, 1938.

Isely, P. J. "Child Sexual Abuse and the Catholic Church: An Historical and Contemporary Review." *Pastoral Psychology* 45, no. 4 (1997): 277–299.

Isetti, R. E. "The Latin Question: A Conflict in Catholic Higher Education between Jesuits and Christian Brothers in Late Nineteenth-century America." *The Catholic Historical Review* 76, no. 3 (1990): 526–548.

Jacq, Brother A. "Brothers and Lay Teachers Associating for the Same Mission. The Policy of the Brothers of the Christian Schools, 1950–2000 (in Britain)." http://www.dlsnet.demon.co.uk/DOCS/ajacq.htm (Accessed March 1, 2005).

Johann, E. "We Are Asking for More Voice." In *Climb along the Cutting Edge: An Analysis of Change in Religious Life*, edited by J. Chittister, S. Campbell, M. Collins, E. Johann, and J. Putnam, 18–28. New York: Paulist Press, 1977.

Joyce, J. *Portrait of the Artist as a Young Man*. Harmondsworth, England: Penguin, 1972.

Judge, H. *Faith-Based Schools and the State: Catholics in America, France and England*. Wallingford, Oxford, UK: Symposium Books, 2002.

Keenan, W. J. "Death Culture in Religious Life: Components of Marist Death Culture 1817–1997." *Mortality* 3, no. 1 (1998): 7–26.

Keenan, W. J. "Clothed in Authority: The Rationalization of Marist Dress-Culture." In *Undressing Religion: Commitment and Conversion from a Cross-Cultural Perspective*, edited by L. B. Arthur, 83–100. Oxford: Berg, 2000.

Kehoe, M. T. "Lay Teachers in Melbourne Catholic Parish Primary Schools, 1872–1972." MEd thesis. University of Melbourne, 1982.

Kelty, B. "Catholic Education: The Historical Context." In *The Catholic School: Paradoxes and Challenges*, edited by D. McLaughlin, 9–30. Strathfield, NSW: St. Paul's Publications, 2000.

Kennedy, S. *Faith and Feminism: Catholic Women's Struggle for Self-Expression*. Sydney: Studies in the Christian Movement, 1985.

Keogh, D. *Edmund Rice and the First Christian Brothers*. Dublin: Four Courts Press, 2008.

King A. R. and Brownell, J. A. *The Curriculum and the Disciplines of Knowledge*. New York: John Wiley and Sons, 1966.

Koch, C., Calligan, J., and Gros, J. (eds). *John Baptist De La Salle: The Spirituality of a Christian Educator*. Mahwah, NJ: Paulist Press, 2004.

Koch, C. J. *The Doubleman*. London: Avon, 1955.

Lakeland, P. *Catholicism at the Crossroads: How the Laity Can Save the Church*. New York: Continuum, 2007.

Lateline. "Sins of the Brothers."http://www.abc.net.au/lateline/stories/s17579.htm (Accessed March 2, 2009).

Lawlor, K. "Bishop Bernard D. Stewart and Resistance to the Reform of Religious Education in the Diocese of Sandhurst, 1950–1979." PhD thesis, La Trobe University, 1999.

Ledden, P. J. "Education and Social Class in Joyce's Dublin." *Journal of Modern Literature*, 22, no. 2 (1998–99): 329–336.

Lee, J. M. (ed.). *Catholic Education in the Western World*. Notre Dame, IN: University of Notre Dame Press, 1966.

Lemke. J. L. *Classroom Communication of Science*. Final report to the US National Science Foundation. Arlington, VA: ERIC Documents Reproduction Service No. ED 222 346, 1982.

Lowden, K. "Women Religious and Teacher Education: A Case Study of the Sisters of Notre Dame in the Nineteenth Century." In *Commitment to Diversity: Catholics and Education in a Changing World*, edited by M. Eaton, J. Longmore, and A. Naylor, 67–93. London: Cassell, 2000.

MacGinley, M. R. A. *A Dynamic of Hope: Institutes of Women Religious in Australia*. Sydney: Crossing Press, 1996.

MacSweeney, S. "Poetic Perspectives on Education." MEd thesis, Trinity College Dublin, 1982.

Manion, B. C. *A Centenary of Service: The Christian Brothers in Queensland, 1875–1975*. Sydney: Christian Brothers of Australasia, 1975.

Marist Brothers of the Schools. *Common Rules of the Institute of the Marist Brothers of the Schools*. np: np, 1947.

Massam, K. *Sacred Threads: Catholic Spirituality in Australia 1922–1962*. Sydney: University of New South Wales Press, 1996.

McAvoy, T. T. *Father O'Hara of Notre Dame*. Notre Dame, IN: University of Notre Dame Press, 1967.

McCane, L. *Melanesian Stories: Marist Brothers in Solomon Islands and Papua New Guinea 1845–2003*. Madang: Divine Word University, 2004.

McGarry, P. "Roots of a Warped View of Sexuality." *The Irish Times*, June 20, 2009.

McLaren, P. "Making Catholics: The Ritual Production of Conformity in a Catholic Junior High School." *Journal of Education* 168, no. 2 (1986): 55–77.

McLaughlin, D. "Educating Together in Catholic Schools: A Shared Mission between Consecrated Persons and the Lay Faithful." *Journal of Catholic School Studies* 80, no. 2 (2008): 37–53.

———. *The Price of Freedom: Edmund Rice—Educational Leader.* Melbourne: David Lovell Publishing, 2007.

McLaughlin, T. P. (ed.). *The Church and the Reconstruction of the Modern World: The Social Encyclicals of Pius XI.* New York: Image, 1957.

McLory, R. "Despite Steep Decline, Brothers See Hope for their Vocation's Future." *National Catholic Reporter,* September 20, 2010.

McNamara, J. A. K. *Sisters in Arms: Catholic Nuns through Two Millennia.* Cambridge: Harvard University Press, 1996.

Melville, J. and Bean, P. *Lost Children of the Empire.* Sydney: Harper Collins, 1990.

Mitchell, C. "Exclusion and Integration: The Case of the Sisters of Providence of Quebec." In *Deaf History Unveiled: Interpretations from New Scholarship*, edited by J. Van Cleve, 146–171.Washington, DC.: Gallaudet University Press, 2003.

Monaghan, L., Schmaling, C., Nakamura, K., and Turner, G. H. (eds.). *Many Ways to Be Deaf: International Variation in Deaf Communities.* Washington, DC: Gallaudet University Press, 2003.

Moran, P. F. (ed.). *The Pastoral Letters and other Writings of Cardinal Cullen, Archbishop of Dublin, Vol. 3.* Dublin: Browne and Nolan, 1882.

Morris, J. *Moon in My Pocket.* Sydney: Australasian Publishing Co. Ltd., 1945.

Murphy, D. *A History of Irish Emigrant and Missionary Education.* Dublin: Four Courts Press, 2000.

Murphy, J. F. "Professional Preparation of Catholic Teachers in the Nineteen Hundreds." In *Enlightening the Next Generation: Catholics and Their Schools 1830–1980*, edited by F. M. Perko, 243–253. New York: Garland Publishing Inc., 1988.

Native Womens' Association of Canada. "Institutional Abuse and Public Response." http://www.nwac.ca/sites/default/files/reports/InstitutionalAbusePublicResponse.pdf (Accessed March 2, 2009).

Nelson, V. "My Father's House." In *Sweet Mothers, Sweet Maids: Journeys from Catholic Childhoods*, edited by K. Nelson and D. Nelson, 195–214. Ringwood, VIC: Penguin Books, 1986.

Noll, M. A. *The Old Religion in the New World: The History of North American Christianity.* Grand Rapids, MI: Wm. B. Eerdmans Publishing, 2002.

O'Brien, F. *The Hard Life: An Exegesis of Squalor.* Dublin: Dalkey Archive Press, 1961.

O'Donnell, H. J. "The Lay Teacher in Catholic Education." In *Enlightening the Next Generation: Catholics and Their Schools 1830–1980*, edited by F. M. Perko, 254–266. New York: Garland Publishing Inc., 1988.

O'Donoghue, T. A. *Bilingual Education in Pre-Independent Irish-speaking Ireland, 1800–1922. A History.* New York: Edwin Mellen Press, 2006.

———. "The Catholic Church and the Promotion of a Gaelic Identity in Irish Secondary Schools." *The Australian Journal of Irish Studies* 2 (2002): 149–165.

O'Donoghue, T. A. *The Catholic Church and the Secondary School Curriculum in Ireland, 1922–1962*. New York: Peter Lang, 1999.

———. "Child-Abuse Scandals and the Catholic Church: Are We Asking the Right Historical Questions?" *History of Education* Review 32, no. 1 (2003): 1–15.

———. *Come Follow Me and Forsake Temptation: Catholic Schooling and the Recruitment and Retention of Teachers for Religious Teaching Orders, 1922–1965*. Bern: Peter Lang, 2004.

———. "Rescuing Lay Teachers in Catholic Schools from Anonymity for the Period 1870–1970." *Education Research and Perspectives* 26, no. 2 (2004): 78–93.

———. "The Sacred Heart Mission and Education in Papua 1885–1942." *Journal of Educational Administration and History* 25, no. 1 (1993): 58–71.

———. *Upholding the Faith: The Process of Education in Catholic Schools in Australia, 1922–1965*. New York: Peter Lang, 2001.

O'Donoghue, T. and Harford, J. "A Comparative History of Church-State Relations in Irish Education." *Comparative Education Review* 55, no. 3 (2011): 315–341.

Ó Fáoláin, S. *Vive Moi: An Autobiography*. London: Atlantic Monthly Press, 1965.

O'Grady, D. *Deschooling Kevin Carew*. Melbourne: Wren, 1974.

O'Hagan, F. J. *The Contribution of the Religious Orders to Education in Glasgow during the Period 1947–1918*. Lampeter, Wales: The Edwin Mellen Press.

O'Keefe, B. "Reordering Perspectives in Catholic Schools." In *Catholics in England 1950–2000: Historical and Sociological Perspectives*, edited by M. P. Hornsby-Smith, 242–265. London: Cassell, 1999.

O'Malley, K. *Inside*. Victoria, Canada: Trafford Publishing, 2004.

O'Reilly, K. "Roman Catholic Reactions to the Thomas Committee Report." *New Zealand Journal of Educational Studies* 12, no. 2 (1997): 119–132.

Oakley, B. "Years of Sawdust, the Crack of the Whip." *The Secondary Teacher* (February 1967): 12–14.

Oates, M. J. "The Professional Preparation of Parochial School Teachers 1870–1940." *Historical Journal of Massachusetts* 12 (1984): 60–72.

Orsi, R. "Material History of American Religion Project: The Material World of Catholic Childhood." http://www/materialreligion.org/journal/children.html#Vocations (Accessed May 10, 2006).

Overton, J. "Child Abuse, Corporal Punishment, and the Question of Discipline: The Case of Mount Cashel." *Critical Social Policy* 12 (1993): 73–95.

Passionist Brothers, *Help Wanted: Good Sincere Catholic Young Men to Labour for Jesus Christ as Passionist Brothers*. Marrickville, NSW: Passionist Brothers, nd.

Payer, P. J. *Book of Gommorah: An Eleventh-century Treatise against Clerical Homesexual Practices*. Waterloo, ON: Wilfrid Laurier University Press, 1982.

Peckham-Magray, M. *The Transforming Power of the Nuns: Women, Religion and Cultural Change in Ireland, 1750–1900*. New York: Oxford University Press, 1998.

Perko, F. M. "With All Those Nuns Watching You: Popular Literature and the Culture of Catholic Schooling, 1900–1970." *U.S. Catholic Historian* 6, nos. 2–3 (1987): 199–212.

———. "Religious Schooling in America: An Historiographic Reflection." *History of Education Quarterly* 40, no. 3 (2000): 320–338.

Plowman, D. H. *Enduring Struggle: St. Mary's Tardun Farm School*. Perth, WA: Scholastica Press, 2003.

Plunkett, J. *Farewell Companions*. London: Random House, 1977.

Poage, G. *Recruiting for Christ*. Milwaukee, WI: Bruce Publishing, 1950.

———. *For More Vocations*. Milwaukee, WI: Bruce Publishing, 1955.

Pope Paul VI. "Declaration on Christian Education—Gravisimum Educationis. Proclaimed by His Holiness Pope Paul VI on October 28, 1965." http://www.vatican.va/archive/hist_councils/ii_vatican_council/documents/vat-ii_decree_19651118_apostolicam-actuositatem_en.html (Accessed May 19, 2009).

———. "Evangelisation in the Modern World." In *Vatican Council II*, edited by A. Flannery, np. Collegeville: Liturgical Press, 1982.

Pope Pius XI. "*Divini Illius Magistri*, December 31, 1929." http://www.vatican.va/holy_father/pius_xi/encyclicals/documents/hf_p-xi_enc_31121929_divini-illius-magistri_en.html (Accessed June 21, 2006).

———. "*Vigilanta Cura: On Motion Pictures, Encyclical of Pope Pius XI Promulgated on June 29, 1936*." http://www.papalencyclicals.net/Pius11/P11VIGIL.HTM (Accessed September 12, 2005).

Pope Pius XII. "*Counsel to Teaching Sisters. An Address by His Holiness, Pope Pius XII, given September 15, 1951 to the First International Congress of Teaching Sisters*." http://www.papalencyclicals.net/Pius12/P12T.CHRS.HTM (Accessed July 1, 2009).

———. "*Sacra Virginitas, Encyclical of Pope Pius XII on Consecrated Virginity March 25, 1954*."http://www.papalencyclicals.net/Pius12/P12SACRA.HTM (Accessed July 1, 2009).

Power, P. C. *Once a Brother: An Irish Christian Brother's Story*. Dublin: Appletree Press, 2008.

Powers, J. R. *The Last Catholic in America*. New York: Warner Books, 1973

———. *Do Black Patent Leather Shoes Really Reflect Up?* New York: Popular Library, 1976

Praetz, H. *Building a School System: A Sociological Study of Catholic Education*. Melbourne: Melbourne University Press, 1980.

Quinn, P. A. *Better Than the Sons of Kings*. New York: Peter Lang Publishing, 1989.

Raftery, M. and O'Sullivan, E. *Suffer Little Children: The Inside Story of Ireland's Industrial Schools*. Dublin: New Island Books, 1999.

Redrup, J. *Banished Camelots: Recollections of a Catholic Childhood. A Celebration and a Requiem*. Sydney: Bookpress, 1997.

Rodriguez, R. *Hunger of Memory: The Education of Richard Rodriguez*. Boston: David R. Godine, 1981.

Ryan, J. "Artistic Perspectives on Education." MEd thesis. Trinity College Dublin, 1984.

Safford, P. L. and Safford, E. J. *A History of Childhood and Disability*. New York: Teachers College Press, Columbia University, 1996.

Sammon, S. D. "By Their Fruits you Shall Know Them: The Challenge of Renewal Among Men Religious in the USA Today." *Social Compass* 48, no. 2 (2001): 209–228.

Schneider, S. M. *Religious Life in a New Millenium*. New York: Paulist Press, 2000.

Scott, M. "Masculinities and National Identity in Adelaide Boys' Secondary Schools, 1880–1911." Proceedings of the ANZHES Annual Conference, Auckland, New Zealand, 1998.

Sergent, B. "Paederasty and Political Life in Archaic Greek Cities." *Journal of Homosexuality* 25, nos. 1–2 (1993): 147–164.

Shields, T. E. "Co-education." In *The Catholic Encyclopedia* (1908). http://www.newadvent.org/cathen/04088b.htm (Accessed March 2, 1204).

Sisters of Mercy. *A Guide for the Religious Called Sisters of Mercy*. London: Robson and Son, 1866.

Sisters of Saint Joseph of The Most Sacred Heart of Jesus. *Constitutions of The Sisters of the Most Sacred Heart of Jesus*. Sydney: Sisters of Saint Joseph of The Most Sacred Heart of Jesus, 1949.

Sisters of Saint Joseph of the Most Sacred Heart of Jesus. *Customs and Practices of the Sisters of St. Joseph of the Most Sacred Heart of Jesus*. Sydney: Sisters of Saint Joseph of the Most Sacred Heart of Jesus, 1950

Smyth, E. "Sisters in Culture: Ethnicity and Toronto's Teaching Communities of Women Religious." Proceedings of the ISCHE XXI Conference, University of Sydney, 1999.

Smyth, E. "Teacher Education within the Congregation of the Sisters of St. Joseph of Toronto, Canada, 1851–1920." *History of Education Review* 23, no. 3 (1994): 97–113.

Smyth, E. "Much Exertion of the Voice and Great Application of the Mind: Teacher Education within Congregations of the Sisters of St. Joseph of Toronto, Canada, 1851–1920." *History of Education Review/Historical Studies in Education* (Joint Issue) 6, no. 3 (1994): 97–113.

Stanosz, P. "Reproducing Celibacy: A Case Study in Diocesan Seminary Formation." PhDthesis, Fordham University, 2004.

Stanton, G. "Introduction." In *We Were Brothers: The Stories of Salesian Seminarians Who Followed A Dream*, edited by S. Boudreau and G. Stanton, 1–3. London: Routledge, 1988.

Stark, R. and Finke, R. "Catholic Religious Vocations: Decline and Revival." *Review of Religious Research* 42, no. 2 (2000): 125–145.

Stewart, J. E. *The Education of Catholic Girls*. London: Longman, Green and Co., 1911.

Stone, J. T. *Recruiting for Christ*. New York: Fleming H. Revell Company, 1910.

Strong, D. *Jesuits in Australia*. Richmond, VIC: Aurora Books, 1995.

Sturrock, M. *Women of Strength, Women of Gentleness: The Brigidine Sisters, Victoria Province*. Melbourne: David Lovell Publishing, 1995.

Sullivan, J. *Catholic Boys*. Auckland, New Zealand: Penguin Books, 1996.

Sullivan, R. *Visual Habits: Nuns, Feminism, and American Postwar Popular Culture*. Toronto: University of Toronto Press, 2005.

Swan, W. *Christian Politeness and Counsels for Youth*. Dublin: The Christian Brothers, 1912.

Sweetman, R. *A Fair and Just Solution? A History of the Integration of Private Schools in New Zealand*. Palmerston North, New Zealand: Dunmore Press, 2002.

Tentler, L. W. *Seasons of Grace: A History of the Catholic Church in the Archdiocese of Detroit*. Detroit: Wayne State University Press, 1990.

The Brigidine Congregation. *The Constitutions of the Sisters of the Brigidine Congregation*. New South Wales, Australia: The Brigidine Congregation, 1956.

The Brigidine Sisters. *Directory of the Brigidine Sisters*. New South Wales, Australia: The Brigidine Sisters, 1955.

The Christian Brothers. *Directory and Rules of the Congregation of the Brothers of the Christian Schools of Ireland*. Dublin: The Christian Brothers, 1927.

The Hospitaller Brothers of St. John of God. *Modern Samaritans*. Christchurch, New Zealand: The Hospitaller Brothers of St. John of God, 1958.

The Institute of the Blessed Virgin Mary. *Rules IBVM*. Dublin: IBVM, 1914.

The Religious Hospitallers of Saint Joseph. *Constitutions of The Religious Hospitallers of Saint Joseph*. Montreal: The Religious Hospitallers of Saint Joseph, 1953.

The Sisters of Mercy. *Constitutions of the Congregation of the Australian Union of the Sisters of Our Lady of Mercy*. London: Robson and Son, 1866.

———. *Constitutions of the Congregation of the Australian Union of the Sisters of Our Lady of Mercy*. Canberra, Australia: The Sisters of Mercy, General Motherhouse, 1960.

The Sisters of Saint Joseph of the Sacred Heart, *My Yoke Is Sweet*. Sydney: Sisters of Saint Joseph of the Sacred Heart, 1948.

The Society of Jesus. *Jesuit Brother*. Melbourne: The Society of Jesus, nd.

The Taize Community. http://www.taize.fr./ (Accessed on May 9, 2011).

Thomas, V., "The Role of the Laity in Catholic Education in South Australia from 1836 to 1986." PhD thesis. The Flinders University of South Australia, 1989.
Thompson, M. S. "Sisterhood and Power: Class, Culture and Ethnicity in the American Convent." *Colby Library Quarterly* 25 (1989): 149–175.
Thorpe, O. *Ecclesiastical Vocations.* Sydney: Pelegrini, 1944.
Titley, B. *Church, State, and the Control of Schooling in Ireland 1900–1944.* Kingston, ON: McGill-Queen's University Press. 1983.
Tolerton, J. *Convent Girls.* Auckland, New Zealand: Penguin Books, 1994.
Touher, P. *Fear of the Collar: My Terrifying Childhood in Artane.* Dublin: O'Brien Press.
Towey, J. *Irish De La Salle Brothers in Christian Education.* Dublin: De La Salle Brothers, 1980.
Trimingham Jack, C. *Growing Good Catholic Girls. Education and Convent Life in Australia.* Melbourne: Melbourne University Press, 2003.
———. "The Lay Sister in Educational History and Memory." Proceedings of the Australian and New Zealand History of Education Society Annual Conference, Auckland, New Zealand, 1998.
Tulasciewitcz, W. and Brock, C. (eds.). *Christianity and Educational Provision in International Perspective.* London: Routledge, 1989.
Van Cleve, J. V. (ed.). *Deaf History Unveiled: Interpretations from New Scholarship.* Washington, DC.: Gallaudet University Press, 2003.
Walch, T. "United States Catholic History: American Catholic Education—Historical Contours and Future Directions." *Catechist* 34, no. 6 (2000): 46–51.
Walsh, B. *Roman Catholic Nuns in England and Wales 1800–1937.* Dublin: Irish Academic Press, 2002.
Weafer, J. and Breslin, A. *A Survey of Irish Catholic Clergy and Religious, 1970–1981.* Maynooth: Council for Research and Development, Report No. 17, 1983.
White, D. *Education and the State: Federal Involvement in Educational Policy Development.* Richmond, VIC: Deakin University Press, 1987.
White, J. P. "A Short History of English Catholic Education." In *Catholic Education in the Western World*, edited by J. M. Lee, 211–251. Notre Dame, IN: University of Notre Dame Press, 1966.
Whyte, J. *Church and State in Modern Ireland.* Dublin: Gill and Macmillan, 1971.
Wills, G. *Bare Ruined Choirs: Doubt, Prophecy and Radical Religion.* New York: Doubleday and Co. Inc., 1972.
Winzer, M. *The History of Special Education: From Isolation to Integration.* Washington, DC: Gallaudet University Press, 1993.
Wittberg, P. *The Rise and Fall of Catholic Religious Orders: A Social Movement Perspective.* Albany, NY: SUNY Press, 1994.
Wong, H. K. "An Investigation into the Work of the De La Salle Brothers in the Far East." *Paedagogica Historica* 6, no. 2 (1966): 440–504.

Index